Female Journeys

**Recent Titles in
Contributions in Women's Studies**

Gender and Genre in Gertrude Stein
Franziska Gygax

Rewriting the Word: American Women Writers and the Bible
Amy Benson Brown

Ethnicity and Gender in the Barsetshire Novels of Angela Thirkell
Penelope Fritzer

Women of Courage: Jewish and Italian Immigrant Women in New York
Rose Laub Coser, Laura S. Anker, and Andrew J. Perrin

Contemporary Irish Women Poets: Some Male Perspectives
Alexander G. Gonzalez

Queer Poetics: Five Modernist Women Writers
Mary E. Galvin

White Women Writing White: H.D., Elizabeth Bishop, Sylvia Plath, and Whiteness
Renée R. Curry

The Foreign Woman in British Literature: Exotics, Aliens, and Outsiders
Marilyn Demarest Button and Toni Reed, editors

Embracing Space: Spatial Metaphors in Feminist Discourse
Kerstin W. Shands

On Top of the World: Women's Political Leadership in Scandinavia and Beyond
Bruce O. Solheim

Victorian London's Middle-Class Housewife: What She Did All Day
Yaffa Claire Draznin

Connecting Links: The British and American Woman Suffrage Movements, 1900–1914
Patricia Greenwood Harrison

Female Journeys

Autobiographical Expressions by French and Italian Women

Claire Marrone

Contributions in Women's Studies, Number 180

GREENWOOD PRESS
Westport, Connecticut • London

Library of Congress Cataloging-in-Publication Data

Marrone, Claire, 1962–
    Female journeys : autobiographical expressions by French and Italian women / Claire Marrone.
        p. cm.—(Contributions in women's studies, ISSN 0147–104X ; no. 180)
    Includes bibliographical references and index.
    ISBN 0–313–30727–X (alk. paper)
        1. French prose literature—Women authors—History and criticism. 2. Women authors, French—Biography—History and criticism. 3. Italian prose literature—Women authors—History and criticism. 4. Women authors, Italian—Biography—History and criticism. 5. Autobiography—Women authors. I. Title. II. Series.
    PQ149.M29   2000
    840.9′492072—dc21   99–089162

British Library Cataloguing in Publication Data is available.

Copyright © 2000 by Claire Marrone

All rights reserved. No portion of this book may be
reproduced, by any process or technique, without the
express written consent of the publisher.

Library of Congress Catalog Card Number: 99–089162
ISBN: 0–313–30727–X
ISSN: 0147–104X

First published in 2000

Greenwood Press, 88 Post Road West, Westport, CT 06881
An imprint of Greenwood Publishing Group, Inc.
www.greenwood.com

Printed in the United States of America

The paper used in this book complies with the
Permanent Paper Standard issued by the National
Information Standards Organization (Z39.48–1984).

10 9 8 7 6 5 4 3 2 1

Copyright Acknowledgments

The author and publisher gratefully acknowledge permission to reprint extracts from the following:

Claire Marrone, "Male and Female *Bildung*: The *Mémoires de Céleste Mogador*." *Nineteenth-Century French Studies* 25.3–4 (1997): 335–47.

Claire Marrone, "Cristina Trivulzio di Belgiojoso's Western Feminism: The Poetics of a Nineteenth-Century Nomad." *Italian Quarterly* 34.133–34 (1997): 21–32.

Marie Cardinal, *The Words to Say It: An Autobiographical Novel by Marie Cardinal*. Trans. Pat Goodheart. Cambridge, MA: VanVactor and Goodheart, 1983.

Sibilla Aleramo, *A Woman*. Trans. Rosalind Delmar. Berkeley: University of California Press. Copyright © 1980.

Marie Cardinal, *Les mots pour le dire*. Paris: Grasset, 1975.

Annie Ernaux, "*Je ne suis pas sortie de ma nuit.*" Paris: Gallimard, 1997. © Editions GALLIMARD.

Annie Ernaux, *Une femme*. Paris: Gallimard, 1987. © Editions GALLIMARD.

Annie Ernaux, *A Woman's Story*. Trans. Tanya Leslie. New York: Four Walls Eight Windows, 1991. Reprinted with permission of Seven Stories Press.

For all of my loved ones

Contents

Acknowledgments   xi

Introduction   1

    A Critical Beginning

    Women Writers, Feminism, and Theories of Autobiography: Debates and Trends

    Traditions in French and Italian Autobiography: Women Writing within and against the Canon

    Women's Autobiography as *Bildungsroman*: Gender and Genre

    Common Elements and Distinctions between Autobiography and *Bildungsroman*

Part I: Leaving the Country

1. Cristina Trivulzio di Belgiojoso's *Souvenirs dans l'exil*: The Journey Home   29

2. Belgiojoso's Western Feminism: The Poetics of a Nineteenth-Century Nomad   45

3. The *Bildung* of Céleste Mogador and Lionel de C***: A Sentimental Journey   61

4. The Reformed Harlot in *Un deuil au bout du monde: Suite des Mémoires de Céleste Mogador* — 77

Part II: Leaving the Family

5. The Turning Point: Sibilla Aleramo's *Una donna* — 91

6. Living Freely, Demanding Choice: Oriana Fallaci's *Lettera a un bambino mai nato* — 107

Part III: Leaving the Mother

7. Creativity and Community in Marie Cardinal's *Les mots pour le dire* — 121

8. Annie Ernaux's Auto/biographies: Unfinished Stories? — 143

Conclusion — 157

Works Cited — 161

Index — 173

Acknowledgments

This project has come to fruition as the result of countless formative relationships and numerous experiences both at home and abroad. My interest in women's autobiographical writing was cultivated during graduate school at the University of Pennsylvania. I am indebted to many professors from Penn's Department of Romance Languages, in particular, Frank Paul Bowman, Lucienne Frappier-Mazur, and Victoria Kirkham. Their guidance and inspiration were instrumental in the early stages of my research. I am also grateful to numerous friends whom I met during my graduate studies for their stimulating conversation and insights regarding women writers and feminism.

Through Penn's exchange programs and travel opportunities, I was able to conduct much of my initial research for this project in France and Italy. While living in Paris, I was fortunate to participate in Columbia University's Graduate Research Institute at Reid Hall under the direction of Danielle Haase-Dubosc. The short seminars and lectures held at Reid Hall were particularly helpful as I began to form ideas about life writing.

When I assumed a teaching position at the University of Minnesota, several professors in the Department of French and Italian graciously agreed to comment on my work. I am particularly grateful to Eileen Sivert and Judith Preckshot for their readings of an earlier version of Chapter 2.

My current position at Sacred Heart University has enabled me to expand my thinking about women's autobiography through a series of courses and research opportunities. I would like to thank my students from two classes—Women's Autobiography and Writing Women's Lives—for their energy and enthusiasm, as well as their insights regarding women's writing. I am also indebted to the students in my recent comparative culture course, Franco–Italian Connections. Their perceptive interpretations of Marie Cardinal's *Les mots pour le dire* (*The Words to Say It*) nurtured my analysis of the text.

In addition to allowing me to develop new literature and culture courses, Sacred Heart has been extremely generous in granting me two University Research/Creativity Grants. These grants have been invaluable in allowing me to consult collections in the United States and abroad, including several rare manuscripts at the *Bibliothèque Nationale* and the *Bibliothèque Marguerite Durand* in Paris. Sacred Heart's research grants also have provided me with the release time necessary to complete this project. I extend my thanks to Sacred Heart's dean of the College of Arts and Sciences, Claire J. Paolini, and the chair of the Department of Languages, Literatures, and Media Studies, David Curtis, for their support in this area.

I would also like to express my gratitude to the members of the organization Women in French, particularly to Colette Hall, for the opportunity to collaborate on numerous conference sessions and research initiatives. Women in French has provided a comfortable forum for the development of innovative projects on women writers and feminist thought.

My thinking on the theoretical issues surrounding personal narratives has also been nourished by a National Endowment for the Humanities Summer Seminar on "Literary Biography" held at the City University of New York Graduate Center. I would like to thank the seminar leader, N. John Hall, and all of the participants for their intelligence and lively discussions about life writing.

I am especially grateful to my parents, Laura and Angelo Marrone, to my brothers Joe and John Marrone, and to my extended family for their guidance and constant confidence in my work. Finally, I thank my husband, Tom Mussio, for his love and encouragement, his careful reading of this manuscript, and his passion for engaging in literary and philosophical discussions, all of which have enhanced this project. Several chapters of this book were composed during our memorable sojourns in Rome, New York, Paris, and the southern Italian village of Pisciotta.

Introduction

A CRITICAL BEGINNING

Current trends in autobiography raise engaging questions about conceptions of selfhood and the process of creating literature inspired by life events. Rather than a single, monumental opus that endeavors to encapsulate the spirit of an individual, contemporary autobiographies are often fragmentary, inconclusive, and subject to further revision: an initial life story may be recast in a novel, revised into a film scenario, and rewritten on numerous occasions. The univocal rendering of experience is challenged by hybrid texts such as "collective" autobiographies. The certainty of the subject is clouded in creative auto/biographies. Despite these novelties, autobiography may generally be defined as an exploration of one's *selected* life experiences, language being one of the many codes through which this analysis can unfold.[1] Although for many contemporary critics, the "self" is said to be elusive, "identity" changeable, and the "life" incomprehensible, the outpouring of personal narratives today attests to an ardent desire to reflect upon one's experiences and to communicate one's "truths." In women's life writing, the self is particularly problematic, not only because women writers have had to construct their own versions of femininity in opposition to generations of male portraits but because women's roles and circumstances continue to change radically.

In this study of nineteenth- and twentieth-century French and Italian women's autobiography, protagonists' self-understanding derives from the movement away from oppressive structures. For these women the autobiographical "journey" involves literal and emotional wandering.[2] Some women choose exile in other countries to flee oppressive societal and cultural norms. Their multicultural experiences define who they are. Others escape abusive marriages and confront losing custody of their children. Some refuse traditional marriages and choose single motherhood. Still others evade constraining religious, class, and familial codes. They often rebel against the woman most closely connected to their own identity, the mother. All of these heroines become writers and flee female stereotypes. The crisis of conscience that such displacements provoke has generic ramifications—the life story is often a confession, justification, or meditation about countless border crossings. In the contemporary period, writers challenge conventional autobiographical borders in an effort to express evolving notions of selfhood and the difficulty of encapsulating a life through writing. In addition, the theme of movement connects with a progressive drive in many of these women's stories; their autobiographies pose groundbreaking questions, challenge accepted standards, and enact narrative innovation.

I read selected life stories as *bildungsromane*, or novels of development, for even in today's "new autobiographies"[3] the desire to create a portrait of growth and maturation informs, indeed often incites, life writing, even if that pursuit may at times prove elusive. Such a reading provides a frame for the movements away from oppression and toward self-realization enacted in the autobiographical texts analyzed here. In addition, reading autobiography in light of the features of the *bildungsroman* allows me to explore crucial moments of "awakening" in women's texts. As the nature of both the *bildungsroman* and autobiography frequently involves progression, development, and identity, there are several shared characteristics regarding narrative perspective, character portraits, and structural techniques. Consciously or unconsciously, all of the women autobiographers I study draw on the *bildungsroman* model. While several critics discuss the autobiographical nature of novels of development as well as the emphasis on growth and maturation in many personal narratives,[4] I am unaware of any systematic review of French and Italian women's autobiography read as *bildungsroman*. I examine the formation of female identities through the various life stages: childhood and adolescence, development of interpersonal relationships (sexuality, marriage, motherhood), entry into society, establishment of career (including the significance of writing), and preparation for death. I also concentrate on particular pivotal moments in women's lives connected to maturation and self-discovery. This is not to say that all women experience particular life stages in the same fashion or that women's development is diametrically opposed to men's maturation. However, several shared characteristics in female development manifest themselves in numerous women's autobiographies of given historical moments because of biological, psychological, and environmental factors. Although recent studies challenge notions of "difference" and gendered identities,[5] female autobiographers continue to contemplate "woman" in relation to women, as well as tendencies in women's writing. Today's innovative textual practices provide a forum for such considerations.

I examine both recognized and lesser-known writers. Some were already well-established authors when their texts were published; others were just beginning their literary careers. In addition, some of the autobiographers were

Introduction 3

aristocratic, and others were from poor or middle-class backgrounds. As such, the voices of different classes, perspectives, and experiences are heard. I have selected both canonical and noncanonical texts in an effort both to expand the female corpus and to explore textual authority. In addition, several of the works fall into various subcategories of autobiography: travel writing, letters, autobiographical novel, and diary. This allows for an exploration of why women writers at times have chosen personal forms often labeled as "feminine" (letters, diary)[6] as opposed to straightforward autobiography and why they often express life experiences through semifictional forms. It also permits a consideration of autobiography in various modes—the immediacy of a daily diary contrasts with the reflection of memoirs written in the autumn of life. The protagonists of these works range from writers, to princesses, to prostitutes, yet they all experience "awakening" in some way. The texts I analyze span approximately 150 years, from 1850 to 1997. The works are situated in various countries within and beyond Europe, namely, France, Italy, Turkey, Australia, and Algeria. In covering such a large area with regard to authorial perspective and genre, as well as temporally, geographically, and politically, I am able to articulate some broad conclusions concerning the evolution of women's autobiographical writing in general and French and Italian women's life writing in particular.

In Part I, "Leaving the Country," I analyze Cristina Trivulzio di Belgiojoso's[7] *Souvenirs dans l'exil* (1850; *Memoirs from Exile*) and *Emina* (1856; *Emina*).[8] I also consider Céleste Mogador's *Mémoires de Céleste Mogador* (1854; *Memoirs of Céleste Mogador*)[9] and its sequel, *Un deuil au bout du monde: Suite des Mémoires de Céleste Mogador* (1877; *Mourning at the Ends of the Earth: Sequel to the Memoirs of Céleste Mogador*).[10] Belgiojoso was an Italian princess who lived in exile in France and the Middle East for many years, and Céleste Mogador was a prostitute turned countess who fled to Australia with her husband. Both writers exploit the autobiographical subgenres of travel literature and letters in writing their life stories.

By reading *Souvenirs* and *Emina*, I explore Belgiojoso's Western feminism both in traditional autobiographical narrative (letters) and in veiled personal writing. In *Souvenirs*, written aboard the ship *Mentor* en route to the Middle East, the controversial Italian figure is able to view her past through various "biographical" portraits of selected women. In such a fashion, she strikes Eastern–Western comparisons and also makes social and political observations regarding strife in Italy and intellectual life in France. Her *bildung* is depicted through her reflection on her various exiles throughout her life and the growth that comes from physical and emotional wandering. In *Emina*, one of the Oriental tales that emerged from Belgiojoso's travels across Turkey and Syria, Belgiojoso herself figures as a traveler. She depicts Western culture and its views as superior to the Eastern civilization she encounters and, in fact, superimposes many of her own concerns onto her heroine, Emina. The young harem wife Emina's *bildung* provides an occasion for Belgiojoso to contemplate her own life. The text emerges as a meditation on the problem of sexual oppression in different cultures and a call to political action both at home and abroad.

With Céleste Mogador's fascinating *Mémoires*, an autobiography that reveals the singular experiences of an "exceptional" nineteenth-century heroine, I consider the common feminine practice of portraying a protagonist's *bildung* through her connection to others. Céleste's development is intertwined with the psychological evolution of her lover, Lionel de C***. The embedded male developmental plot parallels that of the heroine and highlights the different trajectories for male and female self-discovery in the mid-nineteenth century. Since French society of the time would not accept the union of a count and a woman of a *passé douteux*, the couple sets off for Australia to create a new life. This physical voyage, an outward manifestation of Mogador's emotional journey, is recounted in the sequel to the *Mémoires*, *Un deuil au bout du monde*. I explore in this text issues of separation and exile also prominent in Belgiojoso's work. Whereas *Mémoires* tells of Mogador's fall into prostitution and struggle to redeem herself, *Un deuil au bout du monde* presents the "reformed harlot." The text is also a *künstlerroman*, or birth-of-the-artist story, and outlines the impact of a writing career on the protagonist's self-definition.

In Part II, "Leaving the Family," I analyze Sibilla Aleramo's *Una donna* (1906; *A Woman*) and Oriana Fallaci's *Lettera a un bambino mai nato* (1975; *Letter to a Child Never Born*). *Una donna* is a pivotal text in that the author presents a modern heroine who breaks the chain of centuries of female suppression by fleeing an abusive marriage. Aleramo also treats the theme of motherhood as institution and the difficulty of successfully combining motherhood with a career. Like Mogador's *Un deuil au bout du monde*, *Una donna* also recounts the birth of a writer. This progressive piece manifests many of the feminist themes that are taken up in postmodern women's literature. As we move further into the twentieth century, not only is rage over gender oppression voiced more easily, but feminine issues, including women's sexuality, childbirth, and motherhood, are discussed more openly.

In *Lettera*, Fallaci responds to many of the topics raised in Aleramo's text. Fallaci's protagonist is a single woman contemplating motherhood. Her innovative monologue/dialogue with her unborn child allows for a discussion of women's roles, motherhood as institution, and abortion. Fallaci's forceful stance on these feminist concerns illustrates the distance women have journeyed from the turn of the century. Thanks to the feminist movement and the influx of women into the workforce, a new autobiographical subject emerges—a more confident self prepared to voice her anger and battle for her rights.

In Part III, "Leaving the Mother," I discuss Marie Cardinal's *Les mots pour le dire* (1975; *The Words to Say It: An Autobiographical Novel by Marie Cardinal*) as well as Annie Ernaux's *Une femme* (1987; *A Woman's Story*) and *"Je ne suis pas sortie de ma nuit"* (1997; *"I Have Not Escaped My Misery"*). In Cardinal's text, we have an exploration of the crucial mother–daughter relationship, a bond treated extensively in contemporary women's literature.

Through the narration of the heroine's maternal complex, extended battle with mental illness, and treatment in psychoanalysis, issues of expression, language, and communication with others come to the fore. The protagonist's journey to health parallels her voyage as a budding writer. In this *künstlerroman*, the healing powers of expression and community are key components to the heroine's liberation.

Annie Ernaux's *Une femme* and *"Je ne suis pas sortie de ma nuit"* again focus on the mother–daughter relationship. Each offers a daughter's account of her mother's life and slow deterioration because of Alzheimer's disease. Both postmodern texts are, in fact, biography and autobiography at the same time—the daughter's account of her spirited, working-class mother and her own story of evolution through education and talent. The writer/narrator's *bildung* can be read "in between" the two texts. Ernaux's introduction to *"Je ne suis pas sortie de ma nuit"* was written in 1996, subsequent to the diary entries that make up the text proper, and published in the 1997 edition of the auto/biography. As we trace Ernaux's development from her original diary excerpts in *"Je ne suis pas sortie de ma nuit,"* to the narrative *Une femme*, and finally to her introduction to *"Je ne suis pas sortie de ma nuit,"* we witness her struggle to situate herself within the literary elite. Through this emotional voyage, Ernaux provides a forum for fascinating discussion regarding class issues, language, and the mother–daughter bond. In this woman writer's tale of growth and maturation, however, the journey toward self-realization, which should include acceptance of her mother's passing, is inconclusive; her texts constitute initial chapters in an ongoing and unfinished story of selfhood.

WOMEN WRITERS, FEMINISM, AND THEORIES OF AUTOBIOGRAPHY: DEBATES AND TRENDS

Various approaches to women's writing have influenced the theory and criticism of female autobiographical production. Certain of these include revising the male-dominated canon, rewriting history and mythology from a feminist perspective, identifying an *écriture féminine* (female or feminine writing), establishing a tradition of women's writing, and employing the tools of postmodern and postcolonial theory and criticism to the analysis of women's texts.

Those who have focused on canon reform make the political claim that texts written by women must receive more attention than they have in the past, simply because until recently the literary canon has been predominantly male.[11] This approach has also been criticized, however, for occasionally favoring feminist values over literary excellence. In other words, who determines which texts enter "the new canon" and which criteria are involved in those decisions? Regardless of these critiques, however, there is still a need to continue to reconstruct the traditionally neglected corpus of women's writing because of what this process tells us about women's experiences and about women's early literary attempts. Akin to canon reformation is the work of "recovery" dear to historians and literary critics alike. This research seeks not only to publish "lost" texts by women (and other marginalized groups) but to rewrite the stories of historical and mythical figures incorporating feminist perspectives and contemporary research. Thus, Anna Banti reimagines and reinvents from scant historical record the life of the Renaissance painter Artemisia Gentileschi in the creative biography *Artemisia*.[12] Marie Cardinal offers a feminist revision of the traditional, negative reading of Clytemnestra in *Le passé empiété*.[13]

Critics who have focused on female specificity and on a particular type of *écriture féminine* in women's texts rely heavily on psychoanalysis as a means of exploring the unconscious.[14] This study of female "difference" is a common perspective among such French thinkers as Hélène Cixous and Luce Irigaray, though several differences of opinion exist. Cixous, Irigaray, and Julia Kristeva have often been grouped together as representatives of "French feminism," yet scholars have questioned the validity of such national labels. In "The Invention of French Feminism: An Essential Move," Christine Delphy even asserts that "French Feminism" is "an Anglo-American fabrication" (195), based more on the agenda of Anglo-American feminists than on actual happenings in France.[15] Critics of female "difference" have focused on the pitfalls of essentialism and its concepts of "woman," "female," or "feminine." In addition, the abstract nature of psychoanalytic and deconstructive endeavors can lead to the neglect of women's real experiences.

Scholars who read women's texts within the context of a female literary tradition find that women have influenced one another and written for and against each other for centuries.[16] Paola Blelloch finds that women read other women's writing as a process of identification. She states: "We women often

Introduction 7

read books by other women to find a confirmation of our identity. . . . Or still for a sense of solidarity after centuries of silence and solitude, or finally to explain sentiments which are still obscure and confused because they have been unexpectedly reawakened" (7).[17] Sidonie Smith and Julia Watson confirm that "women reading other women's autobiographical writings have experienced them as 'mirrors' of their own unvoiced aspirations" (5). This notion of exchange and sharing seems particularly important to women, both as a means of denouncing gender oppression and as an opportunity to voice their unique experiences, which have too often been considered trivial.

In their theoretical introduction to *Life/Lines* Bella Brodzki and Celeste Schenck consider women autobiographers within the context of the male tradition. In the masculine tradition of autobiography beginning with Augustine, the first premise was "the mirroring capacity of the autobiographer: *his* universality, *his* representativeness, *his* role as spokesman for the community" (Brodski and Schenck 1). Brodzki and Schenck posit that because of her "lack of tradition, her marginality in male-dominated culture, [and] her fragmentation" (1), the female autobiographer has "lacked the sense of radical individuality, duplicitous but useful, that empowered Augustine and Henry Adams to write their representative lives large" (1). Yet, not only do scholars continue to establish a female literary tradition, but numerous women's life stories, including George Sand's *Histoire de ma vie* (*Story of My Life: The Autobiography of George Sand*), Aleramo's *Una donna*, and Ernaux's autobiographical novel *Les armoires vides* (*Cleaned Out*), do depict a "sense of radical individuality" in the portraits of their immature protagonists. This is often reflected in the young girl's confidence in her intelligence or uniqueness. However, this self-assurance is frequently cut short for various reasons when the young girl reaches adolescence. Brodzki and Schenck discuss the authority that masculine autobiographies wield because of the assumption held by both author and reader that the life being written and/or read is an exemplary one. They point out that the autobiographies of such noted figures as Augustine, Jean-Jacques Rousseau, and Adams "rest upon the Western ideal of an essential and inviolable self, which . . . unifies and propels the narrative" (5). Although they see a different dynamic in women's life writing and refuse a facile identification between author and autobiographical protagonist, Brodzki and Schenck caution against postmodern theory's erasure of the subject as a perilous move for feminism's political agenda. They explain that "the feminist enterprise should . . . provide the emotional satisfaction historically missing for the female reader, that assurance and consolation that she does indeed exist in the world which a femininity defined in purely textual terms cannot provide" (14).

Brodzki and Schenck posit that the postmodern fragmented, divided self, an intentionally nonrepresentative self, exemplified in Roland Barthes' *Roland Barthes par Roland Barthes* (*Roland Barthes by Roland Barthes*), has much in common with female subjectivity (5–6). They offer as examples the autobiographical ventures of Margaret Cavendish and Gertrude Stein in their discussion of the common feminine practice of replacing singularity with "alterity" and of defining oneself in relation to significant others (7–12). Their premise is much influenced by studies in object relations psychology from the 1970s and 1980s. Critics such as Nancy Chodorow, for example, emphasize the primary attachment between mother and child during the preoedipal phase. In *The Reproduction of Mothering*, Chodorow posits that boys learn to separate themselves from their mothers during the oedipal phase, whereas girls remain bound to that initial relationship. She observes that as a result of different childhood experiences, women's and men's inner object worlds are different—women define themselves and experience themselves more relationally, whereas men feel more autonomous. This vision of self in relation to significant others (parents, husbands, lovers, and friends) is common to several of the autobiographers I study. However, one also finds such connections influential in male autobiographical writing.

Recently, Nancy K. Miller challenged the notion of female "relationality" as opposed to male autonomy ("Representing Others"). Through an examination of such postmodern texts as Jacques Derrida's *Circonfession. Jacques Derrida* and Art Spigelman's *Maus: A Survivor's Tale*, Miller finds that certain male-authored works exhibit "precisely the structure of self-portrayal through the relation to a privileged other that characterizes most female-authored autobiography" ("Representing Others" 4). She encourages more thinking on issues of gender identity and concludes that autobiographical practices might eventually "be mapped along a continuum of relatedness and autonomy which often but not always coincides with gendered signatures" ("Representing Others" 18).

Indeed, much criticism from the 1980s to the present couples interest in women's texts and women's studies with trends in postmodernism. In "Feminism and Postmodernism," Linda Hutcheon discusses the "renewed interest . . . in the socially and historically specific, the particular, the de-centered (or ex-centric) of our culture: the local, the regional, the ethnic, the female" (25). Both feminism and postmodern thought have challenged the liberal humanist notion of Man, including assumptions of autonomy, transcendence, unity, truth, and the essential nature of men and women. According to Hutcheon, feminist practice has "joined with the postmodern in moving us away from general universal *T*ruth, to specific, contextualized *t*ruth*S*" (37). Furthermore, it has also forced us to see gender in relation to the power struggle, "not as natural, unchangeable power relations, but as constructed by particular social, economic and political forces" (Hutcheon 37). It is important to note, however, that as women's roles evolve, their status as marginalized individuals changes as well. More and more women writers today speak from positions of power and influence.

Finally, contemporary postcolonial criticism has impacted the practice of ethnic autobiography, an area that has led to an eruption of numerous women's voices. Smith and Watson discuss studies on Latina women's autobiography,

Native American oral narratives, and working-class writings (*Women, Autobiography, Theory* 14). In French, the area of Francophone studies has celebrated female narratives from Canada, the Caribbean, and Africa, for example, and analyzed the impact of multicultural and postcolonial experiences on women's identities. Scholars in Italian studies have considered exchanges between Italy and Slavic countries and have also incorporated Italian American autobiographical texts into critical discussions of selfhood. Smith and Watson explain that through reconsidering autobiography in terms of the politics of these differences, scholars have "challenged theories that posit a universal woman—implicitly white, bourgeois, and Western—and that presume to speak on her behalf" (26). Indeed, the authors I study are mainly "white, bourgeois, and Western," and yet their wanderings have brought them to lands and cultures beyond Europe, and their self-portraits, specifically in the cases of Belgiojoso and Cardinal, are often represented through non-Western women of color from different classes. The riveting textual dialogue between author and (autobiographically informed) character in their texts speaks to the complicated nature of identity in women who transgress countless borders. Mogador and Ernaux also tackle class issues in representing their humble backgrounds and the tensions that arise when they venture into the world of the literary elite.

TRADITIONS IN FRENCH AND ITALIAN AUTOBIOGRAPHY: WOMEN WRITING WITHIN AND AGAINST THE CANON

As autobiographical writing itself has evolved over the centuries, so has the place of women writers within that genre. They have at times imitated the male-dominated canonical life stories and at other times explicitly marked out alternative agendas. Often women writers have had to dispute stereotypical images of women. More recently, female authors have gone in new directions, not merely responding to, or rebelling against, male autobiographical models or men's representations of women in literature; they have begun to create their own narrative forms and explore feminine themes and character portraits with greater freedom. Germaine Brée reminds us to ask continually what strategies women who write their lives have adopted "to free themselves from the images of role personae and desire encoded in their language[.] How have they moved beyond silence to speech, engendered through writing alternative motives and myths?" (ix).

I do not attempt an exhaustive history of autobiography or of women's writing, but I point to certain types of personal narratives in which women have traditionally excelled. I consider these female autobiographers in the context of the male and female canons of life writing. In addition, I analyze the strategies these women employ in their life stories in order to resist conventional female images. Many of these techniques, because they reflect resistance to the status quo, create great uneasiness. Finally, I examine the radical changes in women's lives and in postmodern autobiographical literature that influence female life writing today.

Although only a limited number of women's texts entered the canon prior to the 1970s, and women writers were far from the norm, one can point to particular forms and predecessors that influenced nineteenth- and twentieth-century female autobiographers.[18] Several women, including Margery Kempe, Catherine of Siena, Teresa of Avila, and Madame Guyon, for example, composed spiritual autobiographies in the tradition of Augustine.[19] However, these women also distinguish themselves from the male tradition. In the medieval text *The Book of Margery Kempe*, for instance, the fact that Kempe is a woman influences her Christianity. According to Janel M. Mueller, Kempe "signals the fulfillment of her spirituality and selfhood through an expansion of her wifely and maternal concerns to encompass all the souls of Christendom in homely love" (67). Letter writing was also a dominant female form until the mid-nineteenth century.[20] Isabella d'Este's extensive correspondence offers a vivid portrait of Renaissance culture, as do the letters of Alessandra Macinghi Strozzi.[21] Macinghi Strozzi's letters to her children, written in Florentine dialect, are "still today, one of the principal sources for sociological and cultural studies on the 1400s in Italy" (Costa-Zalessow 12). Madame de Sévigné's seventeenth-century letters to her daughter are invaluable for their commentaries on interpersonal ties and on the mother–daughter relationship, topics that remains dear to women autobiographers today. Her correspondence also inscribes feelings of "conflict between the mother's love for her daughter and her love of writing" (Goldsmith 97). Memoir writing was also a genre frequently practiced by women in the seventeenth and eighteenth centuries. Caterina Camilla Faà writes in her memoirs of her secret marriage to Duke Ferdinando Gonzaga, a union that was later annulled so that the duke could marry Caterina de' Medici.[22] Faà, who was banished from the court and then spent forty years of her life as a nun, incorporates themes of betrayal and entrapment in her text, issues that continue to emerge in women's life writing today. In these early examples of memoirs and letters, women frequently reveal personal perspectives on history and subtly voice their struggles within a patriarchal society.

Related to letter writing is the *roman par lettres*, or epistolary novel, practiced from the eighteenth to early nineteenth centuries by many women such as Madame Riccoboni, Isabelle de Charrière, Madame de Duras, and Madame de Staël. Consider, for example, Riccoboni's 1757 *Lettres de Mistress Fanni Butlerd* (*Letters from Mistress Fanni Butlerd*), a novel that sparked debate over its possible autobiographical inspiration. In this type of epistolary novel, the letters, which may be fictional, are often presented as "authentic" and serve as a frame within which the novel unfolds. Women also wrote first-person *romans intimes*, a term coined by Sainte-Beuve, which were sometimes in letter form.[23]

The autobiographical novel, popular among such nineteenth-century women writers as Madame de Staël, George Sand, and Matilde Serao, led the way for twentieth-century texts that fuse fictional and autobiographical elements. In the twentieth century, however, writers have further challenged the boundaries between autobiography and fiction in a self-conscious fashion, questioning the possibility of a unified self, the validity of memory, and the notion of "truth."

Although several of these women from previous centuries entered the literary canon through imitating men, female authors also refuted male models. Whereas Madame Roland imitated Rousseau's frankness in her *Mémoires* (*Memoirs*), written while she was in prison in the late eighteenth century, her autobiographical pact has nothing of Rousseau's confidence ("Moi, seul" (33) ["Me, alone"]). Instead, we hear: "Je me propose d'employer les loisirs de ma captivité à retracer ce qui m'est personnel depuis ma tendre enfance jusqu'à ce moment . . . qu'a-t-on de mieux à faire en prison que de transporter ailleurs son existence par une heureuse fiction, ou par des souvenirs intéressants?" (1–2) ("I propose to spend the leisure time of my captivity in retracing my life from my tender childhood until now . . . what better to do while in prison than to transport oneself elsewhere by a happy fiction or by interesting memories?"). Her unassuming tone is, in fact, quite characteristic of women's autobiographies of the time. Furthermore, such self-deprecation persists into the nineteenth century. In her *Dix années d'exil* (*Ten Years of Exile*), for example, Staël writes: "Ce n'est pas pour occuper le public de moi que j'ai résolu de raconter les circonstances de dix années d'exil; les malheurs que j'ai éprouvés . . . sont si peu de chose au milieu des désastres publics dont nous sommes témoins, qu'on aurait honte de parler de soi" (1) ("It is not to occupy the public with me that I decided to recount the circumstances of ten years of exile; the ordeals that I have suffered . . . are so insignificant amidst the public disasters which we have witnessed that one would be ashamed to speak of oneself"). The late-nineteenth-century writer Neera echoes similar views in her letter "A Luigi Capuana." In the letter, which serves as a preface to Neera's autobiographical *Il castigo* (*The Punishment*), she explains that among her many reasons for embarking upon an autobiographical project is the fact that her doctor has forbidden her "occupazioni del pensiero" (8) ("occupations of the mind"). A self-examination constitutes, for Neera, "una occupazione leggiera" (8) ("a light activity"). The modest tone of these eighteenth- and nineteenth-century women can also be read as a frequent female strategy of the era and beyond. They write *comme il faut* so that their stories will be published but at the same time subtly incorporate into their texts discussions of the serious issues of the day and pleas for personal notoriety. Edward Gilpin Johnson notes that her *Mémoires* were Roland's first concern and that she was eager to "secure in history the esteem that her own times had denied her" (19).

Sand, already an established writer by the time she embarks on her life story, again draws on Rousseau in her mid-nineteenth-century *Histoire de ma vie*. Like several of her contemporaries, including Daniel Stern (Marie d'Agoult), Sand still felt pressure to use a male pen name. However, female autobiographical production increased in Sand's era when women of diverse classes took up the pen. A changing society and new roles for women impacted women's autobiographical writing. Sand, for instance, is not afraid to explicitly distance herself from Rousseau. Although both writers emphasize the importance of feelings and sensations as well as the themes of Nature, social justice, spirituality, and the transcendence of the soul, Sand refuses to reveal intimate details of her sexual life in her life story (common to women autobiographers of the time for obvious reasons). She also chooses not to expose compromising information about people who were still alive. She states: "Il n'y a point d'erreur dont quelqu'un ne soit la cause ou le complice, et il est impossible de s'accuser sans accuser le prochain. . . . C'est ce qui est arrivé à Rousseau, et cela est mal" (I: 13; II: 114) ("There is no error to which someone is not the cause or accomplice, and it is impossible to accuse ourselves without accusing the next one. . . . That is what happened to Rousseau, and that is unfortunate").[24]

Because of greater mobility in the nineteenth century, women also experimented with travel writing. In travel literature, autobiographical subjects are situated in a broader context—woman as explorer, foreigner, social reformer. Whereas men could easily travel alone in the name of adventure or politics, women often had to justify their voyages, particularly if they traveled without a husband. Princess Cristina di Belgiojoso and Céleste Mogador are joined by other adventurous women who journeyed beyond European borders, including Flora Tristan and Amalia Solla Nizzoli.

Women autobiographers also responded to the political climate. In France, particularly from the mid-nineteenth century onward, memorialists such as Tristan, Suzanne Voilquin, and Louise Michel explored class issues, labor reform, and socialist and communist themes. In Italy, the *Risorgimento* was recalled by such autobiographers as Antonietta Giacomelli. Women like Staël, followed by Tristan, Stern, Sand, Belgiojoso, and others, began demanding the privilege of writing more extensively in typically "male genres" such as history, politics, and philosophy. In the nineteenth century, they often encountered much hostility, and their writing was subject to biased readings by critics and historians.

Many nineteenth-century women autobiographers and novelists opposed stereotypical images of women and employed various strategies to subtly undercut such prejudices.[25] First, tragic scenarios indirectly criticized gender oppression. Staël expresses the frustration of her very talented heroine in *Corinne ou l'Italie* (*Corinne or Italy*), a novel with significant autobiographical components. The intelligent and flamboyant Corinne knows she will never fit into a traditional marriage and family life with her beloved Oswald. He eventually marries the proper young Lucile, and Corinne's unrequited love leads to her death. This tragic ending presents a critical portrait of the condition of women—the writer, in fact, refuses to allow her heroine to survive in an unjust world. Writers such as the Marchesa Colombi in *Un matrimonio in provincia* (*A Country Marriage*) also confront gender oppression through analyses of the institutions of marriage and motherhood. Next, women cast such "masculine" qualities as ambition or even intelligence into more acceptable "feminine" traits—the clever woman who used her wits to "catch" a husband rather than exercise her influence in a profession or in politics. In addition, female authors discouraged clichéd portrayals of women in literature by creating paired female characters. In texts such as Sand's *Indiana*, the two feminine protagonists reflect different aspects of a woman and hence advocate more realistic female images. Finally, women authors spoke out directly against prejudicial views. For example, Neera criticizes the cliché of woman as angel or whore in her letter "A Luigi Capuana." She writes: "Gli uomini . . . dividono le donne in due categorie. . . . Tu—dicono all'una—pascerai il mio corpo; all'altra: Sarai il raggio dell'anima mia . . . . Ma di queste divisioni la natura non tiene conto" (10) ("Men . . . divide women into two categories. . . . You—they say to one—will nourish my body; to the other: You will be the light of my soul. . . . But nature does not allow for these divisions"). Neera proclaims that the female protagonist in *Il castigo* will represent something new and different: "Laura [nel *Castigo*] è un tipo umano. In lei vivono . . . i palpiti di mille donne. Sicuro non è simpatica, ma passò quel tempo in cui le eroine di un romanzo dovevano essere simpatiche ad ogni costo. Ella è meno e più che simpatica. È infelice" ("A Luigi Capuana" 11) ("Laura [in *Il castigo*] is a human being. In her the heartbeats of thousands of women live.... Surely, she is not nice, but the era in which heroines had to be sweet at all costs has passed. She is more and less than nice. She is unhappy").

It is understandable that the reaction to the nineteenth-century woman writer was often intimidation and uncertainty. The fear that her ideas might incite other women to step outside traditional family roles created quite a stir. Women who ventured outside the domestic circle constituted a threat to family life. By extension, the makeup of society and humanity at large was called into question. In her study on the nineteenth-century woman writer, Christine Planté points out that women's writing "risk[s] proposing other values, other images, and introducing them into the private lives of their readers.... The *author* holds an *authority* which is not granted to just anyone" (37).

Planté explains that because she was a novelty, the nineteenth-century woman writer was often considered "exceptional" (273–82). Certain interpretations of the exceptional, however, led to views of such women as marginal and strange and incited images of the "monstrous" female. Planté discusses the consequences of such ideas in regard to female self-image and identity. Seeing oneself as the exception seems to "admit the existence of the rule" (Planté 276). Women writers were blatantly "different," and for some this isolation led to insecurities about their femininity.

At the same time, many women authors experienced a "nostalgia for the ordinary," a desire to be seen as "not-so-exceptional-as-all-that" (Planté 282).[26] Many women writers valued their roles in the domestic circle and preferred to be seen as wives and mothers first, writers second. Much of this "nostalgia for the ordinary" grew out of a concern regarding readers' impressions. This exceptional/ordinary duality is played out in women's literary texts as well. The exceptional woman becomes a "double," a "negative" of the ordinary one, and the latter is both fascinated by, and contemptuous of, the former (Planté 282). Planté explains that while we find many heroines, like Sand's Lélia, who were considered excessive and scandalous, the nineteenth century also produces banal and mediocre female figures (283). The latter appear not only because women authors wanted to appease their readers but because on a certain level they aspired to be ordinary themselves (Planté 283).

In the early to mid-twentieth century, the evolution of gender roles and feminist consciousness impacted women's notions of selfhood and influenced their life stories. Clichéd views of women persisted, but numerous autobiographers and critics challenged facile assumptions. Aleramo struggles to define womanhood and challenge traditional motherhood in *Una donna*. In *A Room of One's Own*, Virginia Woolf encourages women to express themselves, even in the male-dominated fields of history and politics. Simone de Beauvoir explores "woman" as a cultural creation in her groundbreaking *Le deuxième sexe* (1949; *The Second Sex*).

With the impact of the rebellious 1960s and the women's movement of the 1970s, various oppressed groups begin to express their anger. Women resist sexist female stereotypes and openly seek power. Whereas in the past, women writers manipulated such narrative strategies as the use of a modest tone of voice in order to conceal ambitious aims or subtly seek justice, women of the contemporary era speak out, justify, defend their right to determine their own paths and have an influence over others' lives. Carolyn G. Heilbrun discusses the evolution of female experiences, which has pushed women to find new structures for their life stories and to expand old models that did not accurately or fully portray the events in contemporary women's lives. She considers the 1970s as a turning point in women's autobiographical writing in particular. At this point, according to Heilbrun, women began writing "honest" life stories that told of anger, refused to accept pain without protest, and dared to reveal a desire for power and recognition. Women are also discovering innovative ways to write about their quest for freedom through greater experimentation with feminine themes. The body, for example, is a prevalent focus in much female autobiographical writing in the modern and postmodern periods. However, women's frank depictions of sexuality are still laden with prejudices. Hélène Cixous calls for freedom to explore the female body and promotes an *écriture féminine* in her feminist essays and "autobiographical manifestos," such as "Le rire de la méduse" ("The Laugh of the Medusa").[27] Oriana Fallaci's *Lettera a un bambino mai nato* explores issues of sexuality and abortion. Annie Ernaux's *Passion simple* (*Simple Passion*) delves into the erotic. Whereas among male authors Jean Cocteau explores homosexuality in his life writing, Violette Leduc and Monique Wittig grapple with lesbian identities in their texts.

Contemporary psychoanalytical findings have led to new kinds of women's self-portraiture. First, while Augustine, Petrarch, and Rousseau could situate themselves in a tradition of fathers and sons in literature, the mother–daughter relationship is central to twentieth-century women's personal narratives. Postmodern writers such as Fallaci, Cardinal, and Ernaux reflect on the writings of Aleramo and Beauvoir, not to mention those of Sand and Neera, their literary "mothers." Throughout the century, women writers contemplate the charged mother–daughter relationship, which impacts the understanding and the writing of the self. Next, discoveries that dispute the possibility of a unified subject or of a definitive life story also inform women's autobiographies. Writers such as Cardinal, Ernaux, and Marguerite Duras offer several possible versions of their life stories in an incessant and often inconclusive search for self-understanding.

The evolution of women's autobiography, the "voyage out" of the male-dominated autobiographical canon, is indeed giving birth to exciting new efforts in the area of female subjectivities. We are hearing more and more the voices of mothers, daughters, sisters, and female lovers writing their own experiences.

WOMEN'S AUTOBIOGRAPHY AS *BILDUNGSROMAN*: GENDER AND GENRE

Women writers of autobiography frequently exploit the *bildungsroman* genre in expressing their personal stories. Yet when the protagonist of a *bildungsroman* is a woman, her passage from youth to adulthood consists of different obstacles from those that men encounter, and society has different expectations of her. The various criteria that have come to define the traditional male *bildungsroman*—novel of formation or novel of development—must often be rewritten when it comes to women's texts; gender often clashes with genre. I first present the conventional definition of the *bildungsroman* and discuss the European tradition of the genre. Then, I examine particular criteria that must be considered when dealing with women's texts. In the next section, I discuss some of the similarities and differences between autobiography and novels of development.

From a chronological standpoint, it is generally accepted that Goethe's *Wilhelm Meister's Apprenticeship* is the prototype for the *bildungsroman*, which had been considered a primarily German genre. Recent studies have placed it within a European context, emphasizing variations on the *bildungsroman* theme depending on the national tradition being studied. In Goethe's novel, the young hero undergoes a series of adventures, encounters, and disappointments, all part of the "growing up" process. As he assimilates certain conventional expectations and prejudices, Wilhelm comes to know himself and his place in society. François Jost explains: "The last page of the volume will show us a mature man . . . sure of himself. . . . In fact, these experiences, these ordeals and misfortunes are for Wilhelm . . . the tools which enable him to train himself, keeping in mind the great trials which mark men's lives" (104). And women? How will they be equipped for their "women's lives"? The tools they acquire in their *bildung*, or formation, are necessarily different. These are the issues I consider in detail in this study.

Franco Moretti considers the nineteenth-century *bildungsroman* as a product of a transitional historical moment in Europe. Revolutions, new regimes, and the rising bourgeoisie influenced European mentalities, and individuals adapted to the new era of what Moretti calls "modernity." He therefore sees the changing, growing protagonist of the *bildungsroman* as a reflection of an evolving society. Young, vibrant heroes and heroines live in a world characterized by mobility. With the *bildungsroman*: "is born naturally a new hero—Wilhelm Meister. And after him, Elizabeth Bennett and Julien Sorel, Rastignac and Frédéric Moreau and Bel-Ami, Waverly and David Copperfield, Renzo Tramaglino, Evgenij Onegin, Bazarov, Dorothea Brooke. . . . In sum, youth" (Moretti 9–10). For Moretti, the "novel of formation" becomes the symbolic form of modernity (12–13).

Marianne Hirsch outlines the German, English, and French traditions of this type of writing in her article "The Novel of Formation as Genre: Between Great Expectations and Lost Illusions." She points to several characteristics of the

Introduction

novel of formation that are useful to my study, although they come to be modified when viewed in relation to women's texts. They include the focus on one central character, which incorporates the story of an individual's "*growth and development* within the context of a defined social order"; the emphasis on biographical and social contexts, with society as the novel's "antagonist"; the novel of formation's plot as a version of the quest story; a search for meaningful existence and values that allows for the protagonist's inner capacities to unfold; an emphasis on the development of selfhood, which incorporates an apprenticeship rather than a full biography; a narrative point of view and voice characterized by irony and distance vis-à-vis the inexperienced hero rather than nostalgia for youth; the novel's other characters serving as educators, companions, lovers; and finally, the novel of formation as a didactic novel that "educates the reader by portraying the education of the protagonist" ("The Novel of Formation" 296–98). Jerome Hamilton Buckley notes additional important features of the genre, including the importance of reading in the development of the imagination; tensions between the hero and his family, particularly his father; and a flight from "the repressive atmosphere of the home" to independent life in the city (17). In women's novels of formation, heroines share certain components with heroes in the quest for selfhood. However, their journeys differ in specific ways as well. For example, daughters often struggle with mothers, rather than fathers, in their quests for independence. Women may long for growth and fusion in a society that considers them "other" from the outset. As Elizabeth Abel, Marianne Hirsch, and Elizabeth Langland have pointed out, in the female *bildungsroman*, conflict arises between "the assumptions of a genre that embodies male norms and the values of its female protagonists" (*The Voyage In* 11).

In the nineteenth century in particular, women's choices for development are few, and therefore their *bildung* cannot be measured in the same terms as that of male protagonists. The typical developmental path for women does not send them out into the world, and their desires to explore and voyage are frequently stifled. Gender limitations often confine female protagonists to the home, interpersonal relationships, and their influence in the domestic sphere. Nineteenth-century autobiographies and novels offer a variety of developmental stories. In Sand's *Histoire de ma vie*, Aurore's partly aristocratic family and her social milieu trace a certain path that a proper young woman is encouraged to follow. In Mogador's *Mémoires*, Céleste's social circle of prostitutes and entertainers provides quite another. Cristina di Belgiojoso's protagonist in *Emina* is caught in the extremely limited female role of harem wife. This culminates in an impossible situation and leads to the heroine's death. Yet in all of these texts there exist certain common points regarding the protagonists' maturation as women, their relationships with others, and their confrontation with society.

Much critical attention has been dedicated to the split between the male-focused *bildungsroman* and the female-centered "novel of awakening."

Although I do not relegate women's texts to one category or the other exclusively, critics' findings regarding the "novel of awakening," also called the "novel of self-discovery," are useful in analyzing the nineteenth- and twentieth-century texts I have chosen. For example, these works all portray exceptional female characters whose growth occurs through a confrontation with obstacles that are particularly significant for women. In the nineteenth century, these range from presumptions about marriage, to prejudices concerning prostitution, to pressures on women writers. Turn-of-the-century texts treat obstacles ranging from divorce laws to expectations regarding motherhood. Twentieth-century works consider the impact of the abortion debate, psychoanalysis, and new understandings of the mother–daughter relationship. All the protagonists in the autobiographical texts I study undergo learning and achieve heightened self-understanding; they all *change* in some way, though the outcome is not always optimistic. Contemporary texts tend to present increased possibilities for female integration in society and more flexible gender roles. I do not view the categories of *bildungsroman* and "novel of awakening" as exclusive because, especially when reading autobiographical texts, there is a great deal of overlap between them. Life stories often, but not always, take on a linear pattern of the traditional *bildungsroman*. A great many autobiographical texts written by both men and women include a spiritual awakening or conversion similar to that found in "novels of awakening." I discuss the critical distinctions that have arisen concerning these various classifications, and they inform my reading. But rather than limiting women's texts to one category or another, I focus on the important elements in the formation process.

Whereas the traditional *bildungsroman* focuses on an outward, linear movement that allows the male protagonist to achieve self-realization through becoming a contributing member of society, Susan J. Rosowski finds that the "novel of awakening" instead illustrates the heroine's inward, vertical movement toward self-knowledge (49). According to Rosowski, in texts by men and women, such as Gustave Flaubert's *Madame Bovary* and George Eliot's *Middlemarch*, female protagonists often experience an "awakening to limitations"—a realization that their choices for social activity are few in comparison to those available to their male counterparts (49).

In their collection concerning nineteenth- and twentieth-century women's developmental texts, Abel, Hirsch, and Langland similarly identify two dominant patterns: first, the apprenticeship, which mirrors the *bildungsroman's* linear structure, and second, the awakening, in which development is characterized not by stages but rather by "epiphanic moments" or internal "flashes of recognition" (*The Voyage In* 11–12). In both of these structures, a surface plot often conforms to social conventions, while a submerged plot inscribes revolt; there is sometimes a disjunction between "a plot governed by age-old female story patterns, such as myths and fairy tales, and a plot that reconceives these limiting possibilities" (12).[28] Furthermore, women characters, more psychologically embedded in relationships, sometimes share the formative voyage with friends, sisters, or mothers, who assume equal status as protagonists (12).

The twentieth-century *bildungsroman* frequently strays from the traditional model, as notions of growth and development are often satirized, and the idea of a unified subject becomes a necessary fiction rather than a naïvely accepted truth. Rita Felski explains that critics view the *bildungsroman* as "a form inadequate to the modern consciousness," and therefore it "can continue to exist only in a parodied form" (137). However, Felski adds that "novels written by women writers in recent years suggest that the *Bildungsroman* may well be acquiring a new function as an articulation of women's new sense of identity and increasing movement into public life" (137). In the twentieth century, many women writers take on the task of sending their female protagonists out into the world rather than condemning them to the limited interiors of marriage and the family common to texts from the previous century. Aleramo's turn-of-the-century *Una donna* presents a turning point in women's writing. She illustrates how difficult it is for a woman to combine family life and a career, relationship and autonomy. Subsequent examples, such as Ernaux's *Les armoires vides*, Fallaci's *Lettera a un bambino mai nato*, and Cardinal's *Les mots pour le dire*, all published in the 1970s, offer contemporary versions of the female *bildungsroman*.[29] Indeed, Laura Sue Fuderer notes that "[d]iscussions of the female bildungsroman began to appear in the critical literature in the early 1970s, when critics recognized its rise as a reflection of the contemporary feminist movement" (2). The *bildungsroman* is still viable today, though often in a modified form. This is evident in works such as Ernaux's *La honte* (*Shame*), published in 1997, which depicts a mature female narrator's reflections on the impact of a particularly painful moment in her adolescence. Current novels of development illustrate both the new opportunities for female independence and the modern-day prejudices still stifling women's growth. This literary form, which stages individual development and self-discovery, or its parody, which questions such progress, continues to satisfy many women writers as they expand on existing inscriptions of female experiences in their texts and solidify their place in the canon.

In her study of contemporary French and German literature, Elaine Martin discusses the heroine's "confrontation with society" ("Theoretical Soundings" 52). Heroines, like heroes, experience death and rebirth, but the greater self-understanding that leads to rebirth, "awakening," or "resurfacing" for female characters often leads to social alienation ("Theoretical Soundings" 49). Instead of the patterns of "separation-transition-incorporation" envisioned by Joseph Campbell, Martin finds that women's texts, including Christiane Rochefort's *Les stances à Sophie* (*Cats Don't Care for Money*), often display one of "isolation-rebirth-separation" ("Theoretical Soundings" 49).

Felski identifies a range of contemporary novels that "narrate the emancipation of the female protagonist" (132).[30] She gives a thorough analysis of the basic stages in the contemporary female novel of self-discovery. They include opening stages that typically "situate the heroine in a marital or heterosexual relationship which is portrayed as oppressive and alienating" and which often emphasizes the "restrictive nature of female social roles" (Felski 133). Rather than killing off the heroine as a means of social protest, however, which we see in nineteenth-century texts such as Staël's *Corinne* or Belgiojoso's *Emina*, Felski argues that texts from the 1970s and 1980s trace the protagonist's gradual development toward self-awareness. Contemporary novels of self-discovery feature a "new narrative model" that includes "the survival of the heroine" (Felski 134). Similar to Rosowski and Abel, Hirsch, and Langland, Felski employs the term "awakening" to characterize the heroine's consciousness of her potential independence (134). In texts such as Margaret Atwood's *Surfacing* and Marilyn French's *The Women's Room*, this awakening is represented through some sort of departure or act of separation from the repressive environment (Felski 134). Felski adds that the most significant element of this model is that "the impulse comes from within; identity is perceived as internal rather than socially produced" (134). In opposition to the traditional *bildungsroman*, Felski emphasizes that "[a]wakening . . . suggests a self-enclosed moment, rather than a historical process" (141). She describes several recurring motifs in the novel of awakening, such as the escape from history, the overcoming of fragmentation, the rejection of civilization, and language as alienation (141–43). In Atwood's *Surfacing*, for example, the heroine retreats from her unsatisfactory life in society to the Canadian wilderness. According to Felski, the act of departure sets the protagonist on her path of discovery, which cannot be completed until she experiences isolation in nature.

Felski's findings are relevant to the contemporary women writers I study, all of whose heroines journey toward self-knowledge through some type of separation or departure: Fallaci's protagonist "leaves the (patriarchal) family," and Cardinal's and Ernaux's main characters "leave the mother" in their own ways in order to attempt to find themselves. However, my analysis traces protagonists' various forms of separation from oppressive structures as far back as the nineteenth century—departures that make way for the journeys of future heroines.

Introduction

COMMON ELEMENTS AND DISTINCTIONS BETWEEN AUTOBIOGRAPHY AND *BILDUNGSROMAN*

When one reads autobiography through the lens of the *bildungsroman* and examines the various developmental phases in women's individuation, certain features of the two genres coincide, while others remain distinct. In noting the points of intersection between life writing and developmental literature, Jost claims that "there is hardly a *Bildungsroman* which is not, in fact, a sort of slightly fictitious autobiography in which the action grows out of a philosophical and didactic base" (100). For these reasons, he considers Saint Augustine's *Confessions*, Cellini's *Vita* (*Life*), Hobbes' *Vita* (*Life*), and Restif de la Bretonne's *Monsieur Nicolas* as distant models of the *bildungsroman* in some ways, and he pays particular attention to Stendhal's *Vie de Henry Brulard* (*Life of Henry Brulard*). Buckley emphasizes the subjective nature of many *bildungsromane*, which may "[gain] in immediacy and authenticity from the novelist's intimate knowledge of his materials" (26). He calls the genre "the most oblique and richly creative" of the autobiographical forms (27). As I compare the two genres, I pay particular attention to the following elements: narration, character development (including the protagonist's relation to secondary characters and to society), and the structure of the text.

Most autobiographies are in the first person, and a great many *bildungsromane*, including Charles Dickens' *Great Expectations* and Charlotte Brontë's *Jane Eyre*, use this narration as well. Sometimes the "mature narrator's" perspective common to autobiography is also a feature of the *bildungsroman*. Whereas the protagonist of the traditional novel of formation is meant to mature and assimilate his or her societal role, the autobiographer may at times endeavor to represent his or her main character's uniqueness, marginality, or exceptional nature. In autobiographical texts, the assumed identity between the author (even if a pseudonym is used), narrator, and protagonist creates a privileged narrative situation. The self-reflexive nature of autobiographical or pseudoautobiographical texts informs our reading. Techniques of irony and distancing between narrator and inexperienced hero, which are common in the *bildungsroman*, can also be found in life stories such as Stendhal's *Vie de Henry Brulard* in the nineteenth century and in the autobiographical works of Italo Svevo in the twentieth century. This ironic gaze is not necessarily the norm, however, as is exemplified in life writing of Rousseau and François-René de Chateaubriand. Also, certain subgenres of autobiography, such as diaries and letters, tend to illustrate an immediacy rather than temporal distance between narrator and main character.

In women's texts, the first-person narrator has a privileged status. Whereas the omniscient narrator who casts the protagonist as "she" may often succumb to traditional expectations for women, the "agency" of the first-person narrator is able to subvert accepted roles and scenarios more easily because it proposes a subjective viewpoint. In *Living Stories, Telling Lives*, Joanne S. Frye discusses the frequency of first-person narration in women's texts and the potential force of that personal voice. She reiterates the critical notion that women novelists have always been "telling lives . . . not literally telling their own lives, but finding in the flexibility of the novel form a capacity for conveying their subjective perceptions" (8). She explains: "To speak directly in a personal voice is to deny the exclusive right of male author-ity implicit in a public voice and to escape the expression of dominant ideologies upon which an omniscient narrator depends" (51). In women's autobiography, where authors strive to relate lived experiences, the potential for subverting established views is even greater. Frye also points out that women commonly use a palimpsestic narrative, a double-voiced discourse, which has traditionally allowed for an undermining of the dominant text. We recall the *other* voice in Nathalie Sarraute's *Enfance* (*Childhood*), for example, which continually questions, echoes, and subverts the "I." The dialogue between the narrator and her "double" enables the latter to express her hesitation in writing the life story. It also allows Sarraute to explore the act of remembering and challenge the limits of autobiographical form. To a certain degree the play of "I/You" in Oriana Fallaci's *Lettera a un bambino mai nato* is also an example of this type of narration.

With regard to character development, identity formation is somewhat distinct in the two genres. Whereas the *bildungsroman* has a "dual focus, inward toward the self and outward toward society" (Hirsch, "The Novel of Formation" 300), introspection is paramount in autobiography. Identities are often defined according to, or counter to, social conventions and expectations, and personal understanding takes precedence over societal assimilation. The formative role played by secondary characters in the development of the protagonist is significant in both genres. Wilhelm Meister's many friends and lovers contribute to his education. In autobiography, the importance of secondary characters often depends on how influential they have been in the protagonist's life. Parents, mentors, lovers, and children might incite the protagonist to grow and change, for example, to undergo a spiritual conversion, or to write the life story.

Secondary characters have traditionally been seen as particularly significant for women writers in both novels of development and autobiography. If society is considered an "antagonistic character," the fixed social context is one from which women characters must often try to free themselves in both autobiography and the *bildungsroman*. Among the life stories I analyze, for example, heroines are dramatically impacted by a mother (Aleramo, Cardinal, Ernaux), by an abandoned or lost child (Aleramo, Fallaci), by a lover (Mogador), or by an abusive husband (Aleramo). The opinions of male characters frequently influence women's self-image, also evident in certain of the texts to be discussed here. Consider, for example, the relationship between the heroine and her therapist in Cardinal's *Les mots pour le dire*. It has already been noted that many feminist critics find the "relational aspect" of female personality central to women's texts, works that are often family-oriented or, in the contemporary period, erotic. A strict division between female relationality

Introduction 23

and male autonomy, however, is currently in dispute,[31] and these findings must be considered in analyses of protagonists' relationships with secondary characters. While Belgiojoso's growth, for example, is influenced by her family, friends, and other writers, and she considers her own character through observation of other women, it is difficult to point to one particular relationship that is central to her personal narratives. She emerges instead as an independent, autonomous figure rather than one intimately tied to a significant other.

Finally, it is important to mention the overlapping elements regarding structure in the two genres. Both are often fundamentally realist and portray a linear development, though, as discussed earlier, this is often challenged in women's "novels of awakening" and in twentieth-century personal narratives. Both genres uphold a belief in the potential growth and development of the central character, though here again, twentieth-century autobiographical texts and *bildungsromane* often portray the impossibility of development or a sense of alienation on the part of the protagonist, in either a serious or satirical mode. They may also call into question narrative time itself. In addition, the structure of such *bildungsromane* as Dickens' *Great Expectations* and Alessandro Manzoni's *I promessi sposi* (*The Betrothed*) allows for strong moral messages to unfold. Frequently, autobiographical confessions or essays also have a significant didactic content, more so than other types of life writing. The major structural similarity in both genres is the frequent exposition of the "stages" of an individual's life. In twentieth-century texts, however, authors often focus on one or only a limited number of these stages.

Susanna Egan analyzes structural similarities between autobiography and fiction in *Patterns of Experience in Autobiography*. She discusses common patterns in both types of writing, including childhood as paradise, or a move from innocence to experience; youth as journey (or pilgrimage in religion or quest in epic); maturity as a type of ascent to rebirth, conversion, or transformation; and finally old age as confession. Egan underscores the interrelation between autobiography and historicism, a connection that is relevant for the *bildungsroman* as well.

Another structural similarity between the two genres is the common "open end" (Jost 100). Jost points out that both exclude "death as a solution to the plot" (100). We should note, however, that in many women's *bildungsromane*, marriage, madness, and suicide represent types of "closure." Although twentieth-century writers tend to subvert these "typical" tragic scenarios inherited from the nineteenth century, feminist critics urge women writers to continue to challenge structures that limit women's lives. Frye finds great potential in the *bildungsroman* for appreciating and rewriting female experience through the feminine subjective eye: "As a blatantly realistic form, modeled on biography or autobiography, [the *bildungsroman*] has a decided place for the experiential base of feminist criticism. And as a dynamic form, committed to the growth of a strong individual, it has a clear relevance to the urgency of female self-definition" (79).

In conclusion, both life stories and novels of development are involved with issues of identity and growth. Therefore, a reading of autobiographical texts via the frame of the *bildungsroman* highlights how women write themselves as subjects, stage their development, and understand their lives.

NOTES

1. I emphasize *selected* experiences not only because autobiographers often summarize, exaggerate, or forget, consciously or unconsciously, in their life stories, but also because of the evanescent quality of experience. An autobiographer can only attempt to recapture a life. Furthermore, contemporary autobiography is often intentionally disjointed and fragmentary.

2. Mary G. Mason and Carol Hurd Green have also studied women's autobiography in the context of the "journey." Their *Journeys: Autobiographical Writings by Women* focuses on the Anglo-American tradition.

3. See Ramsay's *The French New Autobiographies* for a discussion of recent trends in autobiographical writing in France.

4. See, for example, Jost's "La tradition du *Bildungsroman*," Buckley's *Season of Youth*, and Hirsch's "The Novel of Formation as Genre."

5. See, for example, Butler's *Bodies That Matter*.

6. See Planté's chapter "Écrire comme un homme, écrire comme une femme" for a discussion of "genres-femmes" (female genres).

7. One also sees her name spelled Belgioioso. In French, one frequently sees her name as Christine Trivulce de Belgiojoso. Also, the French often refer to Belgiojoso as "la Belle Joyeuse."

8. All English translations of quotations from primary sources in French and Italian are mine unless indicated.

9. The original title of *Mémoires* is *Adieux au monde: Mémoires de Céleste Mogador* (*Good-bye to the World: Memoirs of Céleste Mogador*).

10. Un *deuil* is signed La Comtesse Lionel de Chabrillan. One also sees her aristocratic name as Céleste de Moreton de Chabrillan. The author's various appellations shall be discussed further in Chapters 3 and 4.

11. See the discussion between Peggy Kamuf and Nancy K. Miller in "Replacing Feminist Criticism" and "The Text's Heroine," respectively, for an early version of the debate about women's writing. Also see Miller's more recent "Introduction" to *Subject to Change* regarding women writers and the canon.

12. See my article "Women Writing Auto/biography: Anna Banti's *Artemisia* and Eunice Lipton's *Alias Olympia*" on writing the lives of previously neglected women artists in the context of autobiographical pursuits.

13. A possible translation for this title might be *The Encroached Upon Past*. "Empiéter" also refers to a particular type of embroidery.

14. See Moi, *Sexual/Textual Politics* for an elaboration of this notion. Also see Kamuf's summary of critical practice based on "feminine-centered cultural models" (45).

15. Delphy argues that "French Feminism was invented in order to legitimate the introduction on the Anglo-American feminist scene of a brand of essentialism, and in particular a rehabilitation of psychoanalysis, which goes further than the native kind expressed by Sara Ruddick, Chodorow, or Gilligan" (216).

Introduction

16. Consider, for example, Elaine Showalter's *A Literature of Their Own*.

17. All English translations of quotations from secondary sources in French and Italian are mine unless indicated.

18. See my entry on "Autobiography" in *The Feminist Encyclopedia*. Some of the information from that essay has informed my discussion here of the genre in French literature.

19. See Frank Paul Bowman's article "Suffering, Madness, and Literary Creation in Seventeenth-Century Spiritual Autobiography" for insights on this subgenre.

20. See Planté 234.

21. See Heather Gregory's recent translation *Selected Letters of Alessandra Strozzi*.

22. See Costa-Zalessow (14-15) and Finucci on Camilla Faà.

23. See McCallum Schwartz on the *roman intime*.

24. In the second volume of her life story, the passage is in quotes because Sand is commenting on having written this thought seven years previously. The English translation comes from the following edition: George Sand, *Story of My Life: The Autobiography of George Sand*, a group translation, ed. Thelma Jurgrau (Albany: State U of New York P, 1991) 75-76, 890. Because the English translation of Sand's text is a group project, "mal" is translated differently in the two passages—first as "unfortunate" and next as "bad." All further translations from Sand's *Histoire de ma vie* come from the same edition.

25. Stéphane Michaud affirms the importance of the image of "woman" in the nineteenth-century imagination (*Muse et Madone* [*Muse and Madonna*]). Other critics note that Romantic writers "have dedicated a substantial part of their works to celebrating woman and love" (Rinci and Lecherbonnier 299). The figure of the Virgin Mary of the Catholic Church, for example, was influential as an emblem of maternal devotion in the family. She was also a symbol of liberation for the Saint-Simonians, the *femme messie*, or woman messiah, for many socialist-minded thinkers. The "eternal feminine" in the writings of Goethe, Baudelaire, and others evoked a mixture of desire and contemplation. Michaud notes that the meaning and representation of "woman" in art, literature, philosophy, and politics in the nineteenth century often tended toward a dialectic of a spiritual ideal of purity and perfection, on one hand, versus a sensual, earthy image, on the other. Michaud explains: "This woman who haunts the imaginary of an entire century, this figure both close and inaccessible, Baudelaire named her . . . 'the Muse and the Madonna'" (9-10). Both the Muse, who has pagan roots, and the Madonna, who originates from Christian culture, "participate in the same cult of beauty, in the same sensual perfection. Lover and emblem of poetry, the Muse shares with the Madonna the fact of being at the same time both a carnal and ideal creature" (Michaud 11).

26. See the development of Planté's argument (282-89).

27. See Sidonie Smith's *Subjectivity, Identity and the Body* for a discussion of "autobiographical manifestos" and other progressive practices in life writing.

28. In "The Female Novel of Development and the Myth of Psyche" Mary Anne Ferguson discusses two mythical prototypes for the male and female journeys in novels of development. She likens male *bildung* to Ulysses' experiences in the *Odyssey*, where a young man sets out to find his father. The male character is successful in his quest for identity and undergoes a series of adventures that help him to mature. His journey is a spiral in which the ending represents a new beginning on a higher plane (228). Female

bildung is likened to the character of Psyche in the myth of Psyche and Cupid (Eros); Psyche's journey is a circular one. Her lost love can be restored only after certain trials of initiation, and the mother is the key in her daughter's emotional development. Psyche is eventually reunited with her lover, and their happy union produces a child. Ferguson emphasizes the fact that the male hero retains a sense of integrity and dignity, although as a learner he may have appeared foolish. His adventures send him out into society, and by the end of his journey he is able to look back on his exploits with an ironic gaze. The female character is, however, initiated "at home" through learning the rituals of human relationships (228).

29. See Lazzaro-Weis' chapter on the female *bildungsroman* in *From Margins to Mainstream*, a study that focuses on Italian women's writing from 1968 to 1990.

30. Felski focuses on contemporary women novelists from 1972 to 1985.

31. See Miller's "Representing Others," which has also been discussed earlier in this Introduction.

Part I

LEAVING THE COUNTRY

1

Cristina Trivulzio di Belgiojoso's *Souvenirs dans l'exil*: The Journey Home

> Le parfum de l'âme, c'est le souvenir.
> (The scent of the soul, it is memory.)
> —George Sand, *Lettres d'un voyageur*

The collection of letters entitled *Souvenirs dans l'exil* (1850) stages Princess Cristina Trivulzio di Belgiojoso's developmental journey.[1] The collection was written to friend Caroline Jaubert while Belgiojoso was en route to the Middle East. Although certain letters were altered by editors before publication, one can still trace the impact that living in exile had on Belgiojoso's maturation. Indeed, the farther Belgiojoso journeys into the future and away from her homeland, the more she engages in self-reflection. Importantly, the princess sees herself in others, and her *bildung* is linked, in particular, to the various female portraits offered in *Souvenirs*.[2] The subject of both admiration and slander, Belgiojoso also recalls in the letters relationships with friends and admirers back home in Europe. Ultimately, she is able to forgive those who have wronged her. By the end of *Souvenirs*, Belgiojoso appears a wiser, more mature woman who has come to terms with her past.

A pioneering Italian writer, activist, and journalist, Belgiojoso left an extensive corpus of both French and Italian texts. Her writings include not only travel memoirs, fiction, and letters but also works on religion, history, and politics. Born in Milan in 1808, Belgiojoso devoted her life to both social and political reform. She was avidly in favor of a united Italy under a constitutional monarchy. Such a view was subversive, however, since Italy was divided into several city-states, and the north was largely under Austrian domination until the culmination of the *Risorgimento* from 1859 to 1870. Because of her dissident political views and her unhappy marriage to the philandering Emilio Belgiojoso, the princess left Italy at the age of twenty-two. The nomadic existence that followed included travels in France. She launched an important *salon* in Paris in 1835, where she welcomed expatriates, intellectuals, politicians, and writers (including Alfred de Musset, George Sand, Franz Liszt, Augustin Thierry, and General La Fayette). Her political involvement also included participation in the popular uprisings of the 1840s in Italy. In 1848 she led a shipload of 200 patriots, including Neapolitan countrymen, bourgeois students, and Austrian deserters, to Milan to battle the Austrians. Belgiojoso's political activism led to her compassionate efforts to assist the war casualties. During the Roman Revolutions of 1849, she directed a dozen military hospitals. This was some five years before Florence Nightingale's activities with the British. Belgiojoso was actively involved with contemporary political figures, such as Giuseppe Mazzini and Garibaldi. She met with both Napoleon III and Carlo Alberto of the influential House of Savoy. After her disappointment because of the failed Roman Revolutions, Belgiojoso embarked upon a second exile, this time in the Middle East, where she would remain for several years.[3] Life there inspired further writing and community activity. The princess was also one of the early women journalists and founded several newspapers offering a forum for debate on Italian unification and humanitarian causes.[4] Though her sex denied Belgiojoso due recognition for her political activities, she was eventually honored by Vittorio Emanuele II for her efforts in the Italian unification movement.[5]

Souvenirs represents two important subgenres of autobiography—travel narratives and letters. These subgenres, indeed, have their own distinguishing characteristics: both travel literature and letters may focus on a limited time period, for example, while straightforward autobiography often strives to encapsulate the life span; letters often reflect the immediacy of the moment, rather than the passage of time evident in autobiographies written in old age; travel literature often includes the study of the *other* (foreign peoples, customs, and laws) as equally important as the focus on the self and one's origins. However, both subgenres also share several common concerns with autobiography regarding subjectivity, identity, individual growth, and learning.

Common in women's autobiographical literature, "exceptional," subversive, and, at times, unconventional female figures distance themselves from a hostile, antagonistic society, where they are often judged and misunderstood in order that they might pursue personal growth. Whereas many nineteenth-century female writers situate their stories in enclosed spaces and lament the chains that shackle them, traveling women often overcome societal limitations by transgressing geographical and class boundaries. Writing from exile allows for both a reconsideration of the self and also a new conceptualization of the homeland from a more distant and critical perspective. Putting pen to paper while abroad often enables women writers to express themselves more freely, to comment on, criticize, and remember the land they left behind.

Among the many nineteenth-century women voyagers for whom writing became the medium for social and feminist concerns are Madame de Staël, Flora Tristan, Olympe Audouard, Jane Dieulafoy, Céleste Mogador (discussed in a subsequent chapter), Margaret Fuller, Harriet Martineau, and Lady Hester Stanhope.[6] In addition to Belgiojoso, Italians who voyaged to the East include Amalia Solla Nizzoli, the first Italian woman to travel to Egypt, Carla Serena, who visited Persia, and Matilde Serao, who traveled to Jerusalem.[7] Some of these women traveled with spouses and served as collaborators or secretaries. As such, the desire to participate in the masculine domain of writing is more easily justified.[8] Others, like Belgiojoso, sought new lands alone, with only the company of servants or companions.[9] However, since the princess was already an established writer and because her exile was politically motivated, she was less obliged than other women to explain taking up the pen in *Souvenirs*.

Critics such as Bénédicte Monicat and Sara Mills confirm the substantial body of women's travel writing from the nineteenth century, which distinguishes itself from male travel texts in various ways. Frequently, female texts demonstrate an attention to detail, for example, regarding domestic issues. At the same time, women often inscribe veiled political discourse into their works, particularly concerning feminist issues. Because these female travelers left the domestic sphere and frequently ventured to regions little known to Westerners, they embodied uniqueness, courage, and a pioneering spirit. Monicat notes that women's travel literature concerns itself with writing both everyday events and marginal female experiences ("Écritures du voyage" 25). Women's travel narratives also integrate such typical "genres-femmes" as letters and the diary into their narratives.[10] Belgiojoso chooses the former. Céleste Mogador manipulates both subgenres in *Un deuil au bout du monde*, as certain passages are dated, and letters are embedded within the text. Severe social criticism and feminist commitment appear less harsh in the context of these personal forms than they would in an essay. In addition, women often write their "impressions" of another culture and are hence able to communicate negative views more subtly than their typical male counterparts, proclaiming to write from an "objective" or scientific viewpoint (Monicat, "Problématique de la préface" 68).

Belgiojoso's exile to the Middle East was one of both desire and necessity. Disillusioned because of the failed Roman Revolutions, disappointed with the French alliance with the Catholic Church against a nascent Italy, denied her fortune, and suspected as hostile against both state and church, the princess set sail aboard the ship *Mentor* in 1849. *Souvenirs* was begun immediately upon the princess' departure. We read, "A cette heure je vous écris à bord du *Mentor* faisant voile pour Malte et l'Orient. C'est le 31 juillet dans la nuit que j'ai quitté Rome" (1) ("At this moment I am writing you from aboard the *Mentor* setting sail for Malta and the Orient. It is July 31st on the night that I left Rome"). We note the immediacy of this passage and the sense of new beginnings. Intense drama permeates the opening pages: "Le 31 juillet au soir, je reçus un billet anonyme contenant ces mots: *Fuyez au plus vite*, un dossier qui vous concerne est sur la table du cardinal, et en marge de sa main est écrit: *sentimen[t]s irreligieux*" (1) ("The evening of the 31st of July, I received an anonymous note containing these words: *flee as soon as possible*, a dossier about you is on the cardinal's desk, and he has written in the margin: *irreligious sentiments*"). In this passage, Belgiojoso underscores that she is in danger and hence emphasizes her courage and will.

The collection of letters contains social, anthropological, and geographical insights of the various lands Belgiojoso traverses, such as Malta and Athens, as well as political observations, witty anecdotes, and character profiles. The letters reflect Belgiojoso's era through their depictions of such political figures as Napoleon III and General La Fayette and through portrayals of writers and artists, including Alfred de Musset, Honoré de Balzac, Franz Liszt, and Marie d'Agoult (Daniel Stern). Though many of her initial thoughts in *Souvenirs* are of the siege of Rome and the wounded and dying she consoled in its hospitals, this exile was meant to be a reprieve from politics. *Souvenirs* represents a period of wandering, which would also be one of transition for the author. Belgiojoso explains, "S'il faut renoncer à la réalisation de mes voeux concernant l'Italie, je veux embrasser un genre de vie qui me présente de nouvelles sources d'intérêt; il faut que la nouvelle existence tue le souvenir de l'ancienne" (6) ("If I have to renounce the achievement of my wishes concerning Italy, I want to embrace a type of life which presents new sources of interest to me; this new existence must kill the memory of the old one"). We note a deliberate refocusing of interests away from politics. However, Belgiojoso would not fully embrace this "reprieve." Although she assumes the contemplative writer's life, she also embarks on humanitarian projects and community activity in Turkey aimed at helping the poor, similar to her previous efforts to assist the lower classes of Locate (today called Locate Triulzi), outside Milan.[11]

Souvenirs was not intended to be published in its original form. Beth Archer Brombert explains that had the letters been written for publication, Belgiojoso "would doubtless have been more cautious and in some cases less irreverent" (198). The princess' remarks on the Romans, Roman women in particular, incensed Italian journalists. Luigi Severgnini notes that editors from the French newspaper *Le National*, which published the letters, driven by political opportunism, made modifications in content and structure ("Introduction" 15). Because of these changes, certain passages appeared out of context and were misconstrued, damaging Belgiojoso's reputation. Brombert explains that "[f]aced with the violent reaction of her compatriots to her treatment of Roman women . . . Cristina published an open letter protesting that her statements had been taken out of context from a private correspondence" (197–98). Belgiojoso offended many others, however, including the French, who eventually censured letters critical of them, and the Greeks, because of her descriptions of banditry in their country (Severgnini, "Introduction" 17).

Several other autobiographical texts published in the 1850s emerged from Belgiojoso's Middle Eastern sojourn. In addition to *Souvenirs*, Belgiojoso wrote travel memoirs entitled *La vie intime et la vie nomade en Orient*[12] (*Oriental Harems and Scenery*), published serially in the *Revue des Deux Mondes* in 1855. She also penned various travel novellas, published again in the *Revue des Deux Mondes* as *Récits turcs* (*Turkish Narratives*) in 1856, stories that interestingly highlight aspects of the princess' own life story.[13] One of the tales, *Emina*, is discussed in the next chapter.

In order to understand fully Belgiojoso's developmental journey in *Souvenirs*, it is necessary to consider how the princess was portrayed by various nineteenth-century writers. It will become apparent that rather than tell a straightforward autobiographical narrative, the princess reflects on her past and her evolving selfhood through a series of "biographies," stories of others that come to bear on Belgiojoso herself. The princess' pale beauty embodied many Romantic stereotypes. She was the mysterious figure suspected to have inspired such renowned heroines as Balzac's Féodora, Stendhal's Sanseverina, Musset's Marianne, d'Agoult's Zepponi, and Sand's Princess Cavalcanti. She was described, discussed, and satirized in various contexts as the eccentric mystic, the freedom fighter, the humanitarian, the narcissist, the tease. Biographer Arrigo Petacco laments, "God, how many legends . . . about this woman!" (26). Belgiojoso's relationship with Musset serves as an example.

Musset's experience with Belgiojoso was one of unrequited love. In 1842 he wrote to the princess: "In the love I feel for you . . . there could not be any harm in a sentiment full of respect, based on the most genuine reasons, on the noblest and loftiest thoughts" (qtd. in Brombert 274). That summer, critics claim, Belgiojoso invited Musset to stay in her Versailles country home. According to various sources, the visit was a disaster. Charles Neilson Gattey quotes Musset's version of the episode as follows: "When [Belgiojoso] saw that she was making me miserable, she gave me that irresistible smile of hers . . . which made me feel as if I had been beaten over the head with a stick" (65). Arsène Houssaye quotes Musset's description of the final separation:

One night . . . I went to the home of a princess . . . I declared that I had longed for her enough. I shouted, I abused the lady. . . . Do you know what the princess did? She burst into laughter, saying to me: "Come with me." She took me gently by the hand. I was almost frightened by my triumph. . . . Then, in the bedroom, rather than throwing herself into my arms, she threw me into the arms of a former mistress who wanted me no more than I wanted her. (I: 285–86) [14]

According to various sources, this was no other than the close friend of the princess, George Sand. Hence, prominent in Musset's version of the story is a portrait of the princess as tease, flirt, prankster.

Another fictionalized version of the incident is offered by Louise Colet, longtime mistress of Gustave Flaubert and also romantically associated with Musset. According to Colet, the suffering Musset, limping from a sprained ankle, left Versailles in a huff because of the princess' flirtations with pianist Franz Liszt. In her book *Lui: Roman contemporain* (*Lui: A View of Him*), Albert, who represents Musset, recounts the following story: "J'étais allé la voir à Versailles où elle avait loué près du parc un fort bel hôtel. . . . Un matin où elle m'avait provoqué plus que de coutume . . . elle m'arracha tout à coup sa main, que je la priais de laisser dans la mienne, et voulut me quitter sous prétexte de sa leçon de chant" (80–81)[15] ("I had gone to Versailles where she had rented a very beautiful mansion. . . . One morning when she had been more provocative than usual . . . she suddenly snatched back the hand which I begged her to leave in mine, and wanted to leave on the pretext of taking a singing lesson" 68).[16] The bedridden, languishing lover is outraged when he hears Belgiojoso and Liszt "jeter dans l'air des notes brûlantes et passionnées" (Colet 81) ("trilling burning and passionate notes" Colet 68) in the adjacent room. He limps to the salon only to find his beloved "[qui] appuyait ses lèvres sur la joue du pianiste, qui la regardait dans une pose de vignette anglaise" (Colet 81) ("resting her lips on the cheek of the pianist who was looking at her in a pose right out of an English engraving" Colet 68). The startled princess exclaims that she merely wanted to test Albert (the Musset character), to which he replies: "'Eh bien! princesse, l'épreuve est faite . . . j'ai assez de votre hospitalité'" (Colet 82) ("'Well, Princess, the test is over . . . I've had enough of your hospitality'" Colet 68), and off he goes. In Colet's version of the encounter, we are struck not only by Belgiojoso's flirtation but by Musset's frustration and jealousy because of the arranged love triangle. Brombert notes that Colet bitterly envied Belgiojoso's beauty, her role in Italian politics, and Musset's passion for her and hence offers "a very distorted view of Cristina" (281). Less important than the "truth" of these accounts is the curiosity Belgiojoso inspired, the desire to glimpse beneath her mysterious facade.

Shortly after the Versailles incident, Musset penned a wicked poem about the "cold, unfeeling" princess entitled "Sur une morte" ("About a Dead Woman"). Expressing himself in verse was not enough, however. Musset was audacious enough (and upset enough) to publish his verses in the *Revue des Deux Mondes* in 1842. A fragment of the poem follows:

> Elle aurait aimé, si l'orgueil,
> Pareil à la lampe inutile
> Qu'on allume près d'un cercueil,
> N'eût veillé sur son coeur stérile.
> (*Poésies complètes* 485)
> (She would have loved, if pride,
> Like the useless lamp
> That one lights near a coffin,
> Would not have kept watch over her sterile heart.)

The publication of the poem suspended Musset's friendship with Belgiojoso for several years.

How did Belgiojoso respond to the extravagant images of her in circulation in the nineteenth century? To Musset's poem, she responded with silence, although several years later, after enjoying his new play, *Louison*, she wrote him an amicable letter expressing her appreciation of his Shakespearean talent. Often, rather than producing direct responses to her contemporaries' accusations, Belgiojoso contemplated public opinion about her character in her autobiographical writings and employed various strategies to set the record straight. *Souvenirs* offers several examples.

One of Belgiojoso's female portraits in *Souvenirs* illustrates a cold, unfeeling Moroccan princess en route to Mecca with her entourage. The young royal punishes a handsome slave named Sélim for his penchant and preference for one of the servant girls rather than the princess herself. When the servant pleads with the princess to spare her beloved a terrible thrashing, one that eventually would lead to his death, the princess responds: "Tu l'aimes donc bien, [cet esclave]? . . . Et que ferais-tu s'il lui arrivait malheur?" (5) ("So you love him, [this slave]? . . . And what would you do if something dreadful happened to him?"). The servant responds: "Ah! princesse, je crois que j'en mourrais" (5) ("Ah! Princess, I think I would die of it"). The princess counters: "Tu crois . . . mais tu n'en es pas sûre. . . . Eh bien, dit-elle, de son air le plus sévère . . . au lieu de vingt coups de bâton, tu en feras donner cinquante à Sélim. Par ce moyen . . . tu auras meilleure chance de sortir de l'incertitude" (5) ("You think . . . but you are not sure. . . . Well then, she said, in her most severe manner . . . instead of twenty lashes with a stick, you will have Sélim receive fifty. In this way . . . you will have a better chance of leaving your doubts behind"). Not only does Belgiojoso re-create the love triangle with which she was often associated (Musset–Belgiojoso–Sand, Musset–Belgiojoso–Colet), but we recall that she, too, was a princess, and she, too, was accused of reacting with chilly indifference regarding questions of the heart. We can therefore read Belgiojoso's depiction of the Moroccan princess as a response to negative public opinion. Belgiojoso fights satire with satire. Through such an exaggerated portrait of a cruel Moroccan royal, she deflates portrayals, including Musset's, of her own icy exterior.

In another example, written while Belgiojoso was in Athens, she describes the last mistress of the powerful Greek Ali-Pacha de Jannina. We receive a short biography of the elderly woman in *Souvenirs*. As a young girl, she dared to defy Ali-Pacha as his henchmen slaughtered her family members. He was so impressed with her childish bravado that he spared her life and had her placed in a harem. As he observes her development, he is surprised by her intelligence. The young woman, quick to understand Ali-Pacha's fascination, pursues their relationship by interrogating him on his ideas, plans, and power. Ali-Pachi, in return, enjoys "le plaisir, nouveau pour lui, de la conversation" (18) ("the pleasure, new for him, of conversation"). Belgiojoso explains, "Rien ne saurait peindre l'étonnement du vieux tyran, qui, pour la première fois, se voyait adresser de telles questions. Cette femme appartenait-elle donc à ce sexe; qu'il n'avait jamais connu que chantant, dansant, tremblant ou minaudant?" (18) ("Nothing could depict the astonishment of the old tyrant, who, for the first time, saw such questions addressed to him. This woman belonged then to the female sex; that he had never known but singing, dancing, trembling or simpering?"). In sum, when the young woman requests to leave the harem, Ali-Pacha grants her wish, but he quickly sends her husband away on a secret mission so that he can keep the young woman as his lover more easily.

As in the example of the Moroccan princess, Belgiojoso is drawn to describing characters that reflect her own. Like Ali-Pacha's young lover, the princess, too, was quick to speak her mind and quick to act. She, too, was the young sage who so impressed her elders: General La Fayette, who became "le meilleur des pères" (36) ("the best of fathers") while the young Belgiojoso was exiled in France; historian Augustin Thierry; and likely lover François Mignet. All three served as counselors and guides. The similarities between Belgiojoso and Ali-Pacha's mistress do not stop there, however. After Ali-Pacha's death, his lover is left with wealth and time. Belgiojoso queries, "Quel emploi a-t-elle fait de la liberté depuis lors jusqu'à ce jour? . . . Dimanche dernier, à la promenade, oubliant ses soixante années, elle était au bras d'un jeune dandy" (19) ("What use did she make of such freedom from then until now? . . . Last Sunday, out for a stroll, forgetting her sixty years, she was on the arm of a young dandy"). Belgiojoso goes on to describe the love affair of this young Greek and his "vieille odalisque" (19) ("old odalisque"), thus reversing the older man–younger woman paradigm. At the same time, she once again contemplates her own life through that of another woman. Indeed, several nineteenth-century images depicted Belgiojoso as vulnerable to the love of younger men. As stated previously, it was suspected that Stendhal's Sanseverina, the Italian duchess with a penchant for her younger nephew Fabrice, was inspired by the princess. In addition, rumors had circulated about a possible involvement between Cristina and her younger research assistant Gaetano Stelzi. It was even supposed that she had the young man's body embalmed after his death and hidden for a time on her property outside Milan. Petacco further suspects that Belgiojoso's personal secretary Pietro Bolognini may have fathered her daughter Marie. It becomes clear that the portrayal of the mismatched lovers in *Souvenirs* constitutes an occasion for the princess to reflect on her own past. Belgiojoso fills in the gaps of the sketchy portrait she presents in her letters with her own generalizations: "C'est au jeune homme naïf que cette femme expérimentée s'attache; c'est la femme qui a vécu, qui a souffert, que le jeune homme poursuit et ambitionne. Lorsqu'ils sont ensemble, l'un fait effort pour oublier un passé dans lequel l'autre veut pénétrer" (19) ("It is the naïve young man to whom this experienced woman attaches herself; it is the woman who has lived, who has suffered, whom the young man pursues and seeks. When they are together, one makes an effort to forget a past which the other wants to penetrate"). In these direct, declarative statements, which echo the "truths" of maxims, we hear the voice of experience, the authoritative tone of a woman who feels she has acquired an understanding of people and their interactions. In the evocation of the past that Ali-Pacha's mistress wishes to forget, we also have a commentary on the princess' journey itself and the troublesome past that *she* has fled. In sum, Belgiojoso's veiled response in *Souvenirs* to judgments about her intimate life is a defense. She supports and extols the mistress and, by extension, herself as intelligent in the various seasons of her life: when the mistress was a girl, she submits to allying herself with the power necessary for her survival; as a woman she has earned the right to pleasure. Although Belgiojoso's early relationships with men such as General La Fayette and François Mignet appear to have been genuinely affectionate, one cannot deny the extent to which their influence helped her during the early days in Paris when her fortune was sequestered and her acquaintances limited.

In *Souvenirs*, Belgiojoso also comments on the frequently negative portrayals of strong women who do not conform to societal expectations. She writes to Jaubert, for example, about the spirited duchess of Plaisance who managed to outwit bandits in their attempt to kidnap her and secure a hefty ransom: "Vous ne connaissez pas, ma chère amie, Mme la duchesse de Plaisance, et si quelqu'un vous a tracé son portrait, je crains que ce portrait n'ait été fait en caricature. C'est ainsi que le monde en use à l'égard des femmes dont le caractère n'a point été éffacé par l'éducation" (13) ("You do not know, my dear friend, Mme the duchess of Plaisance, and if someone drew her portrait for you, I fear that this portrait was only a caricature. It is in this way that the world treats women whose character has not been erased by upbringing"). Like the duchess of Plaisance, Belgiojoso, too, had a strong and unconventional personality that inspired many critics. She explains that a pronounced character in men, on the other hand, rouses the reverse response: "on fait un mérite de ce qu'on appelle de l'originalité" (13) ("one makes a quality out of what is called originality"). Because hordes of local villagers come to the duchess' aid, she has a public laundry facility constructed for them at her own expense. Similarly, Belgiojoso served her poor villagers in Locate with the development of an agricultural community. Aware that her independence, intelligence, and social activism were threatening, Belgiojoso indirectly praises her own wit and generosity through her lively portrayal of the duchess of Plaisance.

Whereas several female portraits in *Souvenirs* speak to the princess' reputation in Europe, others parallel the growth and transformation she experiences through remembrance, writing, and exile. In her discussion of the horrors of the Roman Revolutions just before her departure on the *Mentor*, Belgiojoso recounts the "récit véridique des deux mois, juin et juillet, que j'ai passés à Rome" (7) ("true narrative of the two months, June and July, which I spent in Rome"). We recall that the princess was in charge of several military hospitals in Rome. Petacco explains that Belgiojoso's first initiative was "absolutely revolutionary; she rallied the women of Rome together in the goal of constructing a voluntary women's nursing service" (203). To her call for nurses responded roughly 300 volunteers, from aristocrats, to commoners, to prostitutes. In *Souvenirs*, Belgiojoso is initially quite critical of the moral conduct of certain volunteers. As stated previously, publication of these criticisms (albeit out of context because of editors' alterations) stirred the ire of her compatriots. Belgiojoso writes, for example, that "[une femme du peuple] ignore véritablement qu'il y ait une loi morale. . . . Elles volent, elles mentent, et si vous les prenez sur le fait, elles vous regardent en souriant avec une naïveté . . . vraiment angélique" (7) ("[a common woman] is really unaware that there is a moral law. . . . They steal, they lie, and if you catch them at it, they look at you smiling with a naïveté . . . which is really angelic"). Indeed, when the princess left Italy, "a vulgar press campaign was incited . . . against her and against her 'little nurses'" (Petacco 212–13). Belgiojoso denied these accusations at the time, and when the pope expressed dismay that many battle victims died in the arms of prostitutes, she even addressed a letter to him defending the volunteers (Petacco 213). In *Souvenirs*, though Belgiojoso is aware of the women's shortcomings, she again defends them because of the growth she witnessed in them while they worked together. She explains: "[Un] mourant fut-il votre frère ou votre fils confiez-le sans crainte à [une] samaritaine . . . car elle en aura soin, comme si elle était sa soeur ou sa mère" (7) ("[A] dying man, whether it be your brother or your son, entrust him without fear to [a] Samaritan . . . for she will take care of him, as if she were his sister or his mother"). Belgiojoso therefore emphasizes the change and growth of these female volunteers because of dire circumstances. She notes: "Chez presque toutes les femmes que j'ai placées à l'hôpital, j'ai vu ce contraste naître entre le passé et le présent. Toutes se transforment de la même manière, et dans les mêmes circonstances" (7) ("In almost all of the women whom I placed in the hospital, I saw this contrast born between the past and the present. All of them transform themselves in the same manner, and in the same circumstances"). Belgiojoso also uses this example to express her political conviction that through education comes virtue: "Comprenez-vous, chère amie, comme mon coeur saigne en voyant prolonger indéfiniment l'état d'abrutissement de ce peuple, susceptible de vertus héroïques et doué de nobles facultés? Toute éducation lui sera refusée jusques à quand?" (7) ("Do you understand, dear friend, how my heart bleeds in seeing prolonged indefinitely the moronic state of these people, susceptible to heroic virtues and gifted with noble faculties? All education will be denied them until when?"). Although Belgiojoso is unlike these women socially and intellectually, when she recalls their transformation, one understands that she, too, is at a critical juncture in her personal development. Belgiojoso worked with the female volunteers. She ran the hospitals and served the sick in the same manner, and she also matured and grew from the experience. This *bildung* continues throughout her exile as she reflects on her Roman experiences. Furthermore, her displacement coincides with a continued effort and desire to change. In fleeing Italy, she embarks on a period of "transformation" (6) ("transformation"). The *tableau féminin* that the princess paints is both a vast geographical portrait, moving from Europe to the Middle East, and also a temporal and emotional one that constantly points back to the author.

Through nostalgia, a characteristic tone in autobiographical writing that serves as a distancing mechanism between narrator and protagonist,[17] the princess recognizes how much she has grown. Belgiojoso recalls wistfully, for example, the days before the Roman Revolutions. She is astounded that only a few years ago she was "free" to cloister herself in libraries or to play the "poupée de salon" (2) ("salon doll"). She reflects: "Les grands et terribles événemen[t]s auxquels je viens de prendre part remplissent ma vie d'une façon qui ne me permet plus de mesurer le temps. . . . [I]l me semble que vingt ans se sont écoulés depuis" (2) ("The great and terrible events in which I have just taken part fill my life in a way which does not allow me to measure time. . . . It seems to me that twenty years have gone by since then"). Traumatic experiences, rather than the passage of years, age the princess, who is just forty-two when *Souvenirs* is published.

Souvenirs also offers portraits of women in Belgiojoso's artistic circle, depictions that further underscore the princess' *bildung*. One example is that of Marie d'Agoult. Apparently, Franz Liszt, d'Agoult's lover, had begged Belgiojoso to visit his lonely, ailing Marie while he was touring in England in 1840. Belgiojoso writes to Jaubert that she was hesitant to fulfill the obligation, uncertain that d'Agoult desired her company or consolation. Instead of meeting a depressed d'Agoult, however, Belgiojoso finds herself "nez à nez avec une personne radieuse et triomphante" (24) ("face to face with a radiant and triumphant person"). During their conversation, d'Agoult dismisses questions about her health and instead abruptly asks Belgiojoso: "De quoi vous occupez-vous, maintenant, Madame?" (25) ("With what do you occupy yourself now, Madam?"). Belgiojoso remains silent, for when asked such a question, "[i]l est sous-entendu . . . que vous êtes regardée comme une sotte. . . . C'est une tentative pour savoir s'il y a au moins un sujet sur lequel vous puissiez discourir. —. . . quelque théorie apprise par coeur. —Peut-être une dissertation sur la toilette" (25) ("[i]t is understood…that you are regarded as an idiot. . . . It is an attempt to know if there is at least one subject about which you can expatiate. — . . . some theory learned by heart. —Maybe a discourse on grooming"). The princess' sarcasm reveals her hurt pride. Because she is understandably uncomfortable that Liszt placed her in such an awkward situation, she leaves at the first opportunity. Belgiojoso's version of the encounter offered in *Souvenirs* appeared ten years after the incident. Writing from exile, the princess could express her emotions freely, unfettered by the constraints and judgments of home. By including this anecdote in her letters, Belgiojoso reveals that even after a great deal of time she wanted to offer her side of the story.

D'Agoult had written her account to Liszt shortly following the encounter: "La Commédienne sort d'ici et je me hâte de vous dire mon impression sans nulle réticence ni diplomatie. Je l'ai trouvée détruite de visage, presque laide . . . beaucoup moins spirituelle que je ne pensais" (Ollivier I: 424) ("The Actress has just left and I am eager to tell you my impression without any hesitation or diplomacy. I found her face ruined, almost ugly . . . much less witty than I thought"). Liszt is quick to correct this portrayal in his responding letter to Marie: "Vous êtes bien sévère pour la Princesse, elle m'a toujours paru plutôt vraie et bonne que fausse et méchante" (Ollivier I: 428) ("You are quite severe regarding the princess, she always seemed to me true and good rather than false and wicked"). D'Agoult's depiction of Belgiojoso in her autobiography, *Mes Souvenirs* (*My Memoirs*),[18] perpetuates the negative image: "Jamais femme, à l'égal de la princesse Belgiojoso, n'exerça l'art de l'*effet*. . . . Pâle, maigre, osseuse, avec des yeux flamboyants, elle jouait aux effets de spectre ou de fantôme" (356–57) ("Never has a woman exercised the art of *drama* equal to the Princess Belgiojoso. . . . Pale, thin, bony, with flashing eyes, she played the drama of a ghost or phantom"). D'Agoult continues to recount the 1840 meeting with the princess: "[L]orsqu'elle vint me voir, elle ne put cacher son dépit. On m'avait dit mourante, elle accourait à mon chevet . . . elle venait . . . me convertir à la foi: c'eût été un *effet* de soeur de charité. . . . Par malheur, je n'étais qu'enrhumée. Je la reçus debout" (*Mes Souvenirs* 357) ("When she came to see me, she could not hide her vexation. People said I was dying, she ran to my bedside . . . she came to convert me to the faith: that would have been a *drama* of a sister of charity. . . . Unfortunately, I only had a cold. I received her standing"). Thus, d'Agoult admits, beneath her criticisms, that Belgiojoso may have intended to be helpful, but she focuses to a much greater extent on the princess' eccentricity, on her desire to make a dramatic impression.

Exile afforded Belgiojoso the opportunity to reflect on her meeting with d'Agoult and the distance to forgive. Movement thus contributes to her *bildung*. She writes to Jaubert that despite the awkward meeting, d'Agoult is surely "une personne d'une distinction véritable" (25) ("a person of true distinction"). With Belgiojoso's ability to pardon d'Agoult and move on, we see the emotional distance she has traveled. Whereas earlier in *Souvenirs*, the princess needed to combat others' views through satire, toward the conclusion of the collection, she has mellowed. The attention Belgiojoso received from her contemporaries, both positive and negative, ultimately nourished her autobiographical pursuits and helped her along her personal developmental journey.

Toward the end of *Souvenirs*, Belgiojoso once again recalls pivotal moments from the past as she reflects on her first exile in Paris at age twenty-two. She remembers her modest, fifth-floor lodgings where she dared not allow herself the luxury of a servant, where she prepared her own meals "de [ses] blanches mains" (36) ("with [her] white hands"). She states:

Si, à l'époque de mon premier exil, j'avais songé à venir dans ces contrées, j'aurais évité la situation pénible où je me trouvai en France, lorsque j'arrivai d'Italie, où, malgré mon extrême jeunesse, j'avais trouvé le moyen de me brouiller politiquement avec l'Autriche, dont le gouvernement mit le séquestre sur mes biens. . . . Sans appui, ma double qualité de princesse et de réfugiée, servait précisément à me donner des airs d'héroïne de comédie. Riche héritière, élevée selon les usages de l'aristocratie milanaise, je ne savais précisément rien des nécessités de la vie. Jamais je n'avais touché à de l'argent monnayé, et je ne pouvais me rendre compte de ce que représentait une pièce de cinq francs. En revanche, je n'hésitais pas à classer une médaille antique selon son mérite. (36)

(If at the time of my first exile I had dreamed of coming to these lands, I would have avoided the difficult situation in which I found myself in France, when I arrived from Italy, where, despite my extreme youth, I had found a way to quarrel politically with Austria, whose government sequestered my fortune. . . . Without support, my double position as princess and refugee served precisely to give me the air of a comic heroine. Rich heiress, raised according to the customs of Milanese aristocracy, I knew precisely nothing about the necessities of life. Never had I touched coined money. I was unaware of the value of a five-franc piece. On the other hand, I did not hesitate to classify an antique metal according to its worth.)

Modesty aside, Belgiojoso credits her own ingenuity for carrying her through dire straits. She explains, "l'énergie dont je suis douée se ranima.... [Q]uand on n'a pas d'argent, il faut travailler pour en gagner" (36) ("the energy with which I am endowed rekindled itself.... [W]hen one does not have money, one must work to earn some"). She suddenly conceives of selling some of her jewels and painting portraits in order to survive. What might appear common sense to some had to be learned by the privileged princess. In addition, reflecting on such moments through writing these letters constitutes another pivotal moment in Belgiojoso's life, another passage that increases her self-knowledge.

The dawn of Belgiojoso's second exile far from Europe indeed allows for reconsideration of her first exile in Paris. Her early experiences of material deprivation in France foreshadow the financial need she will live out in the Middle East as well, along with the poverty of many of the peoples she will encounter during her travels. She reflects: "Il faut avoir passé sans transition d'une vie splendide, toujours entouré d'amis et de serviteurs, à un état d'isolement absolu pour connaître un genre d'angoisse et de détresse dont l'excès étonne" (36) ("One has to have passed without transition from a splendid life, always surrounded by friends and servants, to a state of absolute isolation to know the type of anguish and distress by which excess is astounded"). Ultimately, in order to grow, it is necessary to have lived. In order to understand other people of many backgrounds, the princess had to have been denied the wealth her social class takes for granted.

By the end of this collection of letters, Belgiojoso has reconstructed either directly or indirectly many of her past experiences. She has observed *others*, often other women, as reflections of her own character. She has contemplated others' impressions of her and reflected on her previous and present exiles. No longer the girl of twenty-two who fled her homeland, she emerges during this new journey as a sagacious and seasoned woman.

As physical distance increases in *Souvenirs*, longing for those she left behind increases. Belgiojoso reveals to Jaubert that "par une douce illusion, j'espérais toujours [vous] voir venir me joindre en Orient" (38) ("by a sweet illusion, I always hoped to see [you] come to join me in the Orient"). When she evokes writer friends such as Balzac and Musset, the princess assumes again a nostalgic tone, remembering "[c]es noms éminemment français" (39) ("[t]hese eminently French names"). Rather than focusing on her voyage, she is drawn to Paris, to her "cercle intime" (39) ("intimate circle"). Severgnini confirms: "Little by little as the voyager distanced herself from France and Italy, political passion calmed, and then the dear figures of faithful friends peeped out, the pleasant memories of Parisian life appeared" (16). Further, sensitivity regarding her controversial reputation back home seems to have mellowed. Even though Belgiojoso was often the misunderstood victim of ridicule, she did not renounce her adopted country. Her personal writings allowed for reflection on life in France and Italy and forgiveness for those who misjudged her. *Souvenirs* launches Belgiojoso's Oriental experience, which takes her very far from Europe. It simultaneously forces her to reflect on herself and her actions and hence brings her very close to home.

NOTES

1. Portions of this chapter were informed by two conference presentations: "Cristina di Belgiojoso's *Souvenirs dans l'exil*: The Journey Home," Nineteenth-Century French Studies Conference, Binghamton, NY, Oct. 1992, and "I See, You See. . . . Portraits of the Princess Belgiojoso," Nineteenth-Century French Studies Conference, Athens, GA, Oct. 1997. French quotations from *Souvenirs* are taken from the 1850 publication in *Le National*. English translations of quotations from *Souvenirs* are mine. For an Italian translation of *Souvenirs*, see Severgnini's *Ricordi dell'esilio*.

2. In her discussion of Belgiojoso's travel writings, Mirella Scriboni finds an interconnectedness between the story of self and the story of others, particularly other women, revealed through a constant movement between internal and external ("Preface" 23).

3. Belgiojoso set sail for the Middle East in 1849 and did not return to Europe until 1855. Her extended exile included an eleven-month voyage through Turkey and Syria to Jerusalem.

4. Belgiojoso was not alone in her efforts to expose injustice in the press. It is important to note the connection between concern for social issues and the birth of feminism in the nineteenth century in Italy and France. An outgrowth of women's efforts for equality was the publication of feminist newspapers and journals. French working-class women Marie-Reine Guindorf and Désirée Véret founded the Saint-Simonian newspaper *La femme libre* (*The Free Woman*) in 1832. It was soon passed on to Suzanne Voilquin, a follower of Charles Fourier, under the title *La tribune des femmes* (*Women's Tribune*), which Christine Planté calls "the first French feminist newspaper" (71). In Italy, writers and activists such as Anna Kulischiff preached socialism, and feminists such as Emilia Mariani and Anna Maria Mozzoni discussed women's emancipation (see Wood 11–15).

5. See Brombert, Petacco, and Spinosa for detailed portraits of the princess.

6. See Monicat's extensive study of nineteenth-century women travelers: *Itinéraires de l'écriture au féminin*.

7. See Scriboni's study "Il viaggio al femminile nell'Ottocento" for details on Belgiojoso, Nizzoli, and Serena.

8. See Monicat's chapter "Du voyage à l'écriture du voyage" in *Itinéraires* for a discussion of women's justification of the act of writing.

9. Included among the princess' traveling associates was her daughter Marie.

10. Once again, see Planté's chapter "Écrire comme un homme, écrire comme une femme" for a discussion of typical "genres-hommes" and "genres-femmes."

11. Belgiojoso's humanitarian efforts in Italy and Turkey are discussed further in the following chapter.

12. This text was later reprinted as *Asie mineure et Syrie, souvenirs de voyages*.

13. See Mills' discussion of "travel novels," which share elements of travel memoirs and fiction (73).

14. Hastier asserts that Houssaye may have embellished the event (302), but it is a frequently cited anecdote.

15. All French quotations from Colet's text are taken from the same edition of *Lui*:

Roman contemporain (Paris: Calmann Lévy, 1880) and cited by page number.

16. All English translations from Colet's text are taken from the same edition of *Lui: A View of Him*, trans. Marilyn Gaddis Rose (Athens, Georgia: U of Georgia P, 1986) and cited by page number.

17. See Lejeune's *L'autobiographie en France* (74–76) on this technique.

18. *Mes souvenirs* is published under the pen name Daniel Stern.

2

Belgiojoso's Western Feminism: The Poetics of a Nineteenth-Century Nomad

The tale *Emina* (1856) emerged from Princess Belgiojoso's peregrinations in the Middle East to regions little known to Westerners at the time—to European women in particular.[1] In this text, certain issues important to *Souvenirs dans l'exil* reappear: women's roles, personal relationships, foreign cultures, and Islamic codes of conduct. Once again, this narrative allows Belgiojoso to grapple with her own developmental journey, this time via her protagonist Emina. Furthermore, rather than through direct autobiographical narrative, the princess addresses her personal concerns circuitously, via fiction with marked autobiographical components. Indeed, autobiographical fiction was already in vogue among such women writers as Madame de Staël and George Sand. At the same time, *Emina* is a novel of development in a more straightforward fashion than *Souvenirs*. The protagonist's "coming-of-age" in a Turkish harem enables Belgiojoso to compare the extreme version of gender inequality she encountered in the East to the sexual imbalance she found so troubling in the West, albeit to a lesser degree.[2] The autobiographical nature of this work and Belgiojoso's use of first-person narration provide a context in which the princess can express nineteenth-century Western values and authority. Importantly, whereas the princess' authoritarian tenor was already evident in *Souvenirs*, in *Emina* Belgiojoso emerges as a colonizer. Through the character of the unnamed narrator/traveler, spokesperson for the author, Belgiojoso prescribes Christian, Western remedies to what she sees as the ills of the Muslim society.[3] The princess, indeed, writes in the spirit of the nineteenth-century female explorer, social reformer, and/or missionary, as did so many of the writers cited in the previous chapter, including Lady Hester Stanhope, Madame de Staël, Flora Tristan, and Carla Serena. Dorothy Middleton explains: "Fortified by a kind of innocent valour, convinced of the civilizing mission of woman . . . the nineteenth-century woman traveller covered thousands of miles—writing, painting, observing, botanizing, missionarizing, collecting, and latterly, photographing" (qtd. in Hamalian xi). In a typical maternal, nurturing fashion, women felt responsible not only to bring morality abroad but also to bring back knowledge to educate the public at home (Hamalian xi). In both *Emina* and many of the princess' travel memoirs, Belgiojoso or her unnamed doubles, indeed, appear as Western, "enlightened" figures "cultivating" the uneducated peoples of the Orient. With these publications, the princess likewise seeks to educate her readers.

"Orientalism" was, of course, a literary trend in the nineteenth century among such authors as François-René de Chateaubriand, Alphonse de Lamartine, Gérard de Nerval, and Gustave Flaubert,[4] and the successful *Arabian Nights* was often cited by travel writers. Some actually voyaged to the Orient, while others merely read about it, and their writing often reflected both Romantic, Orientalist stereotypes and Western political and colonialist agendas. In *Orientalism*, Edward W. Said explains how the "Orient," mainly Turkey and the Middle East during Belgiojoso's era, came to be "Orientalized," that is, studied, discussed, and theorized, according to Westerners' particular views, desires, and projections ("Introduction"). In addition, within the substantial body of "harem literature," men often depict harems as "exotic paradises." Many women writers, however, such as Belgiojoso and Amalia Solla Nizzoli, reveal harems to be filthy, boring cages, microcosms of female imprisonment in society at large (Morandini 62). In her study on Italian women travelers, Mirella Scriboni concurs that Belgiojoso, Nizzoli, and Serena distance themselves from men who wrote about the Orient because these women's descriptions of harems "demythologize the 'Orientalist' image of these places as paradises of sensuality and voluptuousness" ("Il viaggio al femminile" 323). Bénédicte Monicat adds that for traveling women, in particular, who flee constraints the idea of the confinement typical of harems can be horrifying (*Itinéraires* 105).[5] In *Asie mineure et Syrie, souvenirs de voyages*,[6] Belgiojoso explains her privileged status as a woman traveler: "j'étais mieux placée que la plupart des voyageurs pour connaître tout un côté fort important de la société musulmane,—le côté domestique, celui où domine la femme. Le harem, ce sanctuaire mahométan, hermétiquement fermé à tous les hommes, m'était ouvert" (2) ("I was better qualified than most travellers for studying one important side of Mussulman society—the domestic side, that in which Woman predominates. The Harem, the Mahometan sanctuary, hermetically sealed to all men, was open to me" xvii–xviii).[7] She compares the scenes of art and luxury described in the *Arabian Nights* to the real conditions of harem life: "Imaginez des murs noircis et crevassés.... Lorsque j'entrais pour la première fois dans ces charmants réduits, j'en étais choquée" (16) ("Imagine blackened and cracked walls.... When I first entered one of these delightful bowers, it almost sickened me" 28). It is, indeed, common for female travelers to focus on women's lives and roles in their texts, and they often pursue feminist causes in their travel writings.[8]

Belgiojoso's Eastern sojourn included the type of social and political reform efforts she had already begun in Italy in the 1840s. For example, in Locate,

Belgiojoso founded an agricultural community of native workers. There, she created schools for boys and girls, launched artistic workshops, and organized religious celebrations and dances. Community members could receive hot meals, and medicine was distributed without cost. This project reflected a common belief at the time among those in favor of the *Risorgimento*, namely, that by educating the peasants and helping them out of poverty, one could eventually interest them in the national cause (Knibiehler 208). Petacco notes that contemporaries were skeptical about Belgiojoso's activities in Locate, stating that "at that time the 'extravagant' initiatives of Princess Belgiojoso were considered along the lines of a revolutionary endeavor" (148). Later, during her voyage through Turkey and Syria, she bought a piece of land near Safranbolu, north of Andara, with the goal of organizing similar community activity. In buying Ciaq-Maq-Oglou, as the property was called, Cristina "undertook to apply in Asia Minor what she had learned in Locate about farming and administration" (Brombert 201). At Ciaq-Maq-Oglou, she employed Italian expatriates as well as Turkish workers. As with her Italian venture, Belgiojoso's community project in Turkey allowed her to further her political and humanitarian agendas.

Emina and the travel memoirs, letters, and fiction penned during Belgiojoso's Middle Eastern exile "capture the fascination of her discoveries while revealing her keen eye for detail, humor, and the 'human interest' universally sought by journalists" (Brombert 206). Luigi Severgnini affirms that "the princess was inspired by acquaintances and experiences from her travels in the Orient, and she developed above all a sense of social inquiry and representation of people's living conditions. . . . [Her travel writings] were appreciated everywhere . . . even constituting a novelty compared to the usual travel books" (13). Some of Belgiojoso's works from this period were translated into Italian and English and partially serialized in the New York *Tribune* (Brombert 205–6).

In *Emina*, Belgiojoso figures herself as the narrator/traveler who encounters the young protagonist Emina in Turkey. Yet the autobiographical nature of *Emina*, in fact, extends beyond the presence of this foreigner in the text. Whereas in *Souvenirs* the portraits of several female figures allowed Belgiojoso to explore indirectly her own life, in *Emina* the princess projects personal concerns and aspects of her own character onto a single protagonist.[9] For example, Emina spends her days in the fields as a shepherdess and concocts various natural cures for her goats' ailments. She administers her "drugs" to her young shepherd companion Saed and other ill peasant children and hence becomes "un petit docteur" (10) ("a little doctor").[10] In her travel memoirs, Belgiojoso indeed describes her own reputation in Asia Minor for medical prowess. She explains, for example, how an elderly man from Angora seeks her advice on a cure for blindness and how she acts as a physician for a young girl in Kupru (*Asie mineure et Syrie* 28, 44–47). Charles Neilson Gattey adds that Cristina "had learned a great deal about medicine . . . in Rome. [At Ciaq-Maq-Oglou] there was no doctor, and through her having given a few peasants successful remedies, she was now regarded as the physician for the whole province" (151). Beth Archer Brombert confirms that the princess tended to the ill children of Ciaq-Maq-Oglou, and "[h]er fame as a doctor [began] to spread" among the peasants, who marveled at her "powers of healing" (201). A second common point between the protagonist and the author emerges from the narrator's extended criticism of polygamy in Muslim society. The princess' first exilic sojourn in Paris was inspired, in part, by her unhappy marriage to the adulterous Emilio Belgiojoso. At the very least, she would have been sensitive to the problem of multiple partners, which she attributes to Emina. Finally, in keeping with the literary conventions of nineteenth-century realism, the narrator claims to present a "véridique histoire" (4) ("true story"), the tale of a poor Turkish family who lived "dans une des innombrables vallées de l'Asie Mineure" (1) ("in one of the countless valleys of Asia Minor"), emphasizing the fact that Emina's story could have been that of any poor, young girl of this time and place. Belgiojoso surely encountered many young women like the protagonist during her travels, and she visited several harems. Therefore, although the author presents, on one hand, a "simple story," she simultaneously claims that the tale reflects "real" problems that she encountered firsthand. As such, she emerges as a politically committed writer. Ultimately, Belgiojoso is both like and unlike this *other* woman Emina; both are female and thus marginalized, but at the same time Belgiojoso represents the dominant Occidental culture.[11] Monicat explains that there is a unique relationship between "the woman who is other (the traveler) and the other woman (the woman of the other culture)"—the woman travel writer sees both herself and her foil in the foreign woman (*Itinéraires* 29). Belgiojoso's exploration of her own identity through Emina is therefore complex, and we discover traces of the princess' character both through, and in opposition to, her protagonist.

In *Emina*, Belgiojoso speaks via the traveler in a strong first-person voice in order to persuade and influence her readers to favor her feminist principles. Scriboni describes a similar narrative voice in Belgiojoso's *Asie mineure et Syrie*, "a very marked 'I,' which attributes to itself from the beginning the authoritativeness of knowledge" ("Il viaggio al femminile" 317). In *Emina*, such an authoritative narrator also exudes confidence and a sense of superiority, an assurance that may be attributed, in part, to Belgiojoso's noble birth. For example, Belgiojoso continually interrupts the narrative with biting, sarcastic comments, particularly with regard to gender roles. She notes, for instance, that even if Mohammed did not explicitly refuse to give "woman" a soul, he neglected to elaborate on the subject (12). His followers therefore concluded that "il n'avait rien à en dire" (12) ("he had nothing to say about it"). Belgiojoso criticizes the lack of religious education for girls in Islamic doctrine at the time. While she praises Emina's self-education, for example, she is quite critical of her lack of formal education. She reminds the reader that Emina "est femme et Turque . . . on ne lui a rien enseigné de la religion" (12) ("is a woman and Turkish . . . no one had ever taught her anything about religion"). Belgiojoso attributes an intuitive knowledge of religion to her protagonist, which perhaps can be explained by the author's Romantic ideology. Emina is an exceptional young woman, intelligent and curious. Despite her lack of religious instruction, she draws conclusions about God and spirituality from others' remarks. Through "raisonnement" (12) ("reasoning"), Emina comes to believe in eternal life. Belgiojoso, in fact, creates a protagonist who resembles an ideal Western heroine more closely than an Oriental one.

Belgiojoso's analysis of Emina's "coming-of-age" allows for a consideration of both female development and gender oppression in the nineteenth century. *Emina* illustrates female formation in typical nineteenth-century fashion: an innocent young girl is torn from her peaceful, sheltered, childhood world, sent into the "society" of marriage, and expected to adapt to her new role and responsibilities.[12] When she finds that this environment does not allow her to develop as a whole person and that, in fact, there is no socially acceptable manner for her to realize her desire to be an equal partner in marriage and a contributing member of the larger community outside the home or, in this case, the harem, she dies. Certain parallels between the Oriental girl's *bildung* and that of Western heroines—the liberty of youth versus the confinement of marriage, for example—are obvious. Oppositions, such as the legality of polygamy in Turkey at the time versus monogamous marriage laws in Europe, also exist. For these reasons, Belgiojoso accomplishes her dual agenda of warning Westerners against sex discrimination and the lack of formal education for girls in general and condemning Easterners for the extreme gender inequality of harem life and polygamous marriage in particular.

We see very clearly in this text that male and female protagonists confront different societal obstacles and expectations in the growing-up process. Recall that Goethe's prototypical Wilhelm Meister undergoes various adventures, trials, and tribulations on the road to maturity but eventually becomes a contributing member of society, as do Charles Dickens' Pip and Alessandro Manzoni's Renzo. Yet Staël's extraordinary Corinne could never have survived the confines of the typical female path of marriage and motherhood. Like Corinne, Gustave Flaubert's Madame Bovary dies at the end of the novel, the latter being the victim of an all-too-frustrating marriage coupled with a desire for adventure. The plot structure that fixes heroines in stifling marriages is certainly common in nineteenth-century texts. Belgiojoso may have been drawing on two nineteenth-century developmental models for women characters in her portrayal of Emina.[13] First, texts such as Charlotte Brontë's *Jane Eyre* (1847) "taught girls the need to subordinate their individuality and will to others in order to become good wives and mothers through acquiescence, chastity, and self-sacrifice" (Bassanese 135). Flora A. Bassanese notes that such a model also influenced Italian women writers, including Neera and Marchesa Colombi (135). Belgiojoso, indeed, critiques this scenario in *Emina* through the depiction of an extreme version of self-sacrifice—the life of a Turkish harem wife. A second model portrays female characters who are generally more gifted, intelligent, and less conventional. Their *bildung* does not always lead to marriage and maternity. As discussed previously, this "novel of awakening" often depicts women's struggles in male-dominated spheres and frequently leads to pessimistic conclusions. The female protagonist's journey usually culminates in a heightened self-understanding that will, in turn, be frustrated by the lack of appropriate channels allowing her to integrate this awareness into an active social role. *Emina* also echoes this structure, for the intelligent young heroine dies at the end of the tale, apparently the victim of her desire to be her husband's equal and his only wife and also of the jealous first wife's deadly designs.

Emina also shares characteristics with the nineteenth-century French *roman intime*, which Sainte-Beuve saw as "a continuation of the tradition of female memoirs and letters from the XVIIth and XVIIIth centuries" (McCallum Schwartz 221). Lucy McCallum Schwartz explains that these simple love stories often feature a love triangle in which one of the lovers dies at the end of the tale (221). She notes that in several *romans intimes*, "society has placed an obstacle between the lovers—either the financially arranged marriage of the heroine or an inequality of age, race or social class" (221). In *Emina*, the marriage is, indeed, arranged for financial reasons, and Emina and the bey reflect diverse social classes and age groups. However, in the typical *roman intime* there is usually little psychological analysis or commentary by the narrator (McCallum Schwartz 221). In *Emina*, on the other hand, the narrator/traveler assumes an important role and voices her condemnation of arranged marriages.

It is also helpful to read Belgiojoso's tale in the light of studies on archetypical patterns in women's fiction. Annis Pratt discusses the tension between a "concept of liberty," which has ancient roots (she cites the example of the Apollo-Daphne myth, in which Daphne preferred to turn into a tree rather than to submit to Apollo), and the norms of wifely behavior (9).[14] Because of this clash she finds a "pervasive imagery of maiming, dwarfing, and suffocating forced upon young girls as part of 'coming of age'" (9). Pratt identifies several extended metaphors of insanity in women's texts, likening the effects of marriage to madness and incarceration.

Critics have explored the frequent fate of madness or death in female novels of development as well and contend that we must reread these tragic conclusions in light of modern psychology and the female maturation process. Marianne Hirsch argues that "if we look at what adulthood and maturity mean for the female protagonists of these texts, at the confinement, discontinuity, and stifling isolation that define marriage and motherhood, they do not present positive options" ("Spiritual *Bildung*" 27–28). Emina's life will, indeed, be fragmented as she is torn from her safe childhood world, where she experiences a oneness with Nature and possesses a certain dominion, and forced into the harem environment. "Success" in this environment demands a degree of self-effacement. Emina's refusal to conform to harem dictates ultimately leads to her death. Hirsch concludes that "the heroines' allegiance to childhood, pre-Oedipal desire, spiritual withdrawal, and ultimately death is not neurotic but a realistic and paradoxically fulfilling reaction to an impossible contradiction" ("Spiritual *Bildung*" 28). Death and insanity in these texts can therefore be read as affirmations rather than complete renunciations.

Emina is also without a mother in the story, aside from a stepmother, who has no true role. The motherless heroine is, in fact, another common character type in the nineteenth century. Staël's Corinne, Flaubert's Emma Bovary, and Brontë's Jane Eyre are just a few examples. Other nineteenth-century texts grant their heroines only mad or foolish mothers, rather than effective female models. Hirsch traces "a pattern of maternal repression" in British and French texts of the first half of the nineteenth century (*Mother/Daughter* 47). Writing toward the end of this period, Belgiojoso certainly incorporates these models in *Emina*. Emina's mother's death, due to "martyre conjugal" (1) ("conjugal martyrdom"), is a foreshadowing of the protagonist's fate. Hirsch explains that such maternal repression makes way for "surrogate mothers," women characters who "can assume [a] particularly nurturing role" (*Mother/Daughter* 50). The traveler in *Emina* offers one example.

With Emina's marriage, Belgiojoso addresses what she calls "le vrai sujet de notre récit" (49) ("the true subject of our story")—the young shepherdess turned "jeune femme esclave" (49) ("young slave wife"). Whereas marriage is a banal occasion for a Turkish man, it constitutes a turning point in the developmental process of a young woman. Belgiojoso observes in her travel memoirs *Asie mineure et Syrie* as well the importance for women of marriage and producing children. For example, she describes the humility and shame of a childless wife of an important bey. The young woman bows her head and blushes in the presence of the princess and is the victim of the other wives' scorn, for "[r]ien n'est plus honni, plus méprisé, plus délaissé, en Orient qu'une femme stérile" (119) ("[n]o object is so deprecated, none so desolate in the Orient as a sterile woman" 132).

Emina's marriage stems from her father's debts to the rich Hamid-Bey. Emina is offered to the bey as a prize—a means by which Emina's father can *postpone* his debts for another five years. Belgiojoso's criticism of women as objects of exchange in male bartering is quite direct. She comments that one might wonder why the bey preferred a wife to a slave and explains that the reason is quite simple: "[L]'une lui revenait meilleur marché que l'autre" (31) ("[O]ne amounted to a better bargain for him than the other").

In the bey's harem, we are introduced to his first wife, Ansha, the other children and family members, and the slaves. There is an emphasis on the boredom of harem life for women, evoking the limited domestic sphere that so many nineteenth-century female characters experience. Their development is measured in terms of interpersonal relationships rather than through activity in society. A girl's inferior position in this setting is evident from the power boys possess, "traitant leur mère et toutes les femmes du harem comme les dernières des esclaves" (54) ("treating their mother and all the women in the harem like the lowest of slaves").

With the character of Ansha, we get some insight into Belgiojoso's stereotypical views of Oriental women and the rivalry created by the harem setting. Ansha, a "superior woman," is experienced in the domestic circle. She possesses financial savvy and is hence influential in both the personal and economic decisions of her husband. Her experience and shrewdness are contrasted to Emina's naïveté. Ansha, in fact, has arranged the bey's second marriage and in so doing has employed a female strategy, a form of manipulation that allows her to maintain both control over her husband's future and a certain status in the harem environment. We witness the jealousy and competition between Ansha, who can be seen as the "wicked step-mother figure," and Emina, the latter yearning to win the respect and confidence that the bey seems to pay his first wife.

Belgiojoso adds a bit of local color to the story with the inclusion of an external political situation that lends authenticity to the narrative—infighting and brigandage between the Turks and the Kurds.[15] Upon returning from a trip with Emina to baths in a neighboring city, the bey is attacked by Kurdish rivals. Belgiojoso highlights the protagonist's courage as Emina tries to save the bey from being stabbed. Hamid-Bey soon falls ill—a possible metaphor for the ills in Muslim society that Belgiojoso outlines—and Ansha tries frenetically to come between her husband and his second wife. Emina administers one of her "remedies" to her now delirious husband. Similar to the dominion Emina experienced in Nature during her childhood days, this is another instance in which she senses some wholeness and transcendence, for only her touch can relieve the bey's suffering. As a result, Ansha becomes the object of his "profonde indifférence" (103) ("profound indifference"). Here again, however, we are in a realm outside everyday social realities, the world of the bey's delirium and illness.

By establishing the foil Emina/Ansha, Belgiojoso continually emphasizes the contrast between the purity of the heroine and the calculating, malicious nature of her rival. Yet Belgiojoso will later forgive Ansha to a degree and blame unjust marriage laws for a situation that drives women to compete. For the author, the lack of equality between men and women in Muslim marriages forces the latter to scheme against one another in order to maintain the husband's attention and to battle for positions of relative power in the harem hierarchy.

When the bey's illness continues, Ansha proposes to send for the *iman*, a Muslim priest/warlock friend known for his miraculous healing powers. In her portrayal of the bey's illness and the family's reaction, Belgiojoso criticizes the superstitious nature of an "uncivilized" people in need of Western education. She supports this view with her presentation of the ridiculous *iman*, who possesses nothing of what *"nous nous représentons . . . comme le résumé vivant des vertus chrétiennes, ou bien seulement de l'hônnete homme civilisé"* (94; emphasis added) (*"we imagine . . . as the living résumé of Christian virtues, or simply of the civilized gentleman"*; emphasis added).

Belgiojoso may also be projecting onto the *iman* the kinds of attacks of which she, too, was a victim. The princess was a misunderstood and mysterious character and remained so even after her death. Brombert explains that many portraits and caricatures of Belgiojoso appeared during the mid-nineteenth century and beyond. Some depictions were serious. Others were satirical, like that of "la marquise romantique" in *La croix de Berny* (*The Cross of Berny*),[16] an epistolary novel authored by Delphine de Girardin, Théophile Gautier, Jules Sandeau, and Méry. The work appeared in the 1840s and portrayed Belgiojoso as eccentric, theatrical, and mystifying. Brombert notes that another piece, the fictional *Souvenirs du Marquis de Floranges* (1906; *Memoirs of the Marquis of Floranges*), written by *pasticheur* Marcel Boulenger, "provided decades of later writers with details of Cristina's fifth-floor apartment, presumably littered with esoteric volumes in Hebrew and Latin, stilettos, skulls, and a sign on her door reading 'LA PRINCESSE MALHEUREUSE' [the unhappy princess]" (11). The text was actually a farce, drawing many elements from the satiric *Croix de Berny*. Brombert points out that those readers who recognized Cristina from the earlier work were "vastly amused and understood it was a satire" (11). Other readers, who were "less astute, launched the tradition of a macabre conspirator-bluestocking, an image too beguiling to rectify" (Brombert 11).

The bey recovers but forgets the affection that he showed Emina during his illness. Emina, in turn, becomes ill, perhaps purely of unrequited love and perhaps from poisoning by Ansha and the *iman*. As Emina feels death approaching, she turns away from obsessions of love and jealousy and toward the serene days of her childhood and loftier thoughts of God, not unlike virtuous nineteenth-century heroines such as Manzoni's Lucia and Balzac's Madame de Mortsauf. When Hamid finally begins wondering if Ansha could be jealous of his second wife, our narrator is quick to evoke the classic image of the witless male as a victim of female cunning. According to the narrator, the bey's uncertainty regarding Ansha's motivations proves "combien la sagacité de l'homme est aisément déroutée par la malice féminine!" (115) ("how much the wisdom of man is easily diverted by feminine mischievousness!").

It is here that Belgiojoso, through her narrator/traveler, enters the scene: "N'ayant pas [grand] chose à faire dans ma vallée, je pris le parti de visiter la province voisine" (124) ("Not having much to do in my valley, I decided to visit the neighboring province"). With her companions, she happens upon the bey's harem. He recounts the adventure with the Kurds, his illness, the intervention of the *iman*, and his young wife's present condition and asks the traveler to visit and try to cure Emina. Belgiojoso suspects the *iman's* relationship with Ansha, along with the love triangle within the harem. The bey marvels at her perceptiveness and exclaims: "—Je le savais bien . . . que vous autres Européens vous pouvez tout et savez tout!" (126–27) ("—I was quite certain...that you Europeans, you can do all and know all!")—precisely the point Belgiojoso wants to make. Further, she becomes the "doctor" called upon to cure the social ills exemplified by this family. Finally, Belgiojoso subverts the superior male/inferior female paradigm prevalent in nineteenth-century Turkish society. She, the European woman, emerges as the enlightened and progressive figure.

The traveler meets the young girl, who extends the tender welcome "que les femmes turques font d'ordinaire à l'Européenne" (127) ("which Turkish women usually give to the European woman"). She comforts her and answers Emina's questions about Western religious thought, serving as both a maternal substitute and spiritual guide. Through Emina's naïve comments, the narrator is able to criticize a culture that believes in male hegemony. For example, Emina talks of a wonderful place where good Muslims gather with the prophet but where women are not allowed. She has learned that for the "Francs," women are admitted to "les jardins des fidèles" (130) ("the gardens of the faithful"). Belgiojoso, spokesperson for Western ideas and religious beliefs, sets herself up as the voice of knowledge: "je dis à la pauvre enfant tout ce qui me parut clair, facile à saisir, et surtout consolant. . . . A ma place, un membre de la société biblique . . . eût été fort content de lui-même" (130–31) ("I said to the poor child everything that seemed to me clear, easy to grasp, and above all consoling. . . . In my place, a member of the biblical society . . . would have been most happy with himself"). Belgiojoso's heroine may be reserved and meek, but her narrator cannot hide long behind a modest tone. Benjamin Crémieux has analyzed Belgiojoso's personality and her desire and need to serve: "Christine has the need to dominate because she feels superior . . . she has . . . the need to give of herself, but not to a single human being. . . . It is to the whole of humanity that she would like to sacrifice herself" (33). *Emina* tells of a traveler who endeavors to make an impact on one family. Yet Belgiojoso's aspirations are, indeed, much greater. Through the "conversion" and education of Emina, the princess' journey becomes part of a much larger feminist and humanitarian mission.

Belgiojoso, indeed, takes the voice of the Western female explorer/colonizer one step further. Rather than land or an entire people, it is men who are to be "colonized," educated, and brought into the fold of the civilized in this narrative. The female characters in *Emina* are all strong, influential, intelligent, and perceptive. The male characters of all ages and classes, on the other hand, are generally childlike, malleable, ignorant, and in need of guidance. Emina's childhood friend Saed cannot understand her knowledge of God. Emina's father is completely insensitive to her developmental needs. Hamid-bey recognizes only too late the reasons for his wife's suffering. Belgiojoso portrays men as insensitive to loftier spiritual or intellectual understanding. Except for Saed, they are often unsympathetic toward women as well.

After the traveler's meeting with Emina, she explains to an impatient bey that Emina is dying out of love for him. She continues, "à vrai dire je ne voi[s] pas. . . . Non, rien n'est moins fat ni moins irascible qu'un Turc!" (132) ("to tell the truth I don't see. . . . No, nothing is less conceited nor less irascible than a Turc!"). In the ellipses, she implies, "I can't imagine *why* Emina would be in love with you!" Furthermore, she ironically expresses how very irritable and vain the bey, in fact, is. Her condescending attitude toward him is reinforced by the fact that he becomes "nameless" as their conversation continues. He is "mon bey" ("my bey") or "un Turc" ("a Turk"). Finally, she realizes that if she wishes to be understood by the bey and to stir some remorse in this character whom, along with Turkish society, she depicts as the guilty one, she must explain everything to the bey "catégoriquement" (133) ("categorically"), thus implying his limited intellectual capacity. When Hamid protests that he does love Emina, the traveler counters: "[V]ous l'aimiez d'une certaine façon, parce qu'elle était jeune et jolie, et vous auriez aimé de même toute autre femme aussi jeune et aussi jolie qu'elle; mais ce n'est pas ainsi qu'Emina voulait être aimée" (133) ("You loved her in a certain way, because she was young and pretty, and you would have also loved any other woman as young and as pretty as she; but it isn't in that manner that Emina wanted to be loved"). In contrast to the bey's volatile, emotional reaction ("Allah!" 133), we have Belgiojoso's reason: "Il me fallut beaucoup de temps et non moins de patience pour lui faire comprendre qu'Emina souffrait d'être traitée . . . comme une enfant . . . et non pas comme une amie, une égale, une compagne de coeur" (133) ("I needed much time and no less patience to make him understand that Emina suffered from being treated . . . like a child . . . and not as a friend, an equal, a heartfelt companion"). The ideal, then, is Western, Christian, monogamous love, and more specifically, monogamous marriage.[17]

Female rivalry in this text and in this society, according to the author, is the result of circumstances rather than ignorance regarding women's worth as capable individuals. The female characters are exonerated in *Emina*. According to Belgiojoso, they either resemble Western heroines (Emina) or have the potential to do so through their "superior" nature (Ansha). Emina possesses "une intelligence élevée dont [le bey] n'avait aucune idée" (134) ("an elevated intelligence of which [the bey] had no idea"). She is the heroine who approaches a more typically Western conception of womanhood, desiring to be the equal and only conjugal partner. Furthermore, she is very concerned about God and about the afterlife; in this regard she has ideas that are, according to Belgiojoso, much closer to "[les] nôtres" (134) ("ours"). Ansha is, indeed, partially excused for her behavior. In the most dogmatic phrase of the text, the narrator states: "—Ansha n'est pas la seule à blâmer dans tout ceci, dis-je [au bey] un jour, ce sont vos lois sur le mariage qui sont la vraie cause du mal" (139) ("—Ansha is not the only one to be blamed in all of this, I told [the bey] one day, it is your laws regarding marriage which are the true cause of ill"). Through such simple, declarative statements, Belgiojoso continues to draw Eastern/Western contrasts in an authoritative fashion. Similar views are confirmed in Belgiojoso's *Asie mineure et Syrie*: "Que les sages . . . donnent [à leur peuple] une famille en abolissant la polygamie, car si une femme constitue la famille, plusieurs femmes la détruisent. Que sans prononcer le nom du Christ, ils . . . initient [les gens] aux doctrines civilisatrices et à la morale du christianisme" (234–35) ("Let the wise . . . [re-create] the family by abolishing polygamy; for if one wife constitutes the family, more than one destroys it. Without pronouncing the ways of Christ, let the people, however, be initiated in the civilizing doctrines and the moral standard of Christianity" 264). Further, Belgiojoso expresses compassion for Muslim women because of their limited freedom. Again in *Asie mineure et Syrie*, Belgiojoso refutes a Muslim women who has traveled to Europe for admonishing her friends because they tolerate infidelity: "vous parlez presque aussi bien qu'une socialiste d'Europe; mais ces femmes-ci vous disent tout bonnement ce qu'elles éprouvent, et je comprends qu'ayant vecu commes elles, leurs sentiments soient tels qu'elles viennent de nous les exprimer" (415–16)

("You speak on this matter as profoundly as any socialist defender of women's rights. But these women candidly tell you what they experience, and, having lived as they have, I can comprehend how it is that their sentiments are such as they have just expressed to you" 414). It is the bey's point of view, however, that we do not hear in *Emina*. The bey is never pardoned and makes only limited "progress" in his understanding of his relationship with Emina and the ideas she entertains. The male view is only partially represented by the situation, but the fact that there are no explanation of the bey's behavior and no attempt to understand the male code of conduct in Turkish society weakens Belgiojoso's feminist statement. Had the character of the bey been further developed, readers would have had a more balanced portrait of gender divisions.

The princess does not hesitate to inquire about the couple after her departure. She receives such news on several occasions during her sojourn and proceeds to recount three "conclusions" to the story. Perhaps the multiple endings to the narrative, like an open ending, are meant to inspire the reader to draw conclusions about Emina, to make parallels between the oppression of this Oriental girl and that of women in Western culture, past and present, and finally to take action to change such injustice. Perhaps, too, given Belgiojoso's personal investment in the story—Emina's concerns about fidelity and women's roles reflect those Belgiojoso had in her own life—the author is unable to conclude the tale or resolve entirely the problems it treats.[18]

In the first conclusion, which is supposedly relayed to the princess by a traveler six months later, Emina dies as a result of Ansha's plotting and scheming shortly after Belgiojoso's departure. In a second version of this ending, Hamid-bey expects "de fréquentes visites" (142) ("frequent visits") from his dead wife. In the second conclusion, the bey catches Ansha with the *iman*, and a domestic scandal ensues. The couple settles on a divorce, but since such action always requires "un certain temps entre la signature et l'exécution de l'arrêt" (142) ("a certain amount of time between the signature and the execution of the decree"), the divorce is drawn out indefinitely. During this time, Ansha tries to regain her former status. Finally, in the third account, the bey finds another young bride. As the only daughter of the third of five wives of another bey, this young girl had been "élevée à bonne école" (142) ("raised in good hands"). She would neither contest the harem structure nor die a heartbroken victim of her place in it.

In the final pages of her text, then, Belgiojoso refuses closure with regard to the future, positing only potential conclusions to the story. We are left with merely a glimpse of hope for future change in the second version of the first conclusion—Emina's spirit lives on, along with the possibility of reform in harem life. Though Belgiojoso proposes far-reaching changes regarding marriage laws in Muslim society, she realizes that they will come about only gradually. Such tempered optimism reflects Belgiojoso's life experiences; her hopes for Italian unification, for example, and her dreams of a better life for the underprivileged classes were realized only after years of struggle.[19]

Belgiojoso's views are reinforced in one of her later essays entitled "Della presente condizione delle donne e del loro avvenire" (1866; "On the Present Condition of Women and Their Future"). In this feminist study, the princess gives a historical outline of female oppression, beginning in antiquity. She then discusses the injustice of male and female roles in her own era. She laments the destiny of older women, deprived of health and beauty, and of mothers, who devote their lives to children who do not respect them because of the mother's secondary status in the family. Because "la condizione della donna non è tollerabile" (175) ("woman's plight is not tolerable"), Belgiojoso calls for change. Encouraging education for women, she proposes the exercise of their capabilities through the study of literature, history, philosophy, and the sciences and in such professions as teaching. Her appeal is tempered, however, and she refuses to ally herself with the extreme members of the burgeoning feminist movement in France and Italy who request "riforme radicali . . . che disturberebbero la pace della famiglia" (181) ("radical reforms . . . which would trouble family tranquillity"). Instead, "conviene . . . camminare adagio" (182) ("it is better . . . to proceed slowly"). Women must still, in Belgiojoso's view, nurture and educate children. If they are more aware and knowledgeable themselves, this task will produce healthier personal and social relationships. She warns the courageous women who will break new ground of the difficult path they will have to follow: "Le donne che ambiscono un nuovo ordine di cose, debbono armarsi di pazienza e di abnegazione, contentarsi di preparare il suolo, di seminarlo, ma non pretendere di raccoglierne la messe" (183) ("Women who desire a new social order must arm themselves with patience and abnegation, content themselves with preparing the soil, with sowing it, but not aspire to reap the harvest of their efforts"). Belgiojoso's hope is that all women will help to reverse the tide of sexual oppression for generations to come. Although this will be a slow and tedious process, she appeals to women to participate in her feminist crusade.

In conclusion, Belgiojoso brings Western feminism and Western values to an Oriental context in *Emina*. Whereas obvious parallels between the protagonist and the author inform the developmental journey we witness, Belgiojoso also positions herself and her culture as superior to the Oriental one and voices her convictions in an authoritative manner. Though many of the princess' views are dogmatic and her prejudices apparent, her depiction of the female role in Turkish society is compassionate and reflects certain anthropological and cultural insights. Despite the fact that the male point of view is lacking, representation of the unfair female role in harem life found in *Emina* and in other similar texts would have an impact on future women writers.[20]

In her "coming-of-age" Emina experiences many of the common trials and tribulations attributed to her literary contemporaries regarding the relationship between self-education and social education, maturity and development, the role of the wife, and the limitations on women's freedom. Parallels between this Oriental woman's sorry fate and that of other nineteenth-century heroines in tales set in the West serve as a warning to European readers. In effect, Belgiojoso represents the plight of the Oriental woman as the "black fate" of the

Occidental one, an extreme depiction of the issues she saw as problematic at home. The story can, indeed, be read as an argument for monogamous love, and more specifically, monogamous marriage, and the text underscores the tragic consequences that can ensue if such limits are transgressed.

Finally, with the inclusion of the narrator/traveler, spokesperson for the author, in her text, Belgiojoso's narrative reflects a personal commitment to social change. The princess traveled to foreign lands largely unexplored by women and wrote extensively in both fictional and nonfictional contexts about her impressions of class and sexual inequality. Her dedication to social and political activism, indeed, permeated her entire life. Hence, Belgiojoso's political agenda continually merged with her feminist one. As we saw in *Souvenirs*, Belgiojoso frequently expresses her views through the plight of women characters. She again exploits this strategy in *Emina*, which emerges as a meditation on the problem of gender oppression in different cultures and a call for social reform both at home and abroad.

NOTES

1. This chapter constitutes, in part, a revision of my article entitled "Cristina Trivulzio di Belgiojoso's Western Feminism: The Poetics of a Nineteenth-Century Nomad," published in *Italian Quarterly* 34.133–34 (1997): 21–32. All quotations from *Emina* are from the 1858 edition of *Scènes de la vie turque*. English translations of quotations from *Emina* are mine. Flavia Milanese has recently translated the text into Italian.

2. Zonana tackles some similar issues in her study on the "feminist orientalist" discourse in *Jane Eyre*. She notes that Brontë's extended use of the slave/sultan simile allows for the displacement of the root of patriarchal oppression onto an "Oriental" society. As such, British readers are able to contemplate their own problems without jeopardizing their self-image as Westerners and Christians.

3. Although the narrator/traveler is not identified by name in the text, the use of the first person and the narrator/traveler's addresses to the reader identify her as the author's spokesperson. For simplicity's sake, at times I refer to the narrator/traveler as Belgiojoso or the princess. The terms "protagonist" or "heroine" do not fit, as they better represent Emina.

4. See Christopher L. Miller's discussion of these writers in "Orientalism, Colonialism." Also, Mirella Scriboni points out that Belgiojoso would certainly have been familiar with travel narratives by Chateaubriand and Lamartine ("Preface" 21).

5. On the other hand, Monicat points out that certain women travelers, particularly those who visited the harems of the rich, admired the protection and liberty harem inhabitants enjoyed. She states that some women travelers advance numerous arguments "in favor of the harem. Even the concept of confinement implies for Olympe Audouard in particular the idea of protection and that of the preservation of a feminine universe independent of the sphere of men" (*Itinéraires* 97–98).

6. Recall that this text was originally published under the title *La vie intime et la vie nomade en Orient*. All French quotations are from the 1858 edition of *Asie mineure et Syrie* and are cited by page number.

7. All English translations of quotations from *Asie mineure et Syrie* come from the following text: Cristina Trivulzio di Belgiojoso, *Oriental Harems and Scenery*, trans. from the French of Cristina Trivulzio di Belgiojoso (New York: Carleton, 1862) and are cited by page number.

8. For a detailed study of nineteenth-century women travelers in Italy, see Borghi et al.

9. See Monicat's discussion of women travelers' paradoxical analyses of harems and of their self-analyses through portrayals of the Other (*Itinéraires* 94–111).

10. There are certain similarities between the character of Emina and that of Fanchon or "La petite Fadette" ("Little Fadette") in George Sand's novel *La petite Fadette*, published in 1848. Recall that Fanchon, like Emina, is gifted in the natural sciences and granted curative abilities. In addition, *La petite Fadette* illustrates an idealism also common to Belgiojoso. At the conclusion of Sand's novel, inner virtues triumph. The once homely Fanchon marries Landry, founds a school for the needy children of the commune, and revels in her good fortune. As discussed previously, Belgiojoso favored the same type of social reform in her own life.

11. See Monicat's discussion of the woman traveler and her relationship to the women she encounters abroad in *Itinéraires* 29–35.

12. See Annis Pratt et al. (17) for details of the heroine's dominion in the natural childhood world. Pratt's chapter "The Novel of Development" (13–37) is a joint study with Barbara White.

13. My discussion is informed by Bassanese's study of these models (135–36).

14. Pratt discusses the Apollo-Daphne myth throughout her Introduction.

15. In my paper "Crossing Borders: Travel, Transgression, and Self-Discovery in the Works of Cristina di Belgiojoso" (MLA Conference, Chicago, Dec. 1995), I analyzed *Emina* and another tale in the *Scènes de la vie turque* collection: "Un prince kurde" ("A Kurdish Prince"). In both stories, Belgiojoso illustrates conflicts between the Kurds and the Turks. I developed the argument that the princess' comments on the civil strife in Asia Minor were a veiled criticism of the atrocities she witnessed in war-torn Italy between her compatriots and the Austrians.

16. See pages 29-34.

17. In a conversation with me about this study, Lucienne Frappier-Mazur noted that in encouraging a monogamous married situation, Belgiojoso points to the area where Eastern and Western conceptions differed at the time. Whereas a Muslim could repudiate his wives, monogamous marriage, regardless of adultery, gave more dignity to women.

18. A more straightforwardly autobiographical text would also exclude an "ending," of course, or the writing of one's own death (see Jost 100).

19. Note that Belgiojoso, who died in 1871, did live to see Italian unification.

20. Consider the numerous women writers in the latter part of the nineteenth century and the twentieth century who focus on women's roles and women's lives, past and present: Matilde Serao, Sibilla Aleramo, Anna Banti, Oriana Fallaci, and Dacia Maraini, to name only certain Italians. Further, much feminist research continues to be conducted on the harem.

3

The *Bildung* of Céleste Mogador and Lionel de C***: A Sentimental Journey

Mémoires de Céleste Mogador (1854) traces the transformation of Elisabeth-Céleste Vénard (1824–1909) from abused adolescent and prostitute to performer and writer.[1] This first collection of memoirs was signed Céleste Mogador, a name given to her during her days as a performer at the stylish *bal Mabille*,[2] but she would later become the Countess of Chabrillan, wife of the Count Lionel de Chabrillan, whom we meet as Lionel de C*** in *Mémoires*. Though she was not formally educated, Mogador was urged by her lawyers to write her autobiography to defend herself against lawsuits. The text evolves into an occasion to explain and explore her past. One technique for doing so is to incorporate the parallel story of her lover Lionel's *bildung* into her own narrative of development. In *Mémoires*, the protagonist's maturation is nurtured and shaped by her connection with others; Céleste's self-discovery will be intertwined with the psychological evolution of her lover. The embedded male quest for selfhood parallels that of the main character and highlights the gender prejudices of nineteenth-century French society and literature.

Mogador offers a female parallel to the exploits of such leading writers of autobiography as Rousseau, Musset, and Stendhal and of practitioners of *bildungsroman* including Goethe and Flaubert. This "Cinderella story" depicts the developmental journey of an "exceptional" nineteenth-century heroine. Céleste's voyage toward freedom and her quest for a new sense of self constitute a portrait of a woman more gifted and intelligent than many of her nineteenth-century sisters. She confronts a public that has branded her a "fallen woman," and hers is a "success story." Satisfaction occurs, however, only after surmounting serious personal and societal hurdles.

Although Mogador has received little critical attention,[3] her literary career was extensive. Because of her lack of training, her writing contained many spelling and stylistic errors.[4] She employed copyists for assistance, however, and continually strove to educate herself, including efforts to learn English while living in Australia. She composed not only autobiographical works but numerous novels, poems, operettas, songs, and over thirty-five plays.[5] Mogador acted in many of her dramatic productions, even producing some herself, and was a member of the *Société des Auteurs Dramatiques*. Her writing was admired in its day by such figures as Alexandre Dumas *père* and *fils*, Emile and Delphine de Girardin, Camille Doucet, and Théophile Gautier. Her artistic acquaintances also included neighbor Georges Bizet, who lived in a small country home near Mogador's residence, *Le Vésinet*, outside Paris. Bizet enjoyed working at Mogador's comfortable abode (Moser 223–24) and is said to have based his Carmen, in part, on her.[6]

Mogador also witnessed an era of political turmoil, including the Revolution of 1848 and the Commune of 1871. During the Franco-Prussian War, she proposed the formation of a corps of women to train as first-aid nurses. She writes to the mayor of Paris: "Il y a dans la capitale des milliers de femmes énergiques et fortes, appartenant à toutes les classes et surtout à celle du peuple laborieux, qui, sur un mot de vous, sont prêtes à former une légion et à se rendre par divisions à tous les postes qui leur seront indiqués pour soigner les blessés" (qtd. in Moser 250) ("There are thousands of energetic and strong women in the capital belonging to all social classes and particularly the working class. These women, upon your command, are ready to form a legion and go by divisions to all of the necessary posts to attend to the injured"). Her Soeurs de France (Sisters of France), founded in 1870, included some 150 women from diverse backgrounds. The corps of women volunteers recalls Belgiojoso's war efforts in Italy in the 1840s. Mogador also launched a project to turn her home at *Le Vésinet* into an orphanage for homeless girls from Alsace and Lorraine. Françoise Moser explains that Mogador had always resented the lack of guidance she received from her mother and dreamed of concluding her career by protecting young girls from making the unfortunate choices that had tainted her own youth (274). Indeed, Mogador endeavored throughout her life to atone for her past vice through self-improvement and generosity toward others.

Like many female authors of her era, Mogador veils any ambitious tendencies in *Mémoires* with humility—her text is a confession, an explanation of her former days and not an opportunity for self-aggrandizement. In the tradition of Rousseau, Mogador feels compelled to confess even the scandalous details of her past: "j'avais pensé que des mémoires devaient être vrais et qu'on n'avait pas le droit d'arracher à sa fantaisie une page du livre de sa vie" (*Mémoires*, 1858, 1: 3). ("I had thought that memoirs had to be true and that one did not have the right to extract as one pleases one page from the book of one's life"). She confirms to her public a pact of truthfulness: would her pages have but one reader, that person could never accuse her of having concealed "une seule des hontes de [sa] vie" (107) ("even one of the shames of [her] life"). Her forthright narrative voice emphasizes the seriousness of her task and the exemplary nature of this personal story. Finally, as the protagonist of *Mémoires* begins prostituting herself at sixteen, the more mature narrator[7] considers her communicative task as she reflects on her former folly, her youthful self: "Le sentiment qui me guidera dans ce récit est bien supérieur aux divers mobiles qui ont inspité ma conduite" (107) ("The emotion which will guide me in telling this story is quite superior to the various motives which inspired my conduct"). Mogador completes her autobiography with the sequel to *Mémoires*, published over twenty years later, entitled *Un deuil au bout du monde: Suite des Mémoires de Céleste Mogador* (1877). I examine *Un deuil* in the next chapter.

In the French *bildungsroman* tradition, in which society is seen as a corruptive force, Mogador's text represents a reverse response to the masculine model. Whereas the traditional German *bildungsroman* emphasizes the growth of the individual as a gradual process and the substitution of reality and maturity for fantasy and false aspirations, nineteenth-century French and English novels are typically less optimistic (Hirsch, "The Novel of Formation" 302). They depict "not a formation but a deformation of the individual, the corruption of natural impulses and values" (Hirsch, "The Novel of Formation" 302). Marianne Hirsch cites Balzac's Rastignac, who "progresses from moral purity to corruption and thus to a form of delusion" ("The Novel of Formation" 302).[8] In Mogador's text, by contrast, Céleste passes from purity to corruption and back again, her final state being one of awareness of her strengths and qualities despite a difficult youth. Going past her "past," however, will ultimately mean "leaving the country." She must separate from conventional French society, which has no place for her, a woman of a *passé douteux*, and her aristocratic lover Lionel, who has lost his fortune. At the end of the text they prepare to set off for Australia in search of a new life.

From the beginning of *Mémoires*, inconsistent maternal guidance hinders Céleste's development.[9] The loss of her father at age six[10] and the abuse Céleste and her mother endure at the hands of the latter's various lovers add to the youth's vulnerability. One suitor, Monsieur G., captures Céleste and whisks her away to a brothel, an obvious foreshadowing of her future abode. Soon after, another of the mother's suitors, Vincent, attempts to rape Céleste. She narrowly escapes but falls in with Parisian prostitutes, who encourage her to enter the profession and who oversee her initiation. Céleste becomes "inscrite," a prostitute officially "registered" with French authorities and legally permitted to practice the profession. Mogador writes: "J'étais inscrite sur ce livre infernal d'où rien ne vous efface, pas même la mort!" (112) ("I was registered in this infernal book from which nothing obliterates you, not even death!"). Her *Mémoires* will, indeed, be a confession of, and a commentary on, this earlier inscription. Céleste becomes a resident in a Parisian brothel, with her mother's resigned approval to boot. The brothel's feminine universe, with its rules and regulations, recalls the stifling harem environment that oppresses Belgiojoso's Emina. Céleste quickly understands that she has chosen a life of servitude.

The kidnapping motif found in *Mémoires*, a frequent French literary theme, is reminiscent of the abductions that occurred over the centuries, when desired young women were taken away, raped, and forced to marry, either because the "suitors" truly loved them or because they were interested in securing a financial or familial destiny. Kidnapping and induction into prostitution continued to occur in the nineteenth century and beyond.

Céleste's experience, which to us might sound more like fiction than life, would not have been unusual for a woman of her class and time period. Social historians document a high rate of prostitution from 1830 to 1870, for example, years that have been termed "the most grim in the entire history of women's work" (Albistur and Armogathe 313).[11] According to Edmonde Charles-Roux et al., in 1851, 39 percent of the working population in heavy industry was made up of women (qtd. in Albistur and Armogathe 313). Working conditions in factories were often dangerous, illness common, long working hours and poor salary the norm, especially when compared to the wages earned by men. In domestic labor situations, young women were often harassed and sexually abused by rich employers. Maïté Albistur and Daniel Armogathe add that "[s]uch a state of poverty unleashed the outbreak of prostitution in urban areas" (315). They quote Alexandre Parent-Duchâtelet's important study *La prostitution à Paris* (*Prostitution in Paris*), first published in 1836, which states that "[o]ut of 3,120 Parisian prostitutes, only 36 had not previously worked in factories. 4,112 out of 4,222 prostitutes do not know how to write their names, or they do so with great difficulty" (qtd. in Albustur and Armogathe 315).[12] The "cinquième quart" referred to women's "extra hours" after a day's work in order to make ends meet. Because of a lack of education and training for manual or professional work and little legal protection, working women of this period were often the hardest-hit victims of an unfair system. Prostitution as a legal structure within that system was often the only solution, the single means of supporting oneself in dire circumstances.

Susan McClary notes that prostitution was nurtured by the patronage of men from all social classes, including artists. Further, she explains: "Much of the high art of this period—major works and personal letters by Balzac, Baudelaire, Zola, Courbet, Manet—exploits prostitution as a central theme. Moreover, the art world itself was saturated with prostitution: women who modeled, danced or sang in public were assumed to be and were treated as whores" (38). The prostitute is, indeed, quite common in nineteenth-century literature among such novelists as Balzac, Sand, Flaubert, and Emile Zola. Charles Bernheimer offers a valuable analysis into nineteenth-century representations of prostitution in male writing and art. He finds the prostitute "ubiquitous in the novels and the paintings of this period not only because of her prominence as a social phenomenon but, more important, because of her function in stimulating artistic strategies to control and dispel her fantasmatic threat to male mastery" (*Figures of Ill Repute* 2). A comparison between the manner in which male and female writers endeavor either to restrict the harlot's power in narrative or to confront her threat to bourgeois society and marriage would be an engaging study. I underscore the fact that Mogador, whether or not she was representing her own story, was writing within a given literary tradition. Artistic portrayals of prostitution invoked both fear and fascination in this time period. The fact that these representations conjured up particular preconceptions about the lifestyle is evident in the scandal and censure produced by the publication of Mogador's text.

Bernheimer claims that firsthand descriptions of the experiential aspect of prostitution in the nineteenth century are few and far between: "[W]ith the exception of a few autobiographical writings by great courtesans of the period, we have no nineteenth-century accounts written by French prostitutes themselves" (*Figures of Ill Repute* 3). He may have had Mogador in mind in his mention of great courtesans, as she did eventually have clients and contacts in high society. Neither Mogador nor her life story, however, is mentioned in Bernheimer's study. Yet her debut in the profession was as a poor girl in a stifling brothel, and these experiences are described in some detail in *Mémoires*. She likens the brothel to a prison, for example, and after eight days can think of only one thing: leaving (112). Mogador recounts her humiliation after her scarring first experience with a customer (106). In addition, she tells of a mortifying evening when one client—described as a "un des plus grands littérateurs du siecle" (114) ("one of the greatest writers of the century")[13] and known by critics to be Musset—invites her to dinner only to drench her from head to toe with seltzer water.[14] Hence, some firsthand accounts of typical brothel life do exist. Bernheimer, nonetheless, offers valuable insights into the male writer and male artist's depictions of the frightening *femme fatale*.

The theme of prostitution in Mogador's text exemplifies society's function not only as an antagonist, as in the male *bildungsroman*, but as a stifling agent, common to women's developmental literature, especially in the nineteenth century. Mogador blames society for her downfall: "Autant il est difficile à une jeune fille, dans la position où j'étais, de se créer une existence honorable par le travail, autant il lui est aisé de glisser sur la pente du mal" (109) ("It is as difficult for a young girl, in my position, to create an honorable existence for herself by working as it is easy for her to slide down the slope of evil"). She emphasizes, for example, her desire to learn and work hard but laments her lack of resources; at nearly fifteen, she could barely read (63). She continues: "La loi, qui ne permet pas d'administrer ses biens avant vingt et un ans, laisse une fille de seize ans vendre son corps" (117) ("The law, which does not permit managing one's possessions before the age of twenty-one, allows a young girl of sixteen to sell her body"). She furthermore criticizes society's treatment of certain kinds of women. We hear the story of Lise, a well-known dancer and courtesan known as "la Reine Pomaré" ("Queen Pomaré"), infamous through her portrayal in Zola's *Nana*. Mogador scorns newspaper writers who shower Lise with insults and scoffs, and she notes: "Les journalistes traitent les femmes comme les gouvernements" (148) ("Journalists treat women like governments"). She later recounts Lise's death, her train of lovers nowhere in sight, and entitles the section with the biting "Quand la courtisane n'a plus rien à vendre" (234) ("When the courtesan has nothing more to sell").

Over the course of her observations and analyses, however, we become aware that the protagonist is developing a growing sense of self-appreciation. Pride and self-love begin to emerge as Céleste starts to make her own way in life. Mogador gives several examples of her generosity and goodness. For instance, reflecting on her friend Lise's death, she contrasts her own compassion to the indifference of Lise's former friends: "Je fus au cimetière huit jours après, espérant de trouver une pierre. . . . Rien. . . . Je revins au bout de dix jours. Rien. On avait abandonné la morte, comme on avait abandonné la malade. Je commandai un entourage en fer, un mausolée en marbre, avec ces deux lignes: *Ici repose Lise . . . née le 22 février 1825, morte le 8 décembre 1846. Son amie Céleste"* (237–38) ("I went to the cemetery eight days later, hoping to find a tombstone. . . . Nothing. . . . I returned ten days later. Nothing. They had abandoned the dead woman as they had abandoned the ill woman. I ordered an iron frame, a marble mausoleum, with these lines: *Here lies Lise . . . born 22 February 1825, died 8 December 1846. Her friend Céleste"*). Such simple declarative statements with repetition of the first-person subject emphasize the active function of the "I" and Céleste's pride in her own efforts. Additional examples include Céleste's repeated attempts to offer refuge to abandoned women as soon as her own financial condition and social status improve. She also agrees to be the godmother of her maid's child, the mother dying of cholera shortly after childbirth. The goddaughter, who appears throughout the rest of the work and in the sequel, will give Céleste the opportunity to "mother," and the relationship will provide a comforting haven when others abandon her. She muses that though she is at times alone, her goddaughter "n'a [qu'elle] sur la terre" (379) ("has [only her] on earth"). The child also creates a feminine continuity insofar as Céleste hopes to provide a better environment for her godchild than she had herself. She promises her maid that she will raise her child and make "une honnête femme" (335) ("an honest women") of her.[15] Rather than the self-indulgent autobiographer patting herself on the back, Mogador vindicates herself against a society that shuns poor and abandoned women. Her ingenuity and ambition have allowed her to leave poverty; she does not forget her roots, however, when she sees other women in need. We see in the previous examples that positive character traits that had long been buried, even to the protagonist herself, come to the fore. It is this self-love that Céleste must rediscover in order to feel "worthy" of the life and relationships she desires.

Mogador's self-awareness is further heightened after a dramatic questioning of her own life, a common feature in autobiography. Céleste sees her mother again, and the two attempt to open a boutique together. Initially, this reunion brings back peaceful sensations of the harmonious mother–child union prior to the tragic events at the hands of the mother's lover. Céleste then realizes that her mother is still involved with the vile Vincent. At the same time, Céleste is being pursued by the police for debts she has accrued and risks being sent to prison if she does not pay them. She lights two charcoal furnaces and awaits death but at the last minute fears the consequences of her actions. She is saved but has lived through "the dark night of the soul." The experience leads to an awakening: from now on, she must truly rely on herself alone.

Another important influence in Céleste's maturation process is her relationship with Lionel de C***.[16] Their liaison and its impact on both characters are described in the second half of *Mémoires*. We can therefore divide the work into two parts: the first includes childhood, disillusionment, going out into the world on her own, and breaking with her mother; the second portrays the development of Céleste the woman, the love relationship that will influence the rest of her life, the continuation of her theatrical career, and her first attempts at writing.

After Céleste meets Lionel at a ball, her passion for him begins to shape a "new Céleste." She still struggles with her past, however, which will be a constant obstacle for the couple, especially for Lionel's aristocratic family. We read: "Je rentrai chez moi, la tête et le coeur remplis de son image. Insensée que j'étais de désespérer de la vie! A vingt ans!" (245) ("I went home, my head and heart full of his image. Crazy as I was to despair of life! At twenty!"). The myriad of experiences Céleste has already undergone and the people she has had to deal with as a prostitute give the reader the impression that she is much older than twenty and much older than Lionel, nine years her senior.[17] Her liaison with Lionel, however, enables her to rediscover an innocence that was too quickly stolen from her. We read: "si perdue qu'elle soit, ou qu'elle ait été, la femme qui aime trouve dans son passé un souvenir de pudeur, de pureté; je l'aimais" (248) ("as lost as she is, or as she was, the woman who loves finds in her past a remembrance of modesty, of purity; I loved him"). The nostalgic tone in this passage emphasizes the fact that the narrative voice we hear is one of wisdom and experience. The declarative, proverbial "la femme qui aime" in the present tense, juxtaposed with the imperfect "je l'aimais," distinguishes the sagaciousness of the mature narrator from the emotion of the young protagonist, all tied together at the hands of the writer.

Mogador emphasizes love's purifying power, adhering to the Romantic myth of redemption by love. George Sand expresses similar sentiments regarding her parents' relationship in her autobiography *Histoire de ma vie*. Toward the beginning of *Histoire*, Sand ascribes to her father's voice this Romantic theme in a letter he writes to his mother: "L'amour purifie tout. L'amour ennoblit les êtres les plus abjects, à plus forte raison ceux qui n'ont d'autres torts que le malheur d'avoir été jetés dans le monde sans appui, sans ressources et sans guide" (I: 362) ("Love purifies everything. It ennobles the most abject beings, and all the more so those whose only wrong consists in the misfortune of having been cast into the world without friends, resources or guidance" 307). Céleste's will, in fact, turn out to be a "Cinderella story," the typical female drama of the "motherless" daughter of lower social standing who is saved by Prince Charming. Lionel will lose his fortune by the end of the text, but he remains noble all the same. Several feminist critics have emphasized the conscious or unconscious influence of such well-known legends and fairy tales on women's writing.

Why do some men choose "fallen women"? Other nineteenth-century literary works such as Madame de Staël's *Corinne* illustrate the desire to "rescue" the loved one. Parallels between this text and Mogador's *Mémoires* include the fact that both Corinne and Céleste are charismatic, talented performers, intelligent women who attract attention. Whereas Oswald agonizes over whether Corinne could be satisfied with a solitary, domestic life in England, Lionel struggles with the fear that Céleste could be swept away by one of her many other suitors. Writing on *Corinne*, Nancy K. Miller discusses the significance of loving the "fallen woman" and draws on Freud's article "A Special Type of Choice of Object Made by Men" (1910) (*Subject to Change* 199). "[L]ove for a harlot," as Freud puts it, reflects a desire by the lover to save the beloved and a certainty that the woman needs him (qtd. in Miller, *Subject to Change* 199). Miller explains that Freud connects the "impulse to rescue" with the child's attachment to his parents (*Subject to Change* 199). In one scene in *Corinne*, for instance, Oswald saves an old man from drowning, a reflection of his guilt over his relationship with his own father. For Freud, such actions enact the "fantasy to repay [the parents] by 'saving' them" (qtd. in Miller, *Subject to Change* 199). In Mogador's text, Lionel's parents are less "active" as defined characters insofar as we know very little of their actual lives. They are present, however, through the letters Lionel receives exhorting him to leave Céleste and pursue a proper marriage. It is when Lionel's father dies that he first distances himself from her.

A final example of Lionel's influence on Céleste's awakening as a woman is their physical relationship. Set in opposition to her disgust with her first sexual experience as a prostitute, Lionel's kiss sparks a contrary reaction: "je l'aimais trop pour lui mentir. Je lui racontai tout ce que j'avais fait. . . . —Je voudrais ressaisir le passé, mais c'est impossible. Voulez-vous le présent? Sa réponse fut un baiser. Il me sembla qu'*une autre femme venait de s'éveiller en moi*" (249; emphasis added) ("I loved him too much to lie to him. I told him all that I had done. . . . —I would like to recapture the past, but it is impossible. Do you want the present? His response was a kiss. It seemed to me that *another woman had just awakened in me*"; emphasis added). In this "novel of awakening," the honesty of her confession and Lionel's acceptance of it allow the more virtuous Céleste to appear. From the moment of her encounter with Lionel, Céleste's past will be a problem for both of them, but she is on her way toward something new. Lionel is not only a lover but a "family" for her.

Lionel's character is one of excesses, extremes, and rage, as well as sensitivity. His need for lavishness is revealed in the luxurious presents he offers Céleste, from precious jewels, to apartments, to fancy carriages. Céleste is objectified when Lionel dresses her up and adorns her with riches, when she becomes the possession he shows off to his friends. He meanwhile loses almost all of his fortune in gambling and incurs debts he is unable to repay.

Direct discourse underscores the volatile, passionate nature of the couple's relationship and moves the narrative along at a rapid pace. The reader witnesses the couple's interactions, especially their arguments, through a great deal of dialogue. As the text is narrated in the first person, we are continually aware of Céleste's interpretations and feelings. The stormy love affair that she and Lionel lead includes many separations, reunions, jealous arguments, rivalries, and even one violent encounter in which Céleste stabs herself and Lionel because of another woman.

Mogador also includes numerous letters in *Mémoires* that the couple exchanged over the course of several years. They highlight the protocol, distance, and oftentimes artificial nature of nineteenth-century society. They also gauge the exchanges at hand; by the time the written representation of feelings, events, and declarations arrives, the state of mind of the sender is often completely contrary to what is stated in the letter. At the same time, they reflect the competitive character of Céleste and Lionel's liaison. Each is constantly trying to get the better of the other, alternately threatening and nurturing the relationship. Letter writing is furthermore continued in *Un deuil*, notably, when Céleste and Lionel travel separately between Australia and France.

When Lionel finally proposes to Céleste in a letter, we realize that her identity as "la Mogador" is meaningful to her. At first, she is ecstatic about his proposal: "Je ne pouvais en croire mes yeux. . . . Mon orgueil me criait: 'Accepte!'" (393) ("I could not believe my eyes. . . . My pride cried out to me: 'Accept!'"). She later responds: *"Mon cher Lionel, je vous renvoie cette lettre, dont je suis indigne et qui ne peut être adressée à une femme comme moi. Votre couronne de comte me ferait une couronne d'épines . . . laissez-moi Mogador, restez Lionel de C***"* (393) (*"My dear Lionel, I return to you this letter, of which I am unworthy and which cannot be addressed to a woman like me. Your count's crown would be a crown of thorns for me . . . leave me Mogador, stay Lionel de C***"*). The letter again illustrates the opposition between the passion of the moment and the reason that comes with reflection and the time it takes to write down one's thoughts. The metaphor of the "crown of thorns" invokes the reader's sympathy, and the Christian symbolism conveys Céleste's suffering. We note that she prefers the controversial title "Mogador," the name she has earned through her talent and her art despite all of the suffering her past brings her, as opposed to the potential appellation "countess" with all of the wealth and social prestige it entails. Although several critics discuss Mogador's efforts to erase this name associated with her days as a dancer and thinly clad "écuyère" ("horsewoman"),[18] I posit that in her *Mémoires* this name carries with it a pride in overcoming her humble beginnings. The sequel to *Mémoires* is signed by the Countess of Chabrillan, yet it is still subtitled *Suite des Mémoires de Céleste Mogador*. As such, we recognize that her past remains an integral part of the countess, an awareness fitting for any autobiographer.

When Lionel blames Céleste's refusal on his "poverty," she subtly portrays herself as superior to her lover because of her honesty. In a letter from Lionel, we read: *"Votre prédiction sera accomplie: vous ne m'aurez quitté qu'avec mon dernier sou. Je viens d'apprendre ma ruine. . . . Ma cervelle rejaillira jusque sur votre robe de théâtre et votre lit de plaisir"* (395) (*"Your prediction will be *accomplished: you will have left me, taking my last cent. I have just learned my ruin. . . . My brain will splash as far as your theater gown and your pleasure bed"*). In his infinite immaturity, Lionel must insult Céleste by metonymy—he reduces her to her "robe de théâtre," stressing the libertine lifestyle assumed of actresses of the era. In addition, he makes reference to their physical relationship. This is, of course, a sensitive issue for Céleste, and Lionel's emphasis on "plaisir" rather than love evokes the following response:

Le premier jour où je vous ai connu, je vous ai dit mon caractère. Je trouve vos accusations tellement exagérées que je m'excuse un peu en pensant que je ne vous ai jamais menti. . . .

Croyez-moi, si mon corps est avili, il y a une place bien pure où je vais renfermer l'offre que vous m'avez faite. . . . Ah! répondez-moi. . . . Je vous aime. (396)
(*The first day I met you, I told you about my character. I find your accusations so exaggerated that I excuse myself a bit in thinking that I never lied to you. . . .*

Believe me, if my body is degraded, there is a very pure place where I will keep the offer that you made to me. . . . Ah! Answer me. . . . I love you.")

Again, the purifying power of love "cleanses" Céleste of her past and renders her worthy in her mind of Lionel's affection. Repeatedly throughout the text, she asks Lionel and, indirectly, her readers to forgive her past: she is open about her sins; hence, she should be absolved.

When Lionel's ruin continues to menace Céleste's life, she stresses her strength and fortitude. For example, when creditors attempt to seize any gifts that Lionel gave her or property he offered or sold to her, she reacts in the following way: "Abbatue cent fois, je me relevai par des efforts surnaturels" (398) ("Worn out a hundred times, I got back up again by supernatural efforts"). After she refuses Lionel's proposal, he sets off for a long journey by ship to Australia to try his luck at gold mining.

Lionel's *carnet de voyage* (*travel book*), letters to Céleste written throughout his journey from France to Australia, includes an outpouring of his love for her, his encounters and experiences at sea, and a chronicle of his itinerary until the moment of his arrival in Australia. Mogador reproduces the *carnet* in her text, along with Lionel's *journal d'un mineur* (*a miner's diary*), a diary that he writes about his exploits in the new land. Both the embedded *carnet* and *journal* represent masculine parallels to *Mémoires* itself.

Time is an important factor in the *carnet*: the voyage to Sydney will take five months, and once in Australia it will take eleven to fifteen days to arrive at the mines. Letters from Europe arrive in three months. Lionel's emphasis on the length of time of his travels parallels his physical distance from Céleste and the long emotional road toward their reunion.

In the *carnet*, Lionel often portrays Céleste as the Baudelairean paradox, the "femme-satan" ("devil woman") and the uplifting "femme vertueuse/bien aimée" ("virtuous woman/beloved") at the same time. Though "le mal est [son] essence" (401) ("evil is [her] essence"), and she is a "femme sans coeur et sans âme" (401) ("woman without a heart and without a soul"), he still forgives and loves her. Céleste is objectified once again not only through such generalizations but also through the portrait Lionel carries with him and the name "Céleste," which he has had tattooed on his arm. There is the living Céleste with whom Lionel interacts, and there is also the image or representation Lionel makes of her through artifacts, in his remembrances, and on the written page.

Céleste's reaction when she receives the *carnet* is mixed. She is, of course, back in Europe and faced with the realities of life there. Lionel is abroad, with all of the romanticism, philosophizing, and illusions that go with "leaving home" for faraway places. She is happy because she has "inspiré à cet homme si bon, si courageux dans son malheur, une passion si tendre et si dévouée" (411) ("inspired in this man, so good and so courageous throughout his hardships, a passion so tender and so devoted"), but at the same time she is facing legal battles.

At this point in her life Céleste begins writing her *Mémoires*, in part to help in her legal struggles: "Un ami m'avait engagée à faire une confession qui pourrait éclairer mes juges. J'écrivis donc ma vie entière, espérant rendre ma défense plus facile" (433) ("A friend urged me to make a confession that could enlighten my judges. So I wrote my entire life, hoping to make my defense easier").[19] Her writing, then, begins with a particular purpose in mind. It already shows, however, signs of becoming a future passion: "Etudier le jour, écrire la nuit, rien ne m'arrêtait. Je me suis mise à ce travail et j'y ai trouvé un intérêt qui m'a surprise et enchantée" (433) ("Study by day, write by night, nothing stopped me. I set about this work, and I found therein an interest which surprised and delighted me"). Finally, writing helps soften the pains of Céleste's youth: "En repassant ma vie, j'étais étonnée de voir les amertumes s'en adoucir" (433) ("In going back over my life, I was amazed to find the bitterness mellow"). Her talent was surely appreciated by friends such as Camille Doucet, Emile and Delphine de Girardin, and Dumas *père*, who read passages from the work and encouraged her to publish it.[20] Moser writes that Emile de Girardin put Mogador in contact with a publisher and drafted the terms of her contract (136). The former prostitute "became a woman of letters" (Moser 136).

In the 1858 edition of *Mémoires*, Mogador includes a preface that reiterates that her life story was also a defense against false accusations (I: i). Further, she includes notes at the end of the fourth volume that include memoirs written by her defense attorneys for the judges in her trial. Finally, she inserts in the 1858 edition written responses addressed to her adversaries. In the context of her *Mémoires*, these documents lend authenticity to the text. Once again, her attempt to justify and explain her actions reflects her desire to be sincere. The documents support Mogador's claim that she wishes to tell her life story in its entirety, however impossible this may be.

The appearance of Lionel's *journal d'un mineur* in the text shortly follows Mogador's description of her own writing debut and, again, functions as a masculine parallel to the woman's story.²¹ He continues to write of his love for her as he did in the *carnet* but focuses to a greater extent in the *journal* on the dangers of his exploits and on the other miners he meets. The self-pity that characterizes the beginning of the *carnet*—"Mogador! Pour laquelle ce pauvre Lionel a tout sacrifié!" (399) ("Mogador! For whom this poor Lionel sacrificed everything!")—is much more tempered in the *journal*. In the latter text, he portrays himself as the worker struggling to establish himself in a new environment. The pains he goes through are, in part, an "atonement" for his past frivolity. This is, hence, Lionel's *bildung*, his voyage out into the world, and lastly his path toward maturity.

The reader sighs an "it's about time" and realizes that Mogador has set up an engaging opposition. While on the surface she has written the story of her own social evolution into a woman worthy of the love and status Lionel will offer her—the development of a self-sufficient woman by virtue of her intelligence, hard work, talent, and experiences—on another, more subtle level she presents an embedded counterpoint by describing Lionel's psychological evolution. The "spoiled rich boy," no matter how charming a prince he may be, must get down in the dirt and use his hands. He must make his own way in order to render himself worthy of the more emotionally mature and ultimately more worldly Céleste. She has already suffered great personal loss, learned to defend herself against ridicule, and improved her own social station. In Australia, Lionel's growing up includes learning to work and to be productive. Masculine *bildung* in the nineteenth century must include not only love adventures but the formation of an individual who will become a contributing member of society.

Lionel discusses, for example, other miners, many of whom have struggled as he has: "Cette population des mines est ce qu'on peut se figurer de plus étrange. On y voit le rebut des villes, des gens immondes, échappés des galères, à côté d'hommes bien élevés, qui ont vécu dans l'élégance . . . et qui, comme moi, ont tout dissipé" (440) ("This population of the mines is what one can imagine as most strange. One sees there the dregs of the cities, vile people, escaped from the galleys, next to well-mannered men, who have lived in elegance . . . and who, like me, have squandered everything"). At another point in the *journal*, Lionel and his companions have reached the zone where "*diggers*" have their "*claims*" (439).²² It is, however, difficult and expensive to secure places in which to dig. Lionel despairs: "Je ne puis rester plus longtemps sans rien faire; toutes mes ressources s'épuisent. . . . Ah! Céleste! Céleste! où m'as-tu conduit?" (440) ("I cannot stay much longer without doing anything; all of my resources are drying up. . . . Ah! Céleste! Céleste! Where have you driven me?").

Céleste had already refused one marriage proposal, and she, indeed, "drives" Lionel away and forces him to mature. In her response to the *journal*, she will express her longing for their reunion. The "véritable réconciliation" (453) ("true reconciliation"), as Mogador calls it, will follow soon after Lionel's imminent return to Paris. When they meet again, the marks of the physical labor that has influenced Lionel's *bildung* are clear. His beard has grown, his face is thin and pale, and "la souffrance était écrite sur ses traits" (449) ("suffering was written on his features").

The conclusion of the text is ruled by two components: preparations for Céleste's departure with Lionel for Australia and the circulation of *Mémoires*. The new life Céleste will undertake with Lionel corresponds, then, to the birth of the author. We learn that although Mogador had submitted her manuscript to a publisher, she dared not discuss the project in detail with Lionel for fear of his reaction. She furthermore refers to Lionel as Robert in the original edition of the text. This discretion is understandable given the fact that *Mémoires* was to appear soon after the couple's departure. Indeed, Mogador opens the 1877 sequel to *Mémoires*, *Un deuil au bout du monde*, with this amendment: "Lionel (car Robert n'était pas le vrai nom de M. de Chabrillan), était parti seul pour Londres, afin d'y faire publier nos bans"(1) ("Lionel [for Robert was not the real name of M. de Chabrillan], had left alone for London in order to have our banns published there"). Despite the numerous nineteenth-century women writers being discovered today, Mogador's venture into the literary domain was still atypical, and the content of her story certainly shocked her contemporaries.

Concerning the first edition of the life story, *Adieux au monde: Mémoires de Céleste Mogador*, Clermont-Tonnerre writes:

This first edition, because of its blunt revelations of the past of an unfortunate girl, later a kept woman, a "devourer of fortunes," who became the wife of a French consul, provoked a scandal . . . the edition was banned and seized. It would be the same for the second edition which appeared after Céleste's return to France (1858). (14)

The censorship may account for the fact that Mogador's *Mémoires* was not appreciated as it might have been in her own time and perhaps explains why it is little known today. According to Moser, after Céleste agreed to marry Lionel, she preferred to break her contract with her publisher and even exhorted Prince Napoleon and her literary friends for help (143–51). Though Moser claims that their influence may have contributed to the first censorship (151), *Mémoires* would certainly have caused a stir all the same, as evidenced by Mogador's description in *Un deuil* of the chilly welcome she received in Australia by those who had heard of her autobiography. The reaction to Mogador's life story thus reflects a conception of women that affected the production and consumption of literary texts.

The decision to leave Europe for Australia recalls similar flights from society life in Paris to the tranquil security of the country earlier in the text. Céleste's legal battles have taken a more fortunate turn, and both she and Lionel are able to pay their debts. Yet they must abandon a society that disapproves of their union. With her lover, Céleste will "leave the country" in order to find, through love, a new abode. She evokes the Neoplatonic myth of kindred souls in a final letter to Lionel: "Je sens que mon âme sera errante jusqu'à ce qu'elle ait retrouvé la tienne" (445) ("I feel that my soul will wander until it has found yours again"). Lionel, too, communicates his devotion to his beloved regardless of national boundaries, proclaiming: "[M]on pays sera partout où tu seras" (453) ("[M]y country will be wherever you will be"). He has also managed to secure a post as a French consul in Melbourne. Mogador writes: "Il voulut refuser à cause de moi; je refusai de partir s'il n'acceptait pas. Il y avait pour lui une question d'avenir; mon avenir, à moi, je m'en inquiétais peu" (455) ("He wanted to refuse because of me; I refused to leave if he did not accept. There was for him a question of the future; *my* future, I worried little about it"). We note the balance of these two sentences and of the clauses within them, the repetition of *il, je, moi, avenir*, and finally the consonantal alliteration with *pas* and *peu* concluding each sentence. The equilibrium of these sentences reflects the equality finally achieved in Céleste and Lionel's relationship. They can set off as a couple only when their maturity as individuals has reached a level that allows for harmonious exchange.

Mogador has concluded her story/their story. In the final paragraphs, she uses present-tense verbs, which give a sense of immediacy to the ending. She only intimates what the future may hold: "J'éprouve quelques terreurs à m'en aller si loin de mon pays, de ma beauté, de ma jeunesse" (455) ("I feel some terror in going away so far from my country, my beauty, my youth"). As she considers her future with Lionel, she realizes that love will grow only if it is based on respect: "On ne peut aimer longtemps que la vertu, les mérites; pour aimer une femme qui vieillit, il faut qu'on l'estime" (455) ("One can love for a long time only virtue, merits; to love a woman who grows old, one must respect her"). She has, indeed, gained esteem in Lionel's eyes and in her own. The conclusion underscores "la volonté de Dieu" (455) ("God's will") as "Dieu seul condamne sur l'Océan!" (455) ("God alone condemns on the ocean!"), outcries that emphasize the emotional nature of the moment and the scope of the decision both she and Lionel are undertaking.

Mémoires ends here, without any detail about discussions in which Céleste would have finally consented to a permanent union with Lionel. Though the bulk of Mogador's writing was completed in 1852, and she continued to present it as such in future editions ("Lorsque j'ai écrit ces Mémoires en 1852" ["Préface," *Mémoires* 1876]) ("When I wrote these Memoirs in 1852"), the fact that she also includes descriptions of the couple's preparations for their departure for Australia seems to date the writing until at least into 1853.[23] In actuality, then, Lionel would likely have already proposed to her. In response to this omission in *Mémoires*, Clermont-Tonnerre ponders, "Ultime pudeur?" (13) ("Final modesty?"). It seems that the life story Mogador wants to recount in this text is the one that she leaves behind in Europe. She writes: "Il ne m'en restera bientôt plus que le souvenir" (455) ("I will soon have nothing left of it but a remembrance"). The sequel—the story of the Countess of Chabrillan—would not appear until 1877.

In *Mémoires*, Mogador reveals the trials of an exceptional nineteenth-century heroine, the *bildung* of a woman who has the strength and determination to succeed despite societal conventions that limit women's lives and dictate proper marriages. Her journey toward selfhood has been intertwined with that of her lover, the man who will also play a role in her future. She remains hesitant about their destiny: "Si Lionel allait redevenir ce qu'il était, violent, emporté! Peut-être mourrai-je abandonnée là-bas" (455) ("If Lionel were to become once again what he was, violent, hot-tempered! Maybe I will die abandoned there"). By the end of *Mémoires*, Céleste is ready for the voyage.

NOTES

1. This chapter constitutes, in part, a revision of my article entitled "Male and Female *Bildung*: The *Mémoires de Céleste Mogador*," published in *Nineteenth-Century French Studies* 25.3–4 (1997): 335–47. Unless indicated, all quotations from *Mémoires* are from the one-volume 1968 edition and cited by page number. English translations of quotations from *Mémoires* are mine.

2. According to François de Clermont-Tonnerre, "the fashion was exotic nicknames," and it is while at the *bal Mabille*, "society's smartest establishment," that the protagonist is crowned "Mogador" by her dancing partner, who quips that it is more difficult to defend her from her admirers than to defend Mogador (now called Essaouira), the Moroccan city attacked by the French (10).

3. Marcia Glidden Parker discusses this lack of critical consideration of Mogador's writing in her doctoral dissertation, "*Céleste de Chabrillan, Nineteenth-Century French Theatre: Woman and Character*." Her study contributes valuable insights to the study of Mogador's plays in particular.

4. Several critics comment on Mogador's writing difficulties, including Curtiss (168) and McClary. McClary notes that Mogador "had no formal education and notated her works phonetically" (38).

5. Glidden Parker examines Mogador's tendency to grant women characters more authority in her plays than did male writers of the time. She states that the author often

redirects the usual melodramatic order by changing who controls dialogue onstage (number of lines, opening and closing lines of the play and of scenes). That is, she redirects the point of view from male characters to female characters. She refuses to present totally male-centered plays by creating active functions for women characters. Chabrillan's choice of play titles [shows] how she finds a subtle means of placing characters outside the restrictive confines of French patriarchal rules into a place where women characters have more opportunities to assert themselves. (viii)

6. See McClary (38–41) and Curtiss (165–71).

7. Note that Mogador was twenty-eight when she began writing *Mémoires* and thirty when it was published.

8. Hirsch emphasizes that while the German *bildungsroman* possesses a utopian tendency that allows the protagonist to retreat from societal conflicts, in such French novels as *Le rouge et le noir* (*The Red and the Black*) and *L'éducation sentimentale* (*Sentimental Education*), the specific political, social, and economic climate constitutes integral forces in the protagonist's development ("The Novel of Formation" 303). In these texts, "[s]ociety is a field of struggle" (Hirsch, "The Novel of Formation" 303).

9. According to Mina Curtiss, Madame Vénard was "a confirmed slum-dweller . . . an ill-tempered woman" (181).

10. Mogador presents her family history as such in the text. In reality, her father abandoned his wife for the military while she was pregnant with Céleste (see Moser 17).

11. See Albistur and Armogathe (313–17) on the frequency of poor working women who turned to prostitution in France during the mid-nineteenth century.

12. See Charles Bernheimer's first chapter of *Figures of Ill Repute*, which offers a parallel between Parent-Duchâtelet's fascination with, and research on, fertilizers, sewer systems, and cadavers while he was a public health official and his subsequent work on prostitution as social decadence to be controlled by the government.

13. "Littérateur" can have a negative connotation, but that does not seem to be the case in this context.

14. See 113–16 of *Mémoires*.

15. In actuality, Solange, Mogador's godchild, accompanied her godmother to Australia and then back to France. Later, Solange ran off with a Prussian soldier during the Franco-Prussian War, and Mogador never saw her again.

16. Mogador does not name Lionel as the Count of Chabrillan in *Mémoires* but does so in the sequel, *Un deuil*.

17. Lionel was actually younger than Mogadar depicts him in *Mémoires*. According to Moser, on the couple's marriage certificate, Céleste's age is stated as twenty-nine, and Lionel's as thirty-two (148). Charlotte Haldane, however, establishes Lionel's dates as December 1818–December 1858 (196). This concurs with the dates given in Mogador's *Un deuil*. Therefore, Lionel would have been thirty-five in January 1854, when the couple married. We recall that Céleste was born in 1824. In any case, in claiming that Lionel was nine years her senior, Mogador exaggerates the age difference between them. Perhaps she wished to underscore her innocence of spirit despite her background, or she may have felt that a substantial age gap between the lovers appeared more proper at the time.

18. Moser and Glidden Parker, for example, take this stand.

19. In Monicat's discussion of women's travel literature, she suggests that many nineteenth-century women authors "shift the responsibility of their decision to write onto friends or relatives who ask them to do so—these works are therefore considered not to be written for the public" (*Itinéraires* 86). One recognizes similar strategies in various forms of women's autobiographical writing of the period.

20. See Clermont-Tonnerre (13); Moser (136).

21. The artist, engraver, and photographer Antoine Fauchery, a friend of Céleste and Lionel's in Australia, also later published a series of autobiographical "Lettres d'un mineur en Australie" ("Letters of a Miner in Australia") in the Parisian newspaper *Le Moniteur* in 1858.

22. The English terms are used in italics in *Mémoires*.

23. *Mémoires* first appeared in 1854, and even the 1968 edition of the text includes the dates 1824–54 after the title. However, the couple received the necessary authorization to marry from Mogador's mother in November 1853. Céleste left France for London on 3 January 1854 to be married (Haldane 109–11). From there, the couple departed for Australia. Hence, it is likely that Mogador completed the actual writing of *Mémoires* in 1853.

4

The Reformed Harlot in *Un deuil au bout du monde: Suite des Mémoires de Céleste Mogador*

In the continuation of Mogador's autobiography, *Un deuil au bout du monde: Suite des Mémoires de Céleste Mogador* (1877), the author offers a rewriting of the typical harlot's story and gives the "reformed prostitute" a place in literature and in history.[1] *Un deuil* was composed largely in the 1850s and published in 1877, when Mogador was a mature woman of fifty-three. In recounting her exile in Australia with her husband, she incorporates components of travel literature into the autobiographical narrative. In *Un deuil*, she challenges the images and fantasies surrounding the "fallen woman" in the nineteenth century, many of them concocted by men, and offers herself as an example of reform. According to Romantic myth, love's purifying power may "save" the prostitute's soul, but "an essential aspect of this myth . . . is the strict limitation of [the prostitute's] aspirations: she may teach an elevating moral lesson, but she must also condemn herself as irredeemably marked by her sexually deviant past" (Bernheimer, "Prostitution in the Novel" 781). Mogador does not deny her past in *Un deuil*, but neither does she restrain her ambition. In *Un deuil*, the former prostitute does not end her life through suicide, as does Balzac's Esther in *Splendeurs et misères des courtisanes* (1845–47; *A Harlot High and Low*), nor does she suffer consumption, as does Marguerite in Dumas *fils*' *La dame aux camélias* (1848; *The Lady of the Camellias*). Rather, she forges a new life. Mogador's revision of the harlot's story succeeds, in part, because she weaves into the account of her moral conversion her own *künstlerroman*, or birth-of-an-artist tale. Therefore, her growth is both personal and intellectual. Mogador not only renounces her former follies but, by staging her artistic career, seeks to persuade her readers that she is now a member of the cultural elite with the power to influence society. Similar to her strategy in *Mémoires*, Mogador again parallels her own story of reform with that of her husband's maturation. Published nearly twenty years after her husband's death, *Un deuil* portrays a devoted and responsible Lionel, implying that his decision to marry Céleste was not merely a youthful indiscretion but actually contributed to his development.

For any woman voyager, writing a legitimate account of her "self" is doubly challenging: she is in exile, far from her origins and her culture, *and* she is a woman, struggling against clichéd images of femininity. Mogador's task is even greater, for she is battling particularly negative stereotypes of the irredeemable prostitute. Because of her past sexual transgressions, she is "exiled" from proper society in the new land as she was in France. Therefore, her efforts to define herself in *Un deuil* and her reflections on her "past self" are intimately tied to her gender. We recall that texts of sexual deviance, including Gustave Flaubert's *Madame Bovary* and Charles Baudelaire's *Les fleurs du mal* (*The Flowers of Evil*), both published in 1857, as well as Mogador's *Mémoires* in 1854, startled conservative French citizens. Shortly after *Un deuil* appeared, Émile Zola shocked readers with his horrific depiction of the decline of the courtesan in *Nana* (1880), a text that draws on the life of Mogador's close friend and dancing partner *la Pomaré* (Lise Sergent) from the *bal Mabille*. Hence, Mogador's works participate in literary representations of sexual appetites.

In *Un deuil*, Mogador portrays herself and her husband as pioneers who have been forced from their judgmental homeland yet are unafraid to accept the hardships of life abroad. We read of Lionel's beginnings as a French consul near Melbourne and of the couple's pains to assist struggling French compatriots in the new land. Early on in *Un deuil*, Céleste expresses nostalgia for her native country. We read: "Ah! Ma chère France! Je crois que rien au monde ne pourra te faire oublier" (62) ("Ah! My dear France! I think that nothing in the world will allow you to be forgotten"). The couple is in debt, and Céleste first returns home alone in search of funds and a transfer for her husband back to France. Shortly thereafter, Céleste falls ill. Lionel briefly joins her there but returns to Australia, where he feels they have a certain social stature, urging Céleste to remain in France until she is well again. She recovers, but as chance would have it, Lionel falls ill in turn and dies, loving Céleste until his "dernier soupir" (254) ("last breath").

Approximately the first third of the text focuses on the couple's voyage from France to Australia via England, where they are wed, and other layover points. The second phase of the narrative treats the couple's life in Australia, where Lionel establishes himself as a consul. The final segment includes the development of Céleste's career as a professional writer and the conclusion of the couple's love story with Lionel's death. Included in this final portion of the work is the correspondence between Céleste and Lionel when they travel separately between France and Australia. Through the incorporation of letters, Mogador not only conveys authenticity but allows us to gauge the evolution of the couple's relationship.

The different phases of Mogador's story are linked by her insistence on immediacy and detail. Characteristic of travel literature, Mogador gives us a full account of her surroundings on board the ship *Crésus*, including its rowdy crew and friendships formed with other passengers, such as Lady Gamby and

Madame Webe. Once the couple arrives in Australia, *Un deuil* exploits the journal format, and several passages are dated. The unadorned diary form communicates spontaneity, emotion, veracity, and attention to daily details. Mogador describes, for example, Melbourne's main street teeming with boutiques and frequented by gold merchants and miners. Several paragraphs consist of only one line, and the exclamatory voice abounds. The style thus communicates the breathless pace of the immigrant's life. We read: "Ici les événements se suivent et s'enchaînent avec tant de rapidité, qu'on ne trouve pas le temps de les écrire avec ordre" (88) ("Here events follow one another and are linked together with such speed that one does not find the time to write them in a systematic way"). Did Mogador revise her diary in the nearly two decades that passed between Lionel's death in 1858 and the publication of *Un deuil* in 1877?[2] One would assume so, but because present tenses and eyewitness accounts pervade the narrative, it communicates immediacy.

In the opening pages of *Un deuil*, Mogador begins her defense of her "new self" by establishing herself in the eyes of her readers as conforming to traditional models of femininity while also insisting on the authenticity of her own sentiments. An important detail appears on the cover page: she is married.[3] She signs her text with her married and aristocratic name, La Comtesse Lionel de Chabrillan, rather than the name Mogador, given to her at the *bal Mabille*.[4] Since Lionel had visited Australia before their marriage and decided that the new land would provide opportunities and a new haven for them, Céleste can assume the role of accompanying her husband. Bénédicte Monicat confirms: "The agreement and presence of the husband . . . guarantee the traditional function of the woman voyager" ("Problématique de la préface" 63). Céleste also brings her adopted goddaughter with her, thus underscoring her status within a conventional family unit.

Even though Mogador did not serve as the typically subordinated collaborator or secretary for her husband's travel writings, as did many nineteenth-century women voyagers, including Adèle Hommaire de Hell and Janè Dieulafoy,[5] she still manipulates feminine strategies of modesty to justify taking up the pen and writing about herself and her new surroundings. Linda Kraus Worley explains that there is an "anxiety" about women's travel narratives—a "compulsion to justify to the reader both the autobiographical elements of their book[s] and the journey itself, an anxiety not shared by . . . male travellers" (41). Sara Mills notes that women travelers often exploit a "discourse of the 'feminine,'" characterized by such elements as humor, self-deprecation, and descriptions of relationships rather than the confident and daring voice of a typical male narrator (22). Once Céleste and Lionel are settled in Australia, Mogador even portrays writing as a mere distraction. Although we know from newspaper quotations previously presented in the text that she has already gained some notoriety as an author back in France, Mogador continues to present writing as an activity that merely distracts her from gloomy thoughts: "quand j'écris, je pense moins à mes peines" (143) ("when I write, I think less of my sorrow"). In addition, she hides her writing from Lionel: "il se moquerait de moi peut-être" (143) ("he would laugh at me perhaps"). Similarly, in Mogador's first novel, *Les voleurs d'or* (*Gold Thieves*),[6] drafted in Australia, the necessary disclaimer appears in the introduction "Au Lecteur" ("To the Reader"). She states that writing is merely a diversion or a "compagnon d'exil" ("companion in exile"). Monicat explains that nineteenth-century women travel writers, in fact, frequently elaborate this type of "negative rhetoric," which minimizes the artistic and professional value of their writing ("Problématique de la préface" 66). They manipulate conventional discourse (in this case the modest tone, the guise of the female writer who is not serious about her craft), while at the same time intimating that the keys to their texts lie elsewhere and that these hidden meanings are subversive because they valorize a "woman's writing which bears knowledge, a knowledge which seeks to be and calls itself other" (Monicat, "Problématique de la préface" 66). Hence, conforming to conventional societal and literary models of femininity, Mogador intentionally portrays herself as less bold in taking up the pen, so that she can more subtly engage in social and feminist critique.

Mogador is careful to show that her self-inscription within traditional women's roles does not contradict or detract from the sincerity of her feelings. She expresses the Romantic ideal that love for Lionel, rather than the social prestige his title offers, inspires her: "Est-ce un rêve, un conte de fée? Moi sa femme!! Je suis moins émerveillée de mon titre de comtesse que de celui d'épouse" (8) ("Is it a dream, a fairy tale? Me his wife!! I am less marveled by my title of countess than that of wife"). Her enthusiastic outpouring communicates honesty, goodness, and naïveté, underscored by the use of interrogative and exclamatory remarks. The "Cinderella story," indeed, continues as the redeeming quality of marriage marks this stage in the protagonist's developmental journey.

Two essential components in Mogador's narrative of conversion are the evolution of Lionel's character and the story of the couple's love. Lionel is continuously presented in a positive light. His emotional development, represented in *Mémoires*, continues in the sequel; in *Un deuil*, he is a competent, compassionate consul and a devoted husband. For example, on several occasions Lionel goes beyond the call of duty to help his French compatriots in Australia: he gives funds to a Frenchman who has been robbed and attacked (84); he secures a job for another who has just lost his wife and child (88–92); although gravely ill himself, he wins a pardon for a compatriot on the verge of being hanged for having killed his unfaithful mistress (235). Lionel's devotion to his wife is depicted as equally valiant. For example, he continually refuses invitations to balls and dinners that might put Céleste, already the object of curiosity in Australia, in a vulnerable position. Mogador portrays him as constantly reminding her of his ardent love. When she must leave for France alone, he declares: "Écoute mes paroles, elle sont solonnelles: *je ne regrette rien, et si tu n'étais pas ma femme je t'épouserais encore*" (156) ("Listen to my words, they are solemn: *I regret nothing, and if you were not my wife I would marry you again"*). Even though he does not encourage her to study and develop her intelligence, he admires her intellectual gifts. After reading her novel *Les voleurs d'or*, he is astonished by her will and skills of organization and admits: "j'étais loin de m'attendre à cette si grande transformation de ton esprit" (238) ("I was far from expecting such a great transformation of your mind"). Lionel's last letter to Céleste closes, "je t'adore et ne rêve qu'à toi" (238) ("I adore you and dream of only you"). In this way, Mogador not only presents herself as a talented writer but also links this talent to moral virtue, seen in her devotion to her work. By stressing Lionel's goodness and his fidelity to his wife, Mogador responds to critics who disapprove of the union of a count and a former "fille inscrite." She demonstrates that she is good for her husband. They mutually support one another and, despite hardship, create each other's happiness.

Céleste's devotion to her husband is equally apparent in the text. When she first leaves him to voyage from Australia to France, she writes: "A toi d'abord toutes mes pensées, toutes mes tendresses!" (158) ("To you first all of my thoughts, all of my tenderness!"). Her adoration of him verges on idolatry, as in the following phrase: "il est si parfait . . . lui!" (139) ("*he* is so perfect!"). When she is gravely ill and fears death, she confesses to Lionel as one would to a minister (197). After Lionel's untimely death, the Chabrillan family tries to bribe Céleste with 6,000 francs to give up her title, yet she does not bend. When called to the Ministry of Foreign Affairs, she courageously defends her right to Lionel's name, claiming: "Je suis habituée aux luttes et aux souffrances, je ne fléchirai pas, et vous ne serez jamais assez fort pour me briser" (250) ("I am used to struggles and suffering, I will not bend, and you will never be strong enough to break me"). Mogador thus presents herself as heroic. In the final sentence of *Un deuil*, we are brought to the present moment of writing, as Mogador assures her readers of the mutual fidelity between herself and Lionel: "Je pris, envers moi-même, l'engagement de porter son deuil toute ma vie, et depuis dix-huit ans, j'ai tenu ma parole, comme il avait tenu la sienne en jurant de m'aimer jusqu'au dernier soupir!" (254) ("I made a promise to myself to mourn him all of my life, and for eighteen years, I have kept my word, as he had kept his in swearing to love me until his last breath!"). Perhaps in writing these concluding words, Mogador's pain was intensified. In any case, we assume that even eighteen years after her husband's death her devotion to him had not faltered. In presenting such a harmonious union, Mogador renders the "new Céleste" worthy of our indulgence and understanding. She fulfills the dictates of the Romantics, who inspired both her and Lionel: true nobility comes from inner virtue. Yet Céleste goes beyond such figures as Victor Hugo's Marion de Lorme, who, in his play by the same name, "never even dreams of marriage to her adored Didier" (Bernheimer, "Prostitution in the Novel" 781). In *Un deuil*, "la Mogador" has metamorphosed herself into a devoted wife and thus deserves the appellation Countess of Chabrillan.

Mogador also depicts her reformation through expressions of regret for her past and for having written of it. For instance, she narrates first her civil marriage and then the religious ceremony. Mogador confides that she could barely speak when she had to confess herself to a priest. Her pain is evident in the following passage: "Je me mis à genoux . . . mais il me fut impossible de rassembler mes idées, de trouver autre chose à lui dire que ces mots: Mon père, je m'accuse. . . . Je le répétai tant de fois que le digne homme eut pitié de moi" (7) ("I knelt down . . . but it was impossible to collect my ideas, to find anything else to say to him except these words: Father, I have sinned. . . . I repeated it so may times that the worthy man took pity on me"). We the readers are also invited to pity her and to believe her contrition regarding her former life. Mogador also discusses her efforts and those of influential friends such as Alexandre Dumas *père* to regain her rights to *Mémoires* and have it destroyed. She quotes Dumas' discussion with Prince Napoleon exhorting him to intercede: "C'est une espece de confession à la Jean-Jacques, très attachante et qui ne peut faire du tort qu'à elle-même" (2–3) ("It is a type of confession in the style of Jean-Jacques, very engaging and which can harm only her"). Lionel had already managed to have Céleste's name removed from the official registry of prostitutes. However, suppressing Mogador's own inscription of her past in *Mémoires* would prove impossible.

Mogador's efforts to restore her reputation and attest to the transformation of her life are evinced in her combativeness in the face of personal attacks. Her reputation and the scandal that ensued after the publication of *Mémoires* follow her to the new land. Aboard the ship *Crésus*, passengers approach Australia and are met with newspaper articles and gossip of the count "qui avait fait la folie d'épouser sa maitresse et de croire pourtant que la société de la colonie de Victoria ferait un bon accueil à la trop célèbre Céleste Mogador, —qui a laissé du reste des Mémoires très curieux" (74) ("who had been mad enough to marry his mistress and to think, however, that the society of the colony of Victoria would welcome the too famous Céleste Mogador—who left, moreover, some very curious Memoirs"). Because Céleste cannot read the English newspapers that the passengers receive, her friend translates for her "les interminables tartines de ces messieurs de la presse anglaise, qui avaient dû les copier de la nôtre" (75) ("the interminable screeds of these men of the English press, who must have copied them from ours"). Mogador thus seizes this opportunity to criticize both the French press for slander and the English for plagiarism. Her native culture is certainly not immune from attack. Later, after Céleste and Lionel have been living near Melbourne for some time, she receives letters stating that she is "talked about" back home. Her reputation as an author continues to grow, for better or for worse. A friend writes to her: "Nous parlons bien souvent de vous comme auteur; vous avez vos partisans et vos ennemis" (94) ("We speak quite often about you as an author; you have your partisans and your enemies"). In response, Mogador would continue throughout the text to battle sexual stereotypes that brand her a "whore" for life and that refuse the prostitute any virtuous qualities or potential for reform. *Un deuil*, then, which outlines this conversion, carries a forceful feminist message, for the author attempts to redefine classic images of women and static female roles.

Mogador continued her defiant self-defense throughout her life. Haldane chronicles Charles Chincholle's interviews with Mogador some years after the publication of *Un deuil*. Chincholle bemoans an unforgiving French society in two articles written for *Le Figaro* in 1885 and 1890. He writes:

The unfortunate young woman attempted the most difficult thing on earth: to rehabilitate herself. The public is in the habit of classifying people. It does not allow anyone to rise above the station one first chose. For more than thirty years the Comtesse Lionel de Chabrillan . . . has been trying to kill Mogador. This she never succeeded in doing. (qtd. in Haldane 239)

Mogador's response to the journalist's observation illustrates her usual fighting spirit: "Well then, let it be Mogador!" (qtd. in Haldane 239). She does not deny her past or shrink from accusations. She does, however, continue to defend her present. With regard to the Chabrillan family's request that she give up her title, she declares: "I refused. Even a woman whose body was a refuse-heap has a soul. Mine belongs alone to him who raised me to his own level. When I go to sleep and make the sign of the cross, instead of saying 'In the name of the Father,' I say 'Lionel, Lionel, Lionel'" (qtd. in Haldane 240). As she does in *Mémoires* and in *Un deuil* with these remarks, Mogador emphasizes her virtues: she portrays herself as worthy of forgiveness, courageous in defying the Chabrillan family, and faithful to an extreme to her husband's memory. Mogador finally defends her reformed life through the example of her writing—her art itself illustrates her virtue. In Chincholle's 1885 interview, which coincided with the production of her new play *Pierre Pascal*,[7] she declares: "Mogador has written her play for honest women. If I wanted to earn hundreds of thousands of francs by publishing pornographic books, couldn't I do it? Is there any horror that I have not known? I would only have to remember" (qtd. in Haldane 240). Referring to herself in the third person, she defiantly hurls the infamous "Mogador" at her readers, proudly evoking the name that stirs such prejudice and mocking those who cannot see the connection between "Mogador," art, and moral rectitude. Chincholle confirms the decorum of Mogador's writing: "She has written more than thirty books in which there is not a single line that could shock an honest women. It has made no difference. The Comtesse de Chabrillan has remained Mogador" (qtd. in Haldane 239).

Despite her combative nature, Mogador also presents a heroine who forgives and is forgiven in *Un deuil*. By extension, we the readers are invited to imitate Céleste's compassion and forgive her past sins. For example, the governor of Melbourne snubs Céleste by not inviting a former prostitute to his ball. On a later occasion, the mayor of Melbourne invites her to dance, saying, "je profite de cette occasion pour prouver aux habitants de Melbourne ma profonde amitié pour M. le comte de Chabrillan et mon respect pour sa femme" (138) ("I take advantage of this occasion to prove to the inhabitants of

Melbourne my profound friendship for the Count of Chabrillan and my respect for his wife"). The governor may be intransigent, but the mayor forgives Céleste for her past. The mayor's wife and sister, "ces deux chères bonnes âmes" (139) ("these two dear good souls"), are also kind to her, "[pour] me venger publiquement de l'affront qui m'avait été fait par le gouverneur" (139) ("[to] avenge me publicly for the governor's affront to me"). Finally, when the governor dies, Céleste is able to pardon him. She writes that she sincerely feels sorry for his grieving wife (143). By way of another example, when one of Lionel's sisters dies (she had never forgiven him for marrying a former prostitute), his other sister writes to Céleste: she forgives Lionel but does not wish to see him. Through all of these examples, we see a parallel in Mogador's fate—there are those who scorn her and her scandalous *Mémoires*, and there are those who recognize her talent and transformation.

By weaving the *künstlerroman* into the story of her personal reform, Mogador offers her successful "new profession" as proof of her respectability and virtue. Although in *Un deuil* Mogador presents herself as a mere amateur passing time through writing, her ambitions as an author reveal themselves in her diligence and productivity. Haldane explains that "Mogador was possibly the only writer in Victoria at the period—certainly the only French writer—and life there gave her much fictional material" (171). Mogador writes, for example, of her various drafts for a first novel on gold mining in the new land (hence, the ultimate title *Les voleurs d'or*). Furthermore, we learn in *Un deuil* that Céleste completes six plays and two novels (192). Her progress as a writer leads to thoughts of earning a living through her craft: "Je me figure;—cela est ridicule,—qu'en cas de malheur . . . je pourrais arriver à gagner quelque argent" (143) ("I imagine;—it is ridiculous,—that in case of misfortune . . . I could manage to earn some money"). Despite her nonchalant tone in this passage, Mogador notes shortly afterward that upon her return to France alone, she did just that—earn "some money" from her best-selling *Mémoires*, reissued in 1858, and from sales of her novels *Les voleurs d'or* and *La sapho*,[8] for which she attained prestigious contracts with the renowned publisher Michel Lévy.

Despite her modest tone, by the time *Un deuil* was published in 1877, Mogador had actually firmly established herself in the writing profession. She carefully crafts her image as an artist by drawing parallels between her texts and those of important writers. First, she elevates herself as an author by stating that *Les voleurs d'or* was published at the same time as Flaubert's *Madame Bovary* (179). By including this detail, we are asked to welcome Mogador into Michel Lévy's family of eminent writers such as Sand, Flaubert, and Balzac. She then gives her writing the stamp of approval by including in *Un deuil* reviews of her first novel by France's intellectual elite. Nestor Roqueplan praises *Les voleurs d'or*, which shows no pursuit of "ces coquetteries du coeur qui appauvrissent les oeuvres féminines" (180) ("these coquetries of the heart which impoverish feminine works"). With this inclusion, Mogador emphasizes her distinction within the limited circle of female writers. Roqueplan concludes that Mogador "a ambitionné deux titres: celui de comtesse et celui d'écrivain;—elle les a conquis" (180) ("sought two titles: that of countess and that of writer;—she won them"). The distinguished author Dumas *père* in his analysis of *Madame Bovary* and *Les voleurs d'or* calls the latter text "extraordinaire" (180) ("extraordinary"). He praises Mogador in this way:

Pendant les quatre ans qu'elle est restée à cinq mille lieues de la France, elle a, au prix des plus grands sacrifices et par un travail obstiné, refait ou plutôt fait entièrement son éducation; elle a [non seulement] appris l'anglais, mais encore réappris le français. . . . Pendant deux nuits, j'ai vu venir le jour en lisant *les Voleurs d'or*. (180–81)
(During the four years she lived five thousand leagues away from France, she, at the expense of the greatest sacrifices and by persistent work, re-educated or rather entirely educated herself; she not only learned English, but relearned French as well. . . . For two nights, I sat up until dawn reading *les Voleurs d'or*.)

In leading up to his positive evaluation of her novel, Dumas makes the link, intentional or not, between the excellence of her art and her capacity to relearn her culture. In this way, he implies that in the process of becoming a true artist, Mogador had to start from the beginning and review and reform her past life. Jules Janin's review of the same text, also included in *Un deuil*, again makes the connection between her talent and intelligence and her ability to change her life: "Il n'y a qu'une femme heureusement douée et très intelligente, qui puisse ainsi se transformer, se réhabiliter par l'intelligence, renoncer à l'aventure, et conquérir une place honorable parmi les femmes distinguées, et les bons écrivains de son temps" (183) ("There is only one woman favorably gifted and very intelligent, who could transform herself in this way, rehabilitate herself by intelligence, renounce promiscuity, and win an honorable place among the distinguished women and the good writers of her time")—precisely the points Mogador would like to convey to her readers. Though posterity remembered the prostitute rather than the countess and writer, Mogador demonstrates in *Un deuil* that she had at least persuaded several of her noted contemporaries of her merits. Through the voice of others, she sings her own praises and invites her readers to do the same. Mogador also includes evidence of her husband's approval of her first novel. In his last letter to his wife before his death, he explains: "j'ai lu ct relu dix fois les *Voleurs d'or*" (238) ("I read and reread ten times the *Voleurs d'or*").

In *Un deuil*, writing provides more than the occasion to discuss the self or the opportunity to entertain readers with impressions of new lands. Mogador's story of evolution is linked to other social and feminist concerns. She seizes a pedagogical opportunity, for example, to denounce such social ills as slander and classism. Unlike many women writers of her day, she does not shy away from societal critique. Although she frequently employs the self-deprecating rhetoric necessary to downplay her importance as a writer and to express her views subtly, at other moments her writing, in the style of Cristina di Belgiojoso, is quite bold. As in *Mémoires*, she continues her attack on journalists. We read: "Aux mines de Bindigat, il y a des journaux, et naturellement, des journalistes si l'on peut appeler ainsi quelques crève-la-faim qui disent du mal de tout le monde pour en tirer de l'argent" (144) ("In the Bindigat mines, there are newspapers, and naturally, journalists, if one can so call a few down-and-out men who say bad things about everyone to make money"). She also presents several portraits of "mismatched" couples, such as the servant Cilia and the young British officer James from "une bonne famille anglaise" (58) ("a good English family"). Though of different social classes, they are bound by love. Through advocating their marriage, Mogador simultaneously denounces classism and justifies her own union with Lionel. Finally, Mogador critiques the role of money in determining social behavior, evident in the following passage: "[Lionel] s'est donné à moi sans compter avec le monde et l'avenir. Quand on est heureux, indépendant, cela peut encore passer; mais si la misère nous arrivait officiellement, bien des gens, qui sont venus à nous quand même, nous tourneraient le dos" (143) ("[Lionel] gave himself to me without regard for society or the future. When one is happy, independent, that is still acceptable; but if we became officially destitute, many people, who came to us despite everything, would turn their backs on us").

Mogador's text also criticizes gender oppression. After Lionel's short furlough in France, for example, he travels through Africa en route back to Australia and pens several letters to Céleste. In his "travel literature," embedded, as in *Mémoires*, in Mogador's larger story, he writes the following: "Un enfant femelle de [Somalie], à l'âge de dix-huit mois à deux ans, subit une opération dont la conclusion est une couture partielle. . . . La fille non cousue ou décousue vaut peu de chose, deux à trois roupies ou cinq à six francs" (218) ("A female child from [Somalia], between eighteen months and two years old, undergoes an operation which concludes in some stitches. . . . The girl who never receives them or who has the stitches undone is worth little, two to three rupees or five to six francs"). Mogador is less direct in her critique of female excision, of women's control over their own bodies, than in her denunciation of class prejudice, for she attributes this remark to Lionel's voice. Indeed, the personal letter form allows Mogador to express her feminist commentary in a subtle manner. Yet her veiled criticism of the female body as property certainly alludes to the widespread problem of Céleste's former profession. Furthermore, in her writings, Mogador constantly critiques laws that allow young women to sell their bodies.

Un deuil presents the reformed prostitute's story, a tale of transformation enabled by personal evolution and by intellectual activity. By manipulating models of feminine conformity—her married status, devotion to her husband—Mogador invites her readers to forgive her past transgressions and believe in her conversion. She offers herself as an example of self-improvement, social mobility, and positive contribution to society. By weaving the birth-of-the-artist drama into her story of reform, Mogador presents her "new profession" as an artist as integral to her new life. Through associating her own experiences with other social and feminist concerns, she appeals to her readers to implement change. In this way, she anticipates the struggles of women writers at the turn of the century, authors who continue to transform female models of selfhood.

NOTES

1. This chapter is based, in part, on a conference presentation entitled "Subtle Subversion: Céleste Mogador's Australian Narratives," Nineteenth-Century French Studies Conference, Wilmington, DE, Oct. 1995. English translations of quotations from *Un deuil* are mine. However, the following translation of the text has recently been published: Comtesse Céleste Vénard de Chabrillan, *The French Consul's Wife: Memoirs of Céleste de Chabrillan in Gold-Rush Australia*, trans. Patricia Clancy and Jeanne Allen (Carlton, Vic.: Melbourne UP, 1998).

2. Clancy and Allen speculate about possible modifications and embellishments in *Un deuil* (8–13).

3. A literary successor to Mogador is the turn-of-the-century author Liane de Pougy. De Pougy spent many years in Paris as an actress, dancer, and courtesan. She renounced her libertine lifestyle when she married Prince Georges Ghika in 1910. She chronicles her experiences in fictional and autobiographical works, including *Mes cahiers bleus* (*My Blue Notebooks*). After Ghika's death and toward the end of her own life, de Pougy became a nun. See Rogers for further details on de Pougy.

4. See the previous chapter for information on how Céleste became known as "la Mogador."

5. See Monicat's *Itinéraires* (78–93).

6. This text is listed in the Works Cited section under Céleste de Chabrillan.

7. This text is listed in the Works Cited section under Céleste de Chabrillan.

8. This text is listed in the Works Cited section under Céleste de Chabrillan.

Part II

LEAVING THE FAMILY

5

The Turning Point: Sibilla Aleramo's *Una donna*

Sibilla Aleramo's *Una donna* (1906) already manifests many of the feminist themes that are taken up in modern and postmodern women's literature.[1] The progressive issues that she tackles remain relevant to contemporary women's quests to inscribe themselves as subjects. With the publication of *Una donna*, Aleramo anticipates the feminists of the 1960s and 1970s who challenge the limits of male language, seek a uniquely female voice, and explore an *écriture féminine*. She deals with such themes as the confines of bourgeois marriages, motherhood as institution, and the extreme difficulty of combining motherhood with a career at the turn of the century. In her preface to *Una donna*, leading Italian feminist Maria Antonietta Macciocchi describes the work as "a book which pushes the battle for women's emancipation forward, *today*, as a revolutionary battle" (5).[2] She admires the courage with which Aleramo tackles "modern" issues and finds the text relevant to today's problems and struggles. Aleramo's story occurs at a pivotal moment in women's literature, between nineteenth-century texts whose women characters often suffer the tragic effects of patriarchal oppression and modern narratives whose heroines refuse these structures and break new narrative ground. *Una donna* is, indeed, the scene of the struggle.

Aleramo, who was born in 1876 as Rina Faccio, was certainly familiar with important women writers. She translated Madame de Lafayette's *La princesse de Clèves* and the love letters of George Sand and Alfred de Musset. Her essays include reflections on Colette, Virginia Woolf, and Katherine Mansfield. Ada Negri, Grazia Deledda, and Annie Vivanti were her contemporaries. *Una donna* emerged at the beginning of Aleramo's career, which would continue to be nurtured by such literary women and which would frequently focus on female characters and artists.

Aleramo divides *Una donna* into three parts. Part One begins in traditional fashion with a presentation of the protagonist's family and early years. It explores her disappointing and abusive marriage and the birth of her son. Part Two focuses on the protagonist's intellectual awakening. Her interests in social issues and feminism blossom, as does her writing career. Part Three centers on the protagonist's break from previous maternal models as she "leaves the family." She abandons her husband and six-year-old son in order to follow her own destiny. Like Cristina di Belgiojoso, Aleramo envisions a societal restructuring beginning with a modification of the family unit. Sharon Wood explains that Aleramo was the first Italian woman writer to be lauded for "a novel which strongly challenged the social, moral and legal condition of the new State, one in which the condemnation of women's oppression is accompanied by a lucid analysis of social and family structures which underpin the stability of the dominant order and keep women in their allotted roles" (75).

The work is an autobiographical novel in that it recounts much of Aleramo's story in the first-person mode common to life writing, but it also includes significant, intentional modifications, for literary purposes, of the author's experiences. In the text, the father is disgusted by the "courtship" of his daughter by a young employee. In life, explains Masolino D'Amico, it was her parents who persuaded Aleramo to marry the young worker after he raped her (qtd. in Angelone 198). Upon her lover Giovanni Cena's suggestion, Aleramo excluded from the text one of her motivations for leaving her family—her affair with Felice Damiani—so as not to weaken its moral force (Drake xv–xvi). In her later autobiographical work, *Il passaggio* (*The Passage*), Aleramo corrects this omission: "Non era per amore d'un altr'uomo ch'io mi liberavo: ma io amavo un altr'uomo" (24) ("It was not for the love of another man that I liberated myself: but I loved another man"). In addition, two levels of narrative are constantly at play in the work. As critics have noted, there is the personal story, the "confession" to her son, and at the same time, there is the universal feminist statement, a type of allegory of "every woman." This duality is underscored by the fact that there are no proper names in *Una donna*. We meet "the husband," "the Norwegian woman," "the mother," all of whom could represent one of many husbands, friends, and mothers in women's lives at the time. The work actually originated in a cluster of diary entries written in June 1901 (Bassanese 131). Flora A. Bassanese explains that the veracity of her writing was significant to Aleramo, for "although her heroine's tale was exemplary, it was also *her* story whose telling was an act of self-revelation" (131). Still, Bassanese concludes that in *Una donna*, "autobiography and novel merge creating a work which is both private and public" (131). Franca Angelini agrees that Aleramo's narrative lies somewhere between autobiography and fiction, self-analysis and generalization (67). This type of first-person narration, according to Angelini, allows for invention, transformation, and "the most ample margin of fiction" (67). She adds that the use of the pseudonym renders *Una donna* a type of "biography" of Rina Faccio, but one "without names" (66–67). Aleramo's employment of the pseudonym also underscores the opportunity for a subjective, slanted narrative vision of this "other woman."

Indeed, Aleramo would continue her efforts to define and understand herself through a fusion of autobiography and fiction in future poems, plays, novels, and extensive diary writing.

From the first chapter of *Una donna*, we find an opposition set up between freedom, curiosity, and strength, on one hand, and imprisonment, withdrawal, and weakness, on the other. Initially, this opposition is reflected in the parental figures. The protagonist prefers and identifies with her father: "L'amore per mio padre mi dominava unico. Alla mamma volevo bene, ma per il babbo avevo un'adorazione illimitata. . . . Era lui il luminoso esemplare per la mia piccola individualità. . . . Nessuno gli somigliava" (19) ("The only thing that dominated me was love for my father. I took my love for my mother for granted, but for him I felt boundless admiration. . . . *He* was my model. . . . There was no one who could equal him" 3). We note the nostalgic tone of the mature narrator's description of the all-consuming love she had for her father as a girl. He is the empowering figure. Similar examples of paternal idealization occur in George Sand's *Histoire de ma vie*. In addition, it is the father who directs the protagonist's studies and reading. We have a foreshadowing early in Aleramo's text of the later dichotomy between a career and motherhood, the "masculine" world of writing incompatible with raising a child.

As opposed to her own "fanciullezza . . . libera e gagliarda" (19) ("active, carefree childhood" 3), the narrator tells us that her mother must have "cresciuta fra le strettezze, poco amata. Cenerentola della casa" (21) ("grown up in poverty, without much love, a family Cinderella" 6). Instead of the "Cinderella story" that Céleste Mogador ultimately experiences, both the protagonist and her mother in *Una donna* are disillusioned by their mates and married life. The narrator continues to describe the path toward her mother's breakdown—her bliss when she first becomes a mother and then her slow decline over the years because of an estranged husband and her psychologically fragile nature.

Common in this type of situation is the daughter's resentment for having to "mother" her mother. This is often coupled with "matrophobia" or the "fear not of one's mother or of motherhood but of *becoming one's mother*" (Rich 235).[3] Such emotions are, in fact, quite characteristic of women's texts in the 1970s, when the mother–daughter relationship becomes central, works such as Marie Cardinal's *Les mots pour le dire* and Annie Ernaux's *Les armoires vides*. In *Una donna*, the mother's attempted suicide marks the beginning of her estrangement from her family and solidifies the protagonist's negative view of her. From this point in the text the mother becomes more childlike: "Pareva tornata bimba, una bimba timorosa che non sa liberarsi dal ricordo di un suo errore" (39) ("She seemed to have returned to us a child, a frightened child, trapped in the memory of her own mistakes" 26).

Disillusionment with the maternal figure couples with disappointment in the father as well. The family leaves Milan and moves to a small village in southern Italy, where the father opens a factory. The protagonist's bourgeois family holds a superior status in this underdeveloped region, and the adolescent protagonist, who has a great deal of responsibility at the factory, is the object of attention and curiosity. A fellow worker is said to be in love with her, as she is becoming a beautiful young girl of fifteen. In an effort to draw the young girl's attention away from her beloved father, he reveals to her that her father is having an affair. This gives the coworker an excuse to comfort her. In an instant, the father becomes a negative figure, though later in the text the protagonist again recognizes his positive influence and regrets her rebellion against him. Initially, she reacts in the following way: "Mio padre, l'esemplare raggiante, si trasformava d'un tratto in un oggetto d'orrore: egli, che mi aveva cresciuta nel culto della sincerità, della lealtà, egli nascondeva a mia madre, a noi tutti, un lato della sua vita" (44) ("Until then Father had been my model; yet in an instant he was transformed into an object of horror, a man who had brought me up to respect sincerity and loyalty but had deliberately concealed a part of his life from Mother, and from us all" 32). When her mother in a moment of "hysteria" lashes out at the father, he responds, "Quella donna impazzisce!" (45) ("That woman is going mad!" 33), to which the protagonist echoes, "Anch'io impazzirei, papà!" (45) ("And I shall go mad as well, papa!" 33). This act of rebellion leads to her dismissal from her father's factory, where she had taken care of administrative tasks and where she had so much enjoyed being part of the working world, dealing with the other employees, and using her mind.

The protagonist's *bildung* will, in fact, be characterized by a series of losses. During the early years, her development resembles the masculine model; her father's factory represents a chance for her to function as an active member of society, a privileged role for a young girl at the turn of the century in this locality. Maria Marotti explains that Aleramo shapes her text as "a bildungsroman in which the protagonist, through initiation into the reality of a male-dominated society, gains insight, strength, and self-discovery" (69). Later, this heroine's *bildung* diverges from the male model. When the young man who had exposed her father's affair learns that she will be leaving, his despair culminates in panic and an uncontrollable desire for the protagonist. This leads to the rape that is a turning point in the story. The confused adolescent hardly understands what has happened, but she realizes that her "vita di fanciulla era finita" (48) ("childhood was certainly at an end" 36). By the end of the third chapter, the protagonist has "lost" her mother, who has become depressed; the precious camaraderie she once had with her father; and her virginity in a brutal fashion. This sequence of losses goes beyond the typical male protagonist's disillusionment in developmental literature. A victim of circumstances and of a mentality that deems that rape may lead to marriage, this heroine's childhood is stolen from her.[4] Instead of typically disappointing experiences leading to maturity, these crucial events are catalysts for even greater difficulties to come. She asks herself: "Appartenevo ad un uomo, dunque?" (48) ("Did this man own me?" 36).

At this stage of a young girl's development and in the social context of Italy at the turn of the century, masculine figures play an influential role. The protagonist asks herself why she never for an instant doubted the young lover's accusations about her father, and she realizes that with his revelation, the *innamorato* appeared different, "un essere nuovo, dotato di tutto ciò che veniva a mancare a mio padre. . . . Non potevo concepirmi vittima d'un calcolo" (48–49) ("a new person, endowed with all the qualities I now felt my father lacked. . . . Never for one moment did I imagine that I might be the victim of a cold-blooded strategy" 37). Because of the young suitor's deception, the main character is suddenly thrust into womanhood. When the parental figures can no longer be models, she allies herself with a lover. She even begins to wonder whether she does love the young man and tries to lose herself in the type of romantic fantasy in which Madame Bovary indulged: "Amarlo, amarlo! Si, lo volevo tenacemente. . . . [V]olevo trovare bello e grande l'amore, quell'amore dei sedici anni che riassume alla fanciulla la poesia misteriosa della vita" (53) ("I was so determined to love him. . . . I wanted love to be a grand and beautiful experience. I was sixteen and wanted a love which would incorporate all the mysterious poetry of life" 42). He persuades her to reveal her love to her parents, and the young man becomes "un fidanzato regolare" (52) ("a typical fiancé"; translation mine).

A certain female identification develops between the mother and the daughter at this point, the mother believing that her child must be experiencing the same premarital bliss that she had once felt: "parve come bere ad una fontana di giovinezza ascoltando la figliuola innamorata. Erano i suoi vent'anni ch'ella rievocava?" (50) ("she . . . seemed to grow young again as she drank in the words of her love-struck daughter. Was she picturing herself at twenty?" 39). Her mother even becomes somewhat optimistic at the thought of occupying herself with grandchildren. The father's aspirations regarding his daughter's education, however, are crushed. He sees that she is taking a "conventional" female path and refuses to speak to her: "Compresi ch'io ero morta per lui, ch'egli dava l'addio a tutto il sogno che aveva costruito sul mio capo nel tempo remoto" (51) ("He realized that he had lost all my sympathy and that all the hopes and dreams he had once built around me were at an end" 40). The protagonist even feels that she is contributing to her father's estrangement from the family. She regrets this, particularly because she realizes that she has inherited so many of her good qualities from him.

The ensuing marriage will, in fact, prove disappointing. The husband's working-class social milieu is foreign to the protagonist. He is less intelligent and refined than she, and he limits her freedom by allowing her very little contact with society. Further, she is constantly haunted by her violent sexual initiation. She is, however, "*una donna maritata*" (55) ("*a married woman*" 45), and costume changes such as her new flannel dresses reflect this. In her listless state, she recognizes parallels between her own life and her mother's and fears a tragic fate: "La sua debolezza, la sua rinuncia alla lotta mi esacerbavano tanto più in quanto ero costretta a riconoscermi ora dei punti di contatto con lei nella mia rassegnazione al destino" (60–61) ("Her weakness, her renunciation of the struggle, exasperated me much more now that I was forced to admit that my own fatalistic resignation to my situation simply demonstrated to me how alike we were" 51).

When the protagonist gives birth to a son, her life changes. She is able for a time to focus on him and find fulfillment in motherhood. She also begins writing. In a small book she notes down "le date maggiori dell'esistenza fragile e preziosa della quale vivevo e che respiravo come se fosse stata la sola aria per me vitale" (76) ("the major events in the life of my fragile, precious child . . . by now I lived and breathed for him alone, as if he was sufficient for me" 68). Indeed, this is her "esordio di scrittrice" (76) ("debut as a writer"; translation mine); giving birth to a child inspires her to give form to the profound sentiments she experiences at this significant moment in a woman's life. Later, as the protagonist struggles between her desire to leave an abusive husband and her fear of losing her son, she will write as a form of therapy: "Oh, dire, dire a qualcuno il mio dolore, la mia miseria" (107) ("Oh, if only I could tell someone about my pain and misery!" 106). The woman seems to reach for a new form and voice to express her suffering, and the novelty of this endeavor is communicated through a tone often characterized by oscillation and hesitation: "dirlo a me stessa anzi . . . *in una forma nuova, decisa*, che mi rivelasse qualche angolo ancora oscuro del mio destino!" (107; emphasis added) ("Even myself! Perhaps if I could tell myself about it *in some new way* it might have the power to shed some light on what had happened and on what would become of me" 106; emphasis added).[5] Such concern for uniquely female expression would continue to occupy women writers throughout the century, from Virginia Woolf and Colette, to Hélène Cixous and Luce Irigaray.

Another turning point in the work occurs when feelings develop between the protagonist and a married male friend. They exchange letters and even meet one evening when the husband is away, yet she is ultimately repulsed by the friend's touch, which reminds her of her first violent sexual encounter. Neighborhood gossip about the protagonist and her friend reaches her husband, and this sets off a series of arguments, insults, and physical abuses. This drives her (like her mother) to a suicide attempt. Her doctor, an intellectual and sensitive friend, rescues the protagonist and watches over her during her convalescence. This healing leads to a moment of conversion, characteristic of autobiography, which marks the beginning of a new existence.

The first lines of the Part Two read: "Avevo dato l'addio alla vita semplicemente, fermamente, benché in un'ora di smarrimento. . . . La mia esistenza doveva finire in quel punto: la donna ch'io ero stata fino a quella notte doveva morire" (95) ("To wish my life goodbye had been a simple decision, even though I had taken it in a moment of great confusion. . . . I had to end my life; the woman I had been until then had to die" 91). Whereas there had been a move from paternal to maternal identification at the time of the protagonist's marriage, after the suicide attempt, the daughter's life takes a dramatic turn. Angelini explains that rather than the self-destruction that grows from the mother's suicide attempt, the daughter's effort to end her life leads to her liberation (68). Marotti adds that the protagonist's suicide attempt is one of several initiation episodes reminiscent of death-rebirth rituals—darkness is followed by a period of insight and moral advancement (69). At this point the protagonist's intellectual awakening begins—a renaissance that will lead her even farther away from the traditional maternal model. Bassanese sees the second section as a contrast to Part One: the first section "document[s] the heroine's integration into the roles society creates for her and their destructive aftermath whereas the [second] stress[es] personal, rather than social, development" (134). We have already seen, however, that in Part One the protagonist is initially allowed access into the male-dominated milieu of the factory. This freedom is then cut short by rape and assimilation into stifling female roles. Part Two, indeed, demonstrates that the ability to become independent is linked to the heroine's intellectual growth.

Common in female autobiography and developmental literature, an inward search precedes self-realization and an outward movement into society. For Aleramo's protagonist, this quest begins with reading, an activity that leads her to an examination of a variety of social and cultural phenomena presented in Part Two.[6] Bassanese notes that "[l]ike Goethe's Wilhelm Meister, [the protagonist] too finds books a means to growth" (142). Aleramo writes: "In quei giorni di infinita solitudine, nel silenzio di ogni richiamo umano, abbandonata veramente ogni speranza e ogni fede, trovai in un libro una causa di salvezza" (102) ("Yet my isolation seemed interminable; no one ever spoke to me; I had given up all hope and trust. When salvation came, it was in the form of a book" 99), a reference to *L'europa giovane* (1898; *Young Europe*) by sociologist Guglielmo Ferrero, which Aleramo did, in fact, read a year after her suicide attempt.[7] Ferrero, a student and colleague of positivist thinker Cesare Lombroso, explains in the work that "peculiar cultural and hereditary factors tended to transform Latin marriages into prison sentences for women" (Drake viii). Richard Drake explains that Aleramo could comprehend the "maddening phenomenon of compulsively philandering husbands . . . who at the same time were pathologically jealous of wives," something that Ferrero's book expressed in the "language of common sense and in the light of science" (viii–ix). Drake adds that Aleramo would have learned of Mona Caird's work through Ferrero as well. Caird had written extensively on family problems, focusing, in particular, on "the loveless, forced marriage in which the woman had been compelled to bear a child without her consent" (Drake ix). Though not an exact mirror of the marital situation in *Una donna*, such ideas would have resonated with Aleramo's feelings of entrapment and betrayal. She offers several examples of oppressed women in *Una donna*, from servants, to prostitutes, from her mother, to her mother-in-law. We read: "Trovavo mia suocera, la sera, accoccolata dinanzi al grande camino, la cui fiamma talora illuminava da sola la buia cucina" (56) ("I would go to see my mother-in-law in the evenings. I would find her crouched beside their great stove, its flame sometimes the only light in the kitchen darkness" 47). Feminist ideas were closely linked to socialist ones at the time, and so it is not surprising that the protagonist, influenced by this cultural context, becomes interested in the working conditions of people of her region. She thus makes connections between class oppression and the subjugation of women.

The protagonist's intellectual journey also parallels her geographical one; her thoughts move from the people of her region to society at large, and her writing activity takes her from the provinces to Rome, the center of cultural and intellectual activity.[8] Female displacement in this text also occurs within the context of cultural and economic divisions between northern, central, and southern Italy, some of which still exist today. The intellectual women of Rome become foils to the oppressed women of the heroine's southern province. Drake points out, however, that Aleramo's concern with "the peculiarly oppressive character of the cumulative cultural heredity in Mediterranean countries" could not be remedied by economic changes alone (x). Indeed, the heroine's discoveries reflect an awareness that feminists of the 1970s would embrace: class equality cannot fully remedy gender oppression or respond to women's particular needs.

In Chapter 13 (Part Two), the protagonist's feminist consciousness comes to the fore. The chapter opens with a discussion of one of her short articles, which includes the word *"femminismo"* (116) (*"feminism"* 115). We read: "E quando la vidi così, stampata, la parola dall'aspro suono mi parve d'un tratto acquistare intera la sua significazione, designarmi veramente un ideale nuovo" (116) ("[A]nd when I saw the austere-sounding word in print it suddenly seemed to take on its full significance. I realised I had discovered a new ideal" 115). In fact, the period from the late nineteenth century to the early twentieth century was crucial for a burgeoning feminist movement in Italy. According to Annarita Buttafuoco, women journalists, writers, and intellectuals like Aleramo, Donna Paola, and Ersilia Majno were intent on redefining "woman" ("Vite esemplari"). At the same time the emancipation movement was concerned with revising women's roles in the family, in society, and in the state (Buttafuoco 146). Buttafuoco discusses the progress women made in producing propaganda aimed at changing public opinion and attaining the vote,[9] in educational initiatives to combat illiteracy, in concessions concerning citizenship rights for women, and in the creation of new journals for a female readership (141). With advances in education, certain women were able to embark on careers as teachers, telegraph operators, bookkeepers, and government clerks.[10] Aleramo's text participated in these efforts to redefine the feminine, change the status of women, and create new opportunities.

With the protagonist's first publications, other writers and intellectuals begin noticing her work. This sparks a series of correspondences. She is disappointed, however, to learn that intellectual women in Italy know very little about feminist ideas and that their writing, which often imitates male models, consists of "grandi frasi vuote, senza nesso e senza convinzione" (120) ("mere rhetoric, without logic, conviction, or ideas of any kind" 120). She asks when these female authors would realize that a woman could justify a place in the already overcrowded literary world only by writing books with "la sua propria impronta" (136) ("her own imprint"; translation mine). Therefore, here again, the protagonist seeks a type of literature with a uniquely female voice or quality.

The Turning Point 99

She continues to write and publish, and at the end of Chapter 13 we read of the heroine's first desire to write her life story:

Un libro, *il libro*. . . . Ah, non vagheggiavo di scriverlo, no! Ma mi struggevo, certe volte, contemplando nel mio spirito la visione di quel libro che sentivo necessario, di un libro d'amore e di dolore, che fosse straziante e insieme fecondo, inesorabile e pietoso, che mostrasse al mondo intero *l'anima femminile moderna*, per la prima volta, e per la prima volta facesse palpitare di rimorso e di desiderio l'anima dell'uomo, del triste fratello. (122; second emphasis added)
(A book, *the book*. . . . Surely I didn't want to write that? But sometimes I felt such urgent longing when I thought about the book which should be written: a book created out of love and pain, compassionate, yet inspired by an implacable logic, heart-rending, yet optimistic. Such a book would show the world for the first time what it was to be *a modern woman*, instilling in the feelings of her unhappy brother, man, regret for the past, and an intense desire for change. 122; second emphasis added)

We see how much feminism, the desire to express the needs of the modern women, is tied to the writing project and to what extent that project is linked to lived experiences. We also note that this woman is aware of doing something new, of expressing a sense of injustice and an anger that women had hitherto repressed. Her poetic creation, which will, indeed, become her "substitute child," constitutes a search for self-understanding, a confession, and a rebirth as a woman.

The name change from Rina Pierangeli Faccio[11] to Sibilla Aleramo is significant for the birth of both the writer and the independent woman. We recall that many writers from the nineteenth century used pen names, including Marie d'Agoult (Daniel Stern), Delphine de Girardin (le Vicomte de Launay), George Sand, and Céleste Mogador. Sand's pseudonym was associated with her lover Jules Sandeau but was nonetheless a different name from that of her family or her husband. Mogador in her *Mémoires* used the name adopted while she was a performer, although she would sign the sequel, *Un deuil au bout du monde*, with her married name. Aleramo's lover Giovanni Cena bestowed upon her the name Sibilla. The Sibyl was a pagan fortune-teller or prophet and also a figure of authority. Angelini notes that Aleramo's articles on feminist issues are generally signed with two names—those of her father and husband (64). Importantly, with *Una donna*, Aleramo renounces both the father's and the husband's names, opting for "a prophetic and poetic name," albeit a name given to her by a man (Angelini 64). Angelini explains that "[t]he passage to the new name . . . marks . . . the passage to personal and creative writing and opens a new period. . . . The loss of the name coincides with birth in literature" (64–65). Like Céleste Mogador, Aleramo refashions herself by becoming a writer, albeit through different circumstances. Writing leads to rebirth for Aleramo's heroine and eventually enables her to separate from oppressive familial forces.

The protagonist's journey toward subjectivity reaches another pivotal moment when her husband loses his job, and, in turn, she gains a position writing for the magazine *Mulier*. There will still be a great deal of struggle before she is able to leave her husband and her son. However, the intellectual stimulation she finds in Rome, the friends she acquires, and, most importantly, the feeling that she is being true to herself—the sense that she can think, write, grow, and live independently—eventually allow her to break free.

A conflict arises when the protagonist's son becomes ill shortly after she assumes her new job. At this point, she still defines herself in terms of her child; her experience of motherhood constitutes her existence. We read: "Perché avevo pensato tanto naturalmente alla morte quando mio figlio era in pericolo? *Non esistevo io dunque indipendentemente da lui.* . . . [U]na cosa sola, ora come tre anni prima, era realmente *viva* in me, viva formidabile: il legame della maternità" (143; first emphasis added) ("I had to ask why I had instantly wanted to die when I realised my son was in danger. *Had I no life of my own?*. . . . [O]nly one thing lived in me: the bond of maternity. And it was still as powerful and commanding as it had been three years before" 146–47; emphasis added).[12] When her husband regains employment in his native town in the *Mezzogiorno*, southern Italy, however, and the protagonist is faced with the impending move back to a sterile and repressive village, she begins to realize that she can no longer deny her individuality. The double life she has been leading is reflected in the following passage: "[Il mio bambino] era la parte migliore di me. . . . Ma l'altra parte, la creatura vegliante, agitata da ricordi e da presentimenti? . . . L'atra viveva d'una vita intensa come non mai" (142) ("[My son] embodied the best of myself. . . . But there was another me, too, a watchful me: she was still being buffeted by the storms of memory and anxiety. . . . What was to become of her? She lived more intensely than ever" 146). Such a sense of division and lack of wholeness, expressed in the preceding passage through the depiction of different "selves" and through the fluctuation between first- and third-person perspectives, becomes even more common in contemporary women's writing when contradictory societal demands and changing female roles create greater anxiety for women in their attempts to define themselves. Because of her internal divisions, the protagonist reveals to her husband the desire to separate. In a letter to him, she significantly calls on the "sibilla" for strength, the name with which Aleramo signs her story: "Tremava, così scrivendo: interrogavo veramente la sibilla. . . . Una voce nell'anima cantava senza posa: 'Sei libera, libera!'" (157) ("I trembled as I wrote: I truly appealed to the Sibyl. . . . A voice in my soul sang incessantly: 'You are free, free!'"; translation mine). At the close of Part Two, however, maternal ties still bind the protagonist to her son, and she is unable to set off on her own.

In turn-of-the-century Italy, a reimagining of the maternal was difficult, not only because of childbirth risks and the limited availability of contraception, but because strict laws prevented wives from leaving their husbands and keeping their children. Wood explains that "[w]ith the Unification of Italy, a new national Civil Code was drawn up and published in 1865" (6). Unfortunately, it showed "disappointingly little progress from the Napoleonic Code imposed during the period of French rule" in Italy (Wood 6).[13] Divorce was inconceivable and was not legalized until 1970. As in France, women could not manage their own property or money, and laws regarding adultery were much more lax for men. In Aleramo's concluding chapter, set one year after the heroine has left her husband and son, the narrator/protagonist (there is little distance between them as we are brought to the moment of writing) laments that her struggle to gain custody of her son has become futile: "Infine anche l'avvocato rinunziò ad ogni trattativa. Io restavo proprietà di quell'uomo, dovevo stimarmi fortunata ch'egli non mi facesse ricondurre colla forza. Questa era la legge" (201) ("Finally, even the lawyers gave up. I must, they said, remain the property of this man, and should count myself lucky if he didn't force me to return to him. Such was the law" 217). Aleramo outlines many of the problems and ideas circulating during her era and endeavors to render her readers more sensitive to the injustices of the female plight. The suffering and sacrifices of her protagonist make way for more positive portrayals of female independence in later texts.

Aleramo's text foreshadows the efforts of women writers of the 1920s and 1930s. Although several critics consider the Fascist years a dim period for female literary production, Robin Pickering-Iazzi points out in her provocative collection *Unspeakable Women* that numerous women wrote and published during the Fascist regime.[14] She notes that their short stories were particularly prevalent on Italy's *terza pagina*, the cultural page of Italian newspapers. Authors such as Grazia Deledda and Ada Negri dealt with issues of isolation and imposed silence, women's roles, marital strife, and the desire for career. Pickering-Iazzi attributes the absence of many of these women writers, such as Maddalena Crispolti, Marinella Lodi, and Pia Rimini, from anthologies and literary histories to postwar male writers and critics who, in the aftermath of Fascism, bolstered only what they deemed politically committed literature.[15] Unfortunately, they did not recognize the political nature of many of these women's feminist stories.

Marianne Hirsch claims that women's texts of the same period, including Woolf's *A Room of One's Own*, employ "circuitous strategies of female modernism" (*Mother/Daughter* 93). She states that "like a number of women's *Künstlerromane* of the twenties, [*A Room*] defines the liminal discourse of a female artist who stands ... both inside and outside of the structures of tradition, representation, and the symbolic" (*Mother/Daughter* 92). Woolf's is a strategy "appropriate to someone who, having been represented as object, strains to define herself as subject" (Hirsch, *Mother/Daughter* 93). With her 1906 *Una donna*, Aleramo already grapples with such issues of female subjectivity. She precedes similar texts by Woolf and Colette, for example, which "feature young and middle-aged women who renounce love and marriage in favor of creative work, who renounce connection in favor of self-affirmation" (Hirsch, *Mother/Daughter* 96). Grazia Deledda treats similar themes in her autobiographical novel *Cosima*, published in 1937.

Hirsch holds that this move toward self-realization for the modern female writer is intimately tied to the relationship with the mother. Like the writers who follow, Aleramo will have to deal with her mother's memory (from the point of her mother's madness, we can consider her emotionally "dead") in order to stake out her own ground. Her struggle to choose career over motherhood illustrates the difficulty of combining the two at the time. Hirsch posits that "*A Room* makes clear that motherhood and achievement were utterly incompatible in previous generations" (*Mother/Daughter* 97). Hirsch exaggerates somewhat, however, as we can think of such exceptions as Sand, d'Agoult, and Cristina di Belgiojoso, who, even in the nineteenth century and albeit with difficulty, managed a career and children. Hirsch also suggests that interest in maternity could emerge only "at a time in history when motherhood had become less life-threatening and more of a choice for women" (*Mother/Daughter* 97). Indeed, remarkable opportunities for many women succeeded the publication of *Una donna*, including increased availability of birth control and innovations in childbirth technology, as well as new independence following World War I. Italy, like France, however, rejected birth control and innovations in childbirth procedures long after England had adopted them. Hirsch points out that the writers of the 1920s attempted to bridge the gap between "two generations separated by a remarkable shift in opportunity for women" (*Mother/Daughter* 97). She explains that whereas Victorian heroines had to maintain a distance between mother and daughter, in the 1920s "connection has become possible. . . . Even while the daughter-artist herself still does not become a mother, the mother's life can be and needs to be known and explored in its details, incorporated into the daughter's vision" (*Mother/Daughter* 97). Hirsch calls such texts "elegies" because "they are not composed by the daughters until the mothers are dead. Only then can memory and desire play their roles as instruments of connection, reconstruction, and reparation. In fact . . . in contrast to the Victorian examples, death here enables the mothers to be *present* rather than *absent*" (*Mother/Daughter* 97). We note, then, the shift from the need to "repress" the mother in many nineteenth-century texts, such as Belgiojoso's *Emina*, to one of communion with the memory of the mother in the twentieth century. In contrast to Hirsch's findings, Aleramo's turn-of-the-century protagonist does "become a mother," and at this point she can sympathize with her own mother's experiences as a neglected wife, as well as her feelings of guilt over not being capable of mothering well. The son is not conceived out of love, however, and he must be sacrificed so that the protagonist can save her own life. The abandonment of the son in *Una donna* becomes perhaps the only possible option for the heroine, excluding death.

In Aleramo's story, images of entrapment and death, which close Part One (the suicide attempt) and Part Two (the trunks she packs as she prepares to leave Rome are like "tante bare" [173] ["so many coffins" 181])[16] persist in Part Three. First, the protagonist's move back to the southern province repeats the pattern of oppression witnessed earlier in the text. Celia Bucci draws on Julia Kristeva's notion of "women's time" and comments on the cyclical and repetitive nature of the woman's life in *Una donna* (202–3). Bucci explains that the protagonist's move from a confident individual to an abused one recurs in the text and that "this model of cyclicality qua determination/

endurance/compromise (both biological and in terms of her role in society) represents this woman's (a woman's) entrapment within patriarchy" (203). Second, visions of the protagonist's mother force her to realize that a loveless and abusive marriage can lead only to spiritual death. When the protagonist finds old letters in which her mother reveals to her own father that her husband no longer loves her and that she must leave him and her children, we have a foreshadowing of the protagonist's impending departure. This section is followed by the cry that epitomizes the main theme of *Una donna*: "Perché nella maternità adoriamo il sacrifizio? Donde è scesa a noi questa inumana idea dell'immolazione materna? Di madre in figlia, da secoli, si tramanda il servaggio. È una mostruosa catena" (182) ("Why do we idealize sacrifice in mothers? Who gave us this inhuman idea that mothers should negate their own wishes and desires? The acceptance of servitude has been handed down from mother to daughter for so many centuries that it is now a monstrous chain which fetters them" 193). Immediately thereafter we hear Aleramo's feminist plea for a woman's dignity: "Se una buona volta la fatale catena si spezzasse, e una madre non sopprimesse in sé la donna, e un figlio apprendesse dalla vita di lei un esempio di dignità?" (182) ("Yet what would happen if this dreadful cycle was broken, once and for all? What if mothers refused to deny their womanhood and gave their children instead an example of a life lived according to the needs of self-respect?" 194). With this realization, the protagonist will not only fracture the bonds that entrap her in her marriage but symbolically break the chains of centuries of maternal sacrifice. The narrative tone becomes didactic, reinforced by the use of the verb *dovere*:[17] "Per quello che siamo . . . devono esserci grati i figli, non perché, dopo averli ciecamente suscitati dal nulla, rinunziamo ad essere noi stessi" (182) ("Children should be grateful to us for being who we are . . . they shouldn't feel indebted because we give birth to them unthinkingly and then react by renouncing our own destiny" 194). The protagonist of *Una donna* knows that she must live out her destiny as not only a mother but a woman, and to do so she must sever her ties with the past.

The conclusion of the text focuses on feminine dignity, on an inner integrity that pushes the protagonist to break out on her own. Her decision, however, is heart-wrenching, because, as noted before, Italian law at the time made it nearly impossible for a woman to leave her husband and take her child with her without his consent.

The protagonist's movement, "leaving the family," is both an emotional and a physical journey. She can no longer tolerate her husband's embrace: "*la carne era stata più ribelle, aveva urlato, s'era svincolata; ad essa dovevo la mia liberazione*" (195; emphasis added) ("I had left it to *my body* to rebel, to cry out, to fight for its freedom. It was to *my body* that I owed my liberation" 209–10; emphasis added). The use of the term "carne" (literally, "flesh") in the original Italian underscores the raw nature of the protagonist's disgust for her husband and the sterility of their forced union. She is able to justify her avoidance of him more easily after his visit to a prostitute and his acquired disease. As she leaves her son, she resembles a sleepwalker, following an inner mechanism in an almost unconscious fashion: "sentii che una forza fuori di me mi reggeva, e che andavo incontro al destino nuovo, e che tutto il dolore che mi attendeva non avrebbe superato quel dolore. Mi trovai sul treno senza sapere come vi fossi venuta"(199) ("I felt urged on by something outside myself, pushing me forward to a different life. And I knew that no future pain could ever equal the grief I felt at that moment. Without knowing how I got there, I found myself on the train" 214). Aleramo illustrates the trauma of separations, in particular, that of mother and child, a relationship laden with emotional, physical, and cultural significance. The protagonist must reject the resignation and pure sacrifice that led to her mother's madness and leave her family in an effort to live. With *Una donna*, Aleramo portrays a new female destiny for one of the first modern women in literature.

The concluding chapter, as noted previously, recounts the woman's thoughts one year later. Efforts on her and her father's part to gain custody of her son have failed, and she reflects: "La mia maternità s'era dunque chiusa veramente con quell'ultimo bacio?" (201) ("I found it hard to accept that my experience of motherhood had ended when I kissed him goodbye" 217). Present tenses bring us to the moment of writing, and the protagonist and narrator become one: "una cosa sola, su tutto, splende: la pace mia interiore" (202) ("one thing is clear. I feel at peace" 219). We realize the growth and transformation this woman has undergone. Through involvement in humanitarian projects, including assistance to underprivileged children, she is able to persevere. This previews some of Aleramo's future concerns regarding social issues, exposed, for example, in her published diaries.

Aleramo closes *Una donna* with her statement of purpose: her book is for her son so that he will understand her motivations for having left him. She addresses her son: "Figliuolo, figliuolo! Ti strinsi, piansi con te" (194) ("Oh, my son! And I held you and wept with you" 208). She cries out that although she may die before they are able to speak again, her writing is for him: "Le mie parole lo raggiungeranno" (203) ("my words will reach him" 219). Such a moving conclusion requests the reader's sympathy and support in seeking equality for women, including changes in unjust child custody laws. In addition, it underscores the moral impact of the work through profound emotional drama.

Aleramo's text sets the scene for the feminist battles to come in contemporary life stories. She dares to voice her desire for freedom, in a subtle and in an aggressive manner at the same time, through confession and also through protest. As we move further into the twentieth century, not only will rage over the female plight be voiced more easily, but feminine issues of sexuality, childbirth, and motherhood will be discussed more openly. Contemporary women's refusal to be defined simply as wives or mothers is evident in such texts as Oriana Fallaci's *Lettera a un bambino mai nato*, discussed in the next chapter, a text that boldly takes on the issue of reproductive choice. Postmodern women autobiographers will break new narrative ground and begin to fill in some of the gaps in the life stories of their female predecessors.

NOTES

1. Unless indicated, English translations of quotations from *Una donna* are from the following edition: Sibilla Aleramo, *A Woman*, trans. Rosalind Delmar (Berkeley: U of California P, 1980).

2. Macciocchi's preface first appeared in 1973.

3. Rich borrows the term "matrophobia" from Lynn Sukenick.

4. The theme of rape is taken up by future Italian writers, both male and female. Consider, for example, Anna Banti's *Artemisia* and Alberto Moravia's *La ciociara*.

5. Note that Delmar, in her translation of *Una donna*, translates "una forma nuova, decisa" as "some new way." An alternative translation, for example, "a new, decisive form" or "a new, decisive style," places greater emphasis on the new female voice or way of writing that the woman seeks.

6. As discussed in my Introduction, Buckley's description of the *bildungsroman* stresses the importance of reading in the development of the imagination (17).

7. See Drake (viii–ix).

8. Bassanese explains that spiritual awakening precedes physical movement as the protagonist leaves the stifling provincial town for the capital (143).

9. Women did not attain the vote in Italy until after World War II.

10. See Buttafuoco; and Wood 5–18.

11. The name Pierangeli Faccio reflects the husband's and father's names.

12. Delmar, in her translation of *Una donna*, condenses the second part of the quotation. A fuller alternative would be: "[O]nly one thing, now as three years ago, was really *alive* in me, tremendously alive: the bond of maternity."

13. See Wood's discussion of the new system of regulations (6–7).

14. See Pickering-Iazzi's "Preface" in *Unspeakble Women*.

15. See Pickering-Iazzi's "Afterword" in *Unspeakable Women*.

16. See Bassanese on this point and on other images of death, including the passing of the Norwegian woman and the "tomb-like decay" of the home of the prophet, the protagonist's friend (144).

17. *Dovere* translates as "must, to have to." In the conditional tense, it translates as "should," which is the term Delmar chooses in her translation.

6

Living Freely, Demanding Choice: Oriana Fallaci's *Lettera a un bambino mai nato*

Oriana Fallaci, a prolific writer and journalist[1] known for her aggressive reporting and interviewing techniques, was drawn to many of the feminist themes regarding women's lives that Sibilla Aleramo had treated earlier in the century. Journalism mingles with life writing in Fallaci's auto/biographical works and interviews, the latter described by the author as "portraits of myself" (qtd. in Amoia 116). According to Santo L. Aricò, Fallaci turns many of her news articles into narratives containing background, story lines, and twist endings (28). Although she is wary of studying "woman" as a distinct category, Fallaci did travel the world for a project on the status of women—a voyage that recalls Cristina di Belgiojoso's analyses of foreign women over a century earlier. In the articles which emerged from this journey, collected in the book *Il sesso inutile* (1961; *The Useless Sex*), Fallaci attacks the patriarchal systems in place at the time in Pakistan, India, Malaysia, and China (Aricò 50). Fallaci, born in 1930 and the daughter of the late Edoardo Fallaci, one of Tuscany's Resistance heroes, is also immersed in politics. According to Alba Amoia, the young Fallaci "ran courier missions for [her father]. . . . She attended her first political rally in Piazza della Signoria at the age of fifteen and ever since has remained politically involved, always on the side of the opposition" (113). Fallaci's admiration for scores of revolutionary leaders attests to her convictions regarding personal freedom and social justice. Her intimate relationship with the Greek rebel Alekos Panagulis in the 1970s is portrayed in her award-winning biography *Un uomo: Romanzo* (1979; *A Man: Novel*).

Lettera a un bambino mai nato, published in 1975, can be read as a contemporary response to many of the topics raised in Aleramo's *Una donna*.[2] As in *Una donna*, *Lettera* once again reflects the quest for freedom through "leaving the family." Fallaci's protagonist leaves conventionally sanctioned love and marriage behind and lives as a single woman confronting motherhood alone. In her case, she did not have to struggle with an abusive marriage or jealous husband. Legally, she had the right to bear a child and raise it by herself. However, Italian society was still hostile toward single mothers. From the first pages of *Lettera*, Fallaci explores several of the seminal themes common to women's writing since the 1970s, including abortion, the woman's body, single parenthood, and the combination of motherhood and career.

Lettera is not a complete life story but rather a segment of a woman's life told in the first-person autobiographical mode. The title also echoes this "moment"—the work is simply a "letter" to the unborn child rather than a lengthy narrative. The text includes flashes of the woman's past, significant relationships, and meaningful events. In fact, contemporary authors often attempt explorations of phases of their lives, fragments that are frequently rewritten or revised in different contexts and published in different works, all part of an ongoing "story." In today's "new autobiographies,"[3] the lines between fiction and nonfiction, reminiscence and invention blur in a self-conscious fashion. The personal and the collective frequently intermingle through shifting narrative perspectives, and the self often merges with the other.[4] As in Aleramo's work, *Lettera* weaves truth with fiction. Fallaci, indeed, miscarried after a long automobile trip to fulfill a journalistic assignment, much like the protagonist in *Lettera*. Aricò explains that *Lettera* grew out of "the trauma, grief, and despair of losing a child" (160). One of Fallaci's several miscarriages "inspired her to write the book" (Aricò 160). In addition, Fallaci had been researching the abortion topic for a piece in the *Europeo* in 1975, and much of that research blossomed into *Lettera* (Aricò 160–61). The text also incorporates imaginative writing and hypothetical situations, hence, the mélange of fact and fiction.

In the story, the narrator/protagonist (the two are hardly distinguishable) addresses herself to her unborn child, whom she speaks to as "tu" (the familiar "you" form in Italian) or "bambino" ("baby" or "child").[5] This exchange unfolds in a monologue/dialogue that serves as an extension of the narrator/protagonist's thoughts, allows her to voice her views and qualms, and permits the reader to witness the pregnant woman's inner development. It is through this "relationship" with her fetus that the heroine's *bildung* occurs. At one of the woman's more negative moments, we read: "Ti ho attribuito una coscienza, ho dialogato con te, ma la tua coscienza era la mia coscienza e il nostro dialogo era un monologo: il mio!" (62) ("I've bestowed a mind on you, carried on a dialogue with you, but your mind was my mind, and our dialogue a monologue: mine!" 70). The text also includes the woman's meditations and imaginings, recalling the associative nature of reminiscences in Marie Cardinal's *Les mots pour le dire*. It is an extreme form insofar as the fetus becomes a character toward the end of the narrative.[6] The unborn child speaks through the voice of a grown man in the context of one of the protagonist's dreams or hallucinations. He expresses his opinions regarding life, death, and his mother's choices. Because the child is eventually miscarried, we have an echo of Aleramo's "lost" child as well. In *Lettera*, the protagonist's pregnancy forces her to confront the scorn of medical professionals who are startled that she is unmarried, the surprise of colleagues who urge her to place her career before motherhood, and the ire of friends who exhort her to abort. All of these encounters contribute to the protagonist's learning.

The radical nature of the monologue/dialogue in *Lettera* underscores Fallaci's belief in the necessity for innovative visions of motherhood and for a reconsideration of mother–child relationships in varied contexts and settings, both of which are possible through narrative experimentation. Robin Pickering-Iazzi observes that in both Dacia Maraini's *Donna in guerra* (*Women at War*), also published in 1975, and *Lettera* "the writers forge alternatives to women's silence, fashioning a new contextual framework for female identity that expands women's designs, as content, form, and intent" ("Designing Mothers" 334).

Central to this contemporary piece is the theme of choice—a topic treated by several women writers today, including Maraini, Cardinal, and Annie Ernaux. As in Aleramo's *Una donna*, the fact that Fallaci uses no proper names in her text underscores its universality. The issues she addresses—heated ones in 1975, when abortion was still illegal in Italy[7]—concern all women.[8] Through various techniques in *Lettera*, all sides of the abortion issue are presented. Although Fallaci goes to great lengths to express these different arguments, her protagonist intentionally decides to continue her pregnancy, emphasizing that the right to make such a choice is hers alone. She makes the decision to keep her child not out of obligation but through her own volition—a desire nurtured by the relationship she develops with her fetus. The narrator "discusses," for example, whether or not she is willing or ready to care for a child and whether the child should or would want to be born, hinting that the birth is not guaranteed (7–9; 9–11).[9] She recounts a dream in which her grandmother is threatened by a priest and policemen because of her many abortions, a procedure this poor woman, who cannot support the eight children she has already, would undergo again (28; 32). Fallaci's views on the unwelcome intrusions of church and state are clear, as well as her sympathy for her female predecessors who did not possess the freedom of choice she enjoys. Finally, we learn that the protagonist herself was an "accident" and that her mother had tried to induce a miscarriage until she felt her child stirring in her womb (8; 10). Cardinal's *Les mots pour le dire* presents a similar situation of a mother's unwanted pregnancy. In Cardinal's text, however, while the mother resents the child she eventually delivers, the daughter/heroine revels in her first perceptions of her own child within her (157–58). In *Lettera*, the protagonist awaits such a sign from her own fetus, until she finally decides on her own: "nascerai" (9) ("you will be born" 11). This again underscores her emphasis on motherhood as a choice. Fallaci recalls Aleramo's *Una donna* as she questions the socially charged significance of motherhood as sacrifice. She pushes her predecessor's argument even further, however, stating that to be a mother is not a profession nor even a duty, but rather one right among many (13; 16).

Pickering-Iazzi discusses Fallaci's "regenerative notion of maternity" ("Designing Mothers" 325). She explains that "when motherhood is a conscious choice the mother/child relationship has the potential to transform the nature of society and culture" ("Designing Mothers" 325). Fallaci's emphasis on intent and responsibility are central to her sense of self and her belief in the individual's potential to have an impact on societal change. In her visions of alternative family configurations and in her questioning of women's roles, Fallaci joins her Italian predecessors Belgiojoso and Aleramo, whose writings and actions challenged conventional patriarchal structures.[10]

In *Lettera*, Fallaci also puts forth feminine "difference" and considers the impact gender would have on the child's life. The narrator upholds, for example, that only a woman can sense the existence of a new life within her, favoring her own intuition over the science embodied by her male doctor. The pregnant woman considers early on in *Lettera* what it will mean for the child to be a man or a woman. She stresses that especially in our patriarchal society, where heroes from Prometheus to Jesus are male, a woman has several challenges to face, including that of proving her intelligence despite her beauty (12–13; 15–16). Yet such challenges render womanhood fascinating. She hopes, in fact, that her child will be a girl so that the daughter can understand what the protagonist experiences (12; 15). This feminine identification is directly followed by a consideration of the woman's own mother, for whom being born female was a misfortune (12; 15). The gap between the ideas of the protagonist and those of her own mother again recalls Aleramo, whose heroine distinguishes her own values from those of her mother's generation. *Lettera* portrays a contemporary perspective and the evolution of views concerning women despite the prejudices that still exist.

Whereas if the child is a girl, the pregnant woman projects a continuation of herself, if the child is a boy, she envisions the kind of man she would respect. The prospect of a male child is not disappointing to her, for he would at least be spared much of the abuse and humiliation that women suffer. Her ideal male image is nonetheless charged with the qualities we are encouraged to associate with an "honorable man"—one who is gentle with the weak and courageous with the arrogant (14; 17). The narrator adds, however, that such as man would be the enemy of anyone who claims that "i Gesù sono figli del Padre e dello Spirito Santo: non della donna che li partorì" (14) ("the Jesuses are sons of the Father and of the Holy Spirit, not of the women who gave birth to them" 17). Hence, her ideal image goes beyond conventional male stereotypes and reflects someone who would recognize female equality.

Fallaci's feminism is also apparent in her discussion of linguistics. The narrator notes that sexual divisions in our society are prevalent even on the level of language: the term *man* refers to men and women (12; 15). For this reason, she finds the word *person* a marvelous, limitless word, for an individual's heart and mind have no sex (14–15; 17).

The protagonist decides to continue her pregnancy, and it is from this point that her "mothering" takes on greater significance. She is obsessed with examining photographs of the fetus, tangible representations of it, and follows its development closely. She endeavors to communicate with her unborn child, to teach, form, and prepare it for life in society. She invents fables for her fetus in which she reveals many of the injustices and struggles in the world.[11] She also describes to her unborn child the strong, principled character she would like it to develop—one which cherishes freedom to the point of self-sacrifice (35; 40), one reminiscent of that possessed by Fallaci's own father and her former lover Panagulis. Pickering-Iazzi notes that Fallaci's "recurrent references to teaching . . . conveyed by her discourse and the repetition of such words as *lezione*, *spiegare*, *insegnare*, *insegnamento*, *imparare*, and *apprendere*, underscore the formative role mothering may play in reshaping ideas, values, and culture" ("Designing Mothers" 338).[12] By subverting the traditional scope of motherhood, the protagonist "undermines such patriarchal institutions, ideals, and myths as the State, the Church, patriarchy, the family, and gender roles. The writer posits new determinants of human conduct, irrespective of gender" (Pickering-Iazzi, "Designing Mothers" 338). The protagonist, indeed, participates in her fetus' *bildung*, encouraging it to become an individual who will reconstruct and transform society rather than merely assimilate values that she finds unacceptable. Fallaci's is, certainly, an idealistic and positive vision, incorporating great confidence in what she sees as enormous human potential.

Whereas in the nineteenth century many women writers expressed dissatisfaction with the female plight and reproached unfair societal conventions, and at turn of the century women struggled with articulating their problems more clearly and attempted both to justify female rebellion and to propose a renewed sense of female dignity, by the 1970s Fallaci can write in a manner that clearly considers inequality between the sexes inadmissible. Therefore, she can focus on workable solutions to gender oppression. The issues of pregnancy and abortion, the institution of motherhood, male and female roles, and female individuality introduced in the opening pages of *Lettera* are elaborated upon throughout the narrative. When looking back on the nineteenth- and early-twentieth-century texts already analyzed in this study, one realizes that Fallaci's forerunners sowed the seeds for the themes presented in *Lettera*. Furthermore, the reader remembers the debates over feminist issues that have taken place in the intertext of both the female and male literary canons of centuries gone by. The tradition of defining and describing female struggles and women's experiences is not new to literature, but issues of motherhood (including single motherhood and surrogate mothering), fertility choices, child care, and female independence are now being expressed in a more open and direct fashion. Experimental literary forms enable contemporary women writers to grapple with these themes and open up a dialogue in order to create alternative solutions to the problems of inequality. These debates echo in the reader's mind as we consider Fallaci's postmodern attempt to explore womanhood.

Through the character of the pregnant woman, Fallaci explores issues of independence and confinement similar to those broached by Belgiojoso in her analysis of the harem, Céleste Mogador in her portrayal of the brothel, and Aleramo in her depiction of an abusive marriage. In *Lettera*, the protagonist is confined to bed rest as the pregnancy becomes more difficult. For someone of her dynamic nature, such confinement is especially tedious. The contrast between enclosed spaces often frequented by women, including the room, home, or harem, and the infinite possibilities of life outside is apparent when the woman is finally allowed to move about again and leave her abode. She rejoices in nature, revels in having contact with people, and triumphs in being independent once more.

At this point, the protagonist becomes more hesitant about her decision to continue her pregnancy, and she calls into question the developing relationship with her unborn child. She argues with her fetus as a tired mother would with those closest to her. Afterward, she queries: "Ti sei offeso? . . . Ti ho detto che anch'io avevo i miei diritti, che nessuno era autorizzato a dimenticarlo e quindi nemmeno te" (51–52) ("Are you offended? . . . I told you that I too had my rights, that no one was entitled to forget it and that meant you as well" 59). Yet this is followed by one of several moments of mother–child fusion: "[V]ieni qui. . . . Dormiamo insieme, abbracciati. Io e te. . . . Nel nostro letto non entrerà mai nessun altro" (52) ("[C]ome here. . . . [W]e'll sleep together, our arms around each other. You and me . . . no one else will ever get into our bed" 59). We note the intimacy between the mother and fetus and the intensity of emotions this relationship inspires. Through introspection, the narrator/protagonist reflects on the origins of human beings and on the magnitude of a woman's life-giving potential.

The mother–child bond is a motif continued throughout the work, at times portrayed as a positive union, at times as an imposition limiting the pregnant woman's freedom. The protagonist informs her fetus early on that she chooses to live alone, without the child's father. When the father hears of her pregnancy, he tries to persuade her to abort, drawing on arguments about the active life she leads and her career. Later, when he comes to visit her, the mother feels that his presence has invaded the mother–child world, and in her mind she excludes him from the experience (52–56; 59–64). Perhaps because she is uncertain if she ever loved the father, perhaps out of an egotistical desire to be the sole link between the child and the world, or perhaps to prove that she can lead her life independently, she conjures up religious images in order to deny the importance of a father. Why, she asks, must Joseph intrude so, when Mary and Jesus are just fine on their own (54; 62)? In contrast to so many of her literary predecessors and even some of her contemporaries, Fallaci's protagonist has little need for the approval of the men in her life.[13]

In a voice appropriate to today's parenting debates, including custody and fertility choices, Fallaci declares that mothers and fathers as well as surrogate or adoptive parents can take on the nurturing role.[14] When the pregnant woman loses patience, she reflects that an older lady with less responsibility and activity in her life, and for whom pregnancy would not be such a burden, might be a better surrogate mother (32–33; 37). As she sifts through the various emotions that accompany her pregnancy, the narrator/protagonist realizes that a "mother" is the one who loves and raises the child, and can, indeed, be a man or a woman.

One of the greatest obstacles for the protagonist is that of her career. Her superior fears that she will not be able to take on an assignment that will require travel abroad. In the end, the protagonist decides to assume the charge, despite warnings from her doctor. After a plane trip and arduous car travel, she realizes that she has lost the child. When she learns that the fetus had stopped developing even earlier than she and her doctor had suspected, we hear: "Creatura della mia fantasia, riuscisti appena a realizzare il desiderio di due mani e due piedi" (98) ("Creature of my imagination, you barely succeeded in realizing the wish for two hands and two feet" 111). At other moments, however, she underscores the fact that the life developing inside of her was unique: "Tutti gli spermii e tutti gli ovuli della terra . . . non potrebbero mai creare di nuovo te, ciò che eri e che avresti potuto essere. Tu non rinascerai mai più. . . . E continuo a parlarti per pura disperazione" (92) ("All the sperm and all the ova on earth . . . could never create a new you, what you were and what you might have been. You'll never be reborn. . . . And I go on talking to you out of pure desperation" 103–4). Dialogue with the unborn child becomes a consolation, even though the desired mother–child reunion can never occur. However, this relationship has begun to teach the protagonist the meaning of love.

We are reminded to what extent the mother–child dyad, a duality reflected in the narrative structure, is also one unit. For example, the woman's inability to cope with the death of the fetus and part from it leads her to suicidal thoughts: the fetus' death must equal her death. By the time the protagonist agrees to the procedure that will remove the dead fetus from her body, her own life is, indeed, in danger. *Lettera* concludes on a positive note, however, as the main character regains the will to live productively. Pickering-Iazzi explains that "[a]lthough the protagonist miscarries and may die, the concluding images of the woman express a life-affirming vision; the daily struggle, to question, to meet and create opportunities, produces a life of committed belief and purposeful action" ("Designing Mothers" 339).

In the concluding scenes, the salient issues of abortion and choice at play throughout the text are highlighted once more. In a dream or hallucination which the protagonist has after she has already lost the child, she finds herself in a cage.[15] This image reflects both the fetus that grows inside the mother and the persistent trappings of traditional womanhood. Members of a "jury" are seated around the cage and must decide whether or not to condemn or acquit the woman. Through the mother's imaginings, we hear other "voices" as each jury member gives his or her opinion. Aside from the views of the protagonist's parents and the fetus, who is granted a male identity, all of the members' opinions are divided along sexual lines. All of the male jurists condemn her. The doctor finds her guilty of murder, stating that she was unwilling to assume her responsibilities as a mother and as a citizen. He believes that the exercise of personal liberty in this case disregards the rights of others, particularly those of the unborn child. The father of the child also finds her guilty. Even her boss, after hearing the doctor's testimony, votes guilty, though he feels that both parents are involved. He reveals that the protagonist feared that the important assignment might go to another colleague and that is why she "era balzata dal letto" (87) ("had jumped out of bed" 98) without any concern for the life inside of her. The female members of the jury, however, support the protagonist. The female doctor who examined her while she was abroad, for example, maintains that pregnancy is a natural event and that if it does not proceed normally, a woman cannot be expected to remain in bed for months "come una paralitica" (83) ("like a paralytic" 94). She values a woman's right to continue an active life just as a man can. The true feminist tirade, however, is expressed by the protagonist's friend. Her friend had originally encouraged her to abort, reminding her of her career and presenting biological arguments: several species of animals, for instance, terminate the lives of their developing offspring. When the friend hears the cowardly reaction of the father, she turns and spits in his face. She defends the right of all women to choose in the name of centuries of discrimination:

Puttana, le dite se ha fatto l'amore con voi. La parola puttano non esiste nel dizionario. . . . *Sono millenni* che ci imponete i vostri vocaboli, i vostri precetti, i vostri abusi. *Sono millenni* che usate il nostro corpo. . . . *Sono millenni* che ci imponete il silenzio e ci relegate al compito di mamme. . . . Dovrei sputare anche su lei, signor dottore. Lei che in una donna vede soltanto un utero e due ovaie, mai un cervello. . . . Qui non si fa il processo a una donna, dottore: si fa il processo a tutte le donne. (85; emphasis added)
(You call her a whore if she's made love to you. There's no male equivalent in the dictionary. . . . *For thousands of years* you've been forcing your words on us, your precepts, your oppression. *For thousands of years* you've been making use of our bodies. . . . *For thousands of years* you've imposed silence on us and consigned us to the job of being mothers. . . . I ought to spit on you too, Doctor. All you see in a woman is a uterus and two ovaries, never a brain. . . . We're not putting one woman on trial here, Doctor: we're putting all women on trial. 95–96; emphasis added)

We are struck not only by the anger of this female friend but by her language. The anaphora—"sono millenni"—fortifies her protest. She not only condemns men for centuries of female oppression but does so in an unabashed fashion, using the terminology of the female body. We recall that only some fifteen years before the publication of *Lettera* the French daily *Le Monde* contested printing the word "vagin" ("vagina") in a description of the rape of the Algerian girl Djamila Boupacha (a case debated by such noted feminists as Simone de Beauvoir and Gisèle Halimi), explaining that the term "ventre" ("stomach") would be less offensive to its reading public.[16] Such a progressive use of language on Fallaci's part, inconceivable for women writers of the nineteenth century, is taken up by other contemporary female authors as well, including Cardinal and Ernaux—women who describe in graphic detail in their texts sexuality, bodily functions, and decay.

The protagonist's parents refuse to judge or condemn her, explaining that no one is able to enter into her mind or soul to understand her motivations or actions. Do the parental voices, so much a part of an individual's sense of self, exonerate the main character? It seems that their refusal to judge their daughter reflects Fallaci's notion of the relativity of truth and the need to weigh each individual woman's choice within a given context. The protagonist's mother further points out that only one testimony would be valid, that of the fetus itself, and it is, in fact, that voice that we hear next.

At this point in the text, as previously stated, the fetus speaks in the voice of a grown man.[17] The protagonist feels dizzy, empty, "hollowed out,"[18] because for the first time she hears herself referred to as "mother." Since the child has the voice of a man, she fears that he will judge her guilty as well. This is, however, not the case. The voice of the fetus states that each of the jury members has spoken a truth, and that this is fitting for his mother had taught him that truth is made up of "molte verità differenti" (89) ("many different truths" 100). We note the echo here of the subjective "truths" that make up biographical and autobiographical narratives as well, and the numerous possible "stories" of an individual's life. Pickering-Iazzi affirms that Fallaci's pluralistic vision is based on the fact that there are "many realities, many truths, and many kinds of consciousness, dependent upon experience and contextuality" ("Designing Mothers" 339). The child continues that once he observed his mother's hesitations and fears, he decided on his own to die. He remarks that her fables always concluded with a question: was it really time for him to leave his peaceful nest to enter the world (90; 101–2)? The child explains that once the mother realized this and began presenting a more hopeful picture he was already committing suicide. He forgives the mother, however, realizing that she was trying to prepare him for life. The child concludes that in his world, there was a clear goal in birth, but in her world the only goal was death. After the trial, the woman grapples with the meaning of her ordeal and realizes that all of the voices she had imagined were in fact a part of herself. We understand that in her mind she is both guilty and not guilty, that a single judgment is impossible. The text, indeed, underscores the various possible interpretations an individual may have of an action or of his or her own life story. We realize, too, the emotional journey and soul-searching the woman has undergone.

Despite the fact that the protagonist loses her child, she has grown from the experience and is willing to go on, reflecting the perseverance of so many autobiographical heroines, past and present, including those of Mogador, Aleramo, Cardinal, and Ernaux.[19] This "awakening" teaches Fallaci's protagonist that she has more to learn about love—not sexual or romantic love, but the love she approached with her unborn child. She also believes in life and feels a vitality within her that brings her out of her illness. She refutes her fetus who had claimed during the trial that she did not believe in life. She counters that, in fact, she enjoys life, even with its infamies, and declares: "intendo [vivere la vita] ad ogni costo. Io corro, bambino" (97) ("I mean to live [life] at all cost. I'm running, Child" 110). The agency of "intendo [vivere la vita]" and the use of the verb "correre" ("to run") underscore the protagonist's will and zest for living. Whereas in a nineteenth-century text, a single mother might have resorted to suicide or madness, and in a turn-of-the-century work, her plight would have conjured up even more societal disapproval than it does in *Lettera*, this contemporary piece has an optimistic conclusion. According to Pickering-Iazzi, Fallaci's conceptualization of motherhood endeavors "to reconcile the disjuncture between domestic and social spheres described in *Una donna*" ("Designing Mothers" 339). *Lettera* posits that life itself is to be valued above the importance of individual beings. This is evident in the concluding lines of the text: "altrove nascono mille, centomila bambini, e mamme di futuri bambini: la vita non ha bisogno né di te né di me. Tu sei morto. Forse muoio anch'io. Ma non conta. Perché la vita non muore" (101) ("elsewhere a thousand, a hundred thousand children are being born, and mothers of future children: life doesn't need you or me. You're dead. Maybe I'm dying too. But it doesn't matter. Because life doesn't die" 114). In this sense, the protagonist's story takes on new significance. As Fallaci states in her dedication, "questo libro è dedicato da una donna per tutte le donne" ("this book is dedicated by a woman for all women"). Rather than the autobiographical story of an individual woman, it is a chapter in a potential biography of contemporary female experience.

NOTES

1. Alba Amoia explains that Fallaci covered the Persian Gulf War for *Corriere della sera* in 1991 (114).

2. Unless indicated, English translations of quotations from *Lettera* are from the following edition: Oriana Fallaci, *Letter to a Child Never Born*, trans. John Shepley (New York: Simon and Schuster, 1976).

3. I once again borrow the term from Ramsay's *The French New Autobiographies*.

4. Consider such hybrid texts as Fausta Cialente's contemporary *Le quattro ragazze Wieselberger* (1976; *The Four Wieselberger Girls*) and Luisa Passerini's *Autoritratto di gruppo* (1988; *Autobiography of a Generation: Italy 1968*).

5. Fallaci's mastery of the second-person narrative in *Lettera* is demonstrated once again in *Un uomo: Romanzo*.

6. One possible literary analogue is Sterne's *Tristram Shandy*, where much of the narrative takes place before the hero is born.

7. Abortion was legalized in Italy in 1978. The issue remained controversial, however. Aricò explains that a referendum to appeal the abortion law was defeated in 1981 (160).

8. Critics are divided as to Fallaci's viewpoint on abortion in *Lettera*. Aricò states that pro-life advocates and radical feminists alike study the work and "claim it as their own to justify their positions on abortion" (Preface). He notes that, on one hand, the beauty of the lyrical passages describing the developing fetus supports life, while, on the other hand, the protagonist's refusal to sacrifice her own life and career for her unborn child advocates choice (161–62). Pickering-Iazzi, whose claims are further analyzed in this chapter, finds Fallaci's notion of maternity "regenerative" precisely because it includes a conscious choice ("Designing Mothers" 325).

9. The first set of page numbers refers to the Italian edition of *Lettera*, and the second, to the English translation, in this and subsequent examples that refer to scenes

without offering specific quotations.

10. Interestingly, when she travels to other countries, Fallaci also shares some of Belgiojoso's condescending, judgmental attitudes. In *Il sesso inutile*, Fallaci visits a young Pakistani bride and moralizes about the woes of arranged marriages in which children become mothers. Belgiojoso expresses similar views in *Emina*. In addition, Fallaci's male guide, who easily reveals his belief in women's inferiority, is reduced in stature through such nameless tags as "my Pakistani" (23), a label reminiscent of Belgiojoso's condescending "my bey" in *Emina*. Fallaci also shares the intensity and political involvement characteristic of Belgiojoso and her nineteenth-century socialist sisters. Aricò explains that in her role as a correspondent, Fallaci "allows opinions, ideas, and commitments to permeate projects so intensely that her reporting merits comparison to the active zeal of missionaries" (106). Fallaci's writings on the Vietnam War, for example, stand as "classic examples of journalistic activism" (Aricò 106).

11. See Aricò's analyses of Fallaci's fables in his chapter on *Lettera*, "To Be or Not to Be," in *Oriana Fallaci* (158–75).

12. The italicized words translate as follows: lesson, to explain, to teach, teaching, to learn, and to learn/grasp.

13. As discussed in the next chapter, Cardinal's heroine in *Les mots pour le dire* responds positively to male approval.

14. In another current interrogation into the maternal role, Denise Bonal explores surrogate motherhood in her recent play *Légère en août* (*Light in August*).

15. Regarding the dream or hallucination scene, see pages 76–94 in *Lettera* and 86–106 in the English translation.

16. See Bair's discussion of Beauvoir and Halimi's involvement in this case (480).

17. According to Aricò, the idea that the fetus speak came from Fallaci's little sister Elisabetta, who also modeled the fetus' "voice" itself (172).

18. Fallaci uses the phrase "mi son sentita svuotare" (88), which Shepley translates as "I felt a sense of loss—of emptiness" (99).

19. In the next two chapters, I discuss Cardinal's *Les mots pour le dire* and Ernaux's works: *Une femme* and *"Je ne suis pas sortie de ma nuit,"* texts that continue the discussion of contemporary women's struggles and female self-discovery.

Part III

LEAVING THE MOTHER

7

Creativity and Community in Marie Cardinal's *Les mots pour le dire*

[J]e ne crois pas que notre désir de naître cesse dès l'instant où nous quittons le corps de notre mère.
(I do not believe that our desire to be born ceases from the moment that we leave our mother's body.)
—Annie Leclerc, Postscript to *Autrement dit*

In Marie Cardinal's most celebrated text, *Les mots pour le dire*, the protagonist's *bildung* and self-discovery involve a journey that is intimately linked to creativity and connection with others.[1] The main character evolves from an upset, desperate, and miserable woman besieged by a mental illness, which is ambiguously labeled "la chose" ("the thing"), to a more confident, aware, and "whole" one as the story unfolds. The heroine remains nameless, as did the protagonists of Sibilla Aleramo's *Una donna* and Oriana Fallaci's *Lettera a un bambino mai nato*. Yet unlike these texts, *Les mots pour le dire* does not reflect a potentially universal female experience, although certain feelings that the protagonist encounters—tensions in her relationship with her mother, ambiguity regarding traditional marriage and motherhood, and insecurities about entering the working world—are common to many women. Rather, it is the story of an individual who experiences mental problems, certain manifestations of which are particularly female. Because the protagonist's sense of self is harmed by a detrimental maternal figure, the process of developing a healthy identity means separating from the mother. Cardinal's protagonist "leaves the mother," the character most intensely connected to the formative years, in order to shed what she perceives as the cause and symbol of her neurosis. In *Les mots pour le dire*, Cardinal outlines the mother's criticism and distaste for the daughter, feelings that develop, in large measure, because the child was conceived while the mother was in the midst of divorce proceedings, and suggests that this antipathy stifles the daughter, preventing her from developing normally. Eventually, Cardinal's contemporary heroine is able not only to reject the mother's values, as did Aleramo's turn-of-the-century protagonist in her refusal of maternal resignation and self-sacrifice, but to forge a new life for herself with family and career intact. The text maps out the protagonist's progress toward overcoming her mental illness by highlighting the interpretive work of psychoanalysis and the cathartic benefits of communication. In the second part of the narrative, Cardinal develops the analogy between telling one's life experiences and writing them. However, it is not just writing creatively that helps the protagonist to heal; it is the community that artistic production anticipates, from family, to colleagues, to the society of readers, that ultimately cures her.

Les mots pour le dire was published in 1975, when numerous women's voices entered the literary scene, and it already anticipated many of today's trends. As evidenced in the works of Fallaci, Hélène Cixous, and Luce Irigaray, women writers questioned the type of language that could appropriately voice their sexuality and their evolving roles. Feminist writers discussed controversial issues such as abortion, single parenthood, and lesbianism. In addition, the outpouring of women's autobiographical texts from the 1970s to the present has led to innovative narrative experimentation. Through Cardinal's practice of "autocitation,"[2] for example, shared by many contemporary female authors, including Marguerite Duras and Annie Ernaux, characters, scenes, and even specific passages in a given text reverberate in later works. The mentally ill woman we meet in *Les mots pour le dire* already had a precursor in Cardinal's *La souricière* (1965; *The Trap*). The woman writer born in Algeria and living in France found in *Les mots pour le dire* resembles the more mature protagonist in the author's recent *Amour . . . amours . . .* (1998; *Love . . . loves . . .*).[3] Furthermore, the scene in which the protagonist of *Les mots pour le dire* recalls her mother's attempts to induce a miscarriage already had textual model. In the conclusion to *La clé sur la porte* (1972; *The Key in the Door*), we find a comparable scene in very similar language, this time in the context of a poem about an unwanted pregnancy written by a young female character. As discussed in the previous chapter, such "rewriting" in contemporary autobiography is further complicated by the fact that today's personal narratives often transgress generic boundaries. Present-day autobiographers, including Cardinal, often revise life stories as novels, rework novels into film scenarios, or create hybrid auto/biographies.[4]

The publication of *Les mots pour le dire* also coincided with heightened interest in the mother–daughter relationship by feminist and psychoanalytical critics. By the 1970s theorists such as Irigaray and Nancy Chodorow established that a woman's self-definition is intimately linked to her identification with the parent of like gender.[5] In her discussion of Cardinal and Jeanne Hyvrard, Marguerite Le Clézio explores the attempts by these authors "to find an identity, either as liberated from or symbolically tied to the mother" (383). Whereas Cardinal's protagonist chooses separation, Hyvrard's heroines often opt for a return to the womb, a refusal of separation, and thus madness.[6] In *Ce sexe qui n'en est pas un* (*This Sex Which Is Not One*), published in 1977, shortly after *Les mots pour le dire*, Irigaray revisits Freud's theory of the unconscious and states that "what has been singularly neglected . . . is woman's relationship to the mother and women's relationships among themselves" (qtd. in Le Clézio 383). In her study of twentieth-century literature of madness written by women, Marilyn Yalom finds that the mother–child connection is represented in *Les mots pour le dire*, among other texts, as "the primary [relationship] in human life" (67). In *Autrement dit* (*In Other Words*, 1977), an innovative text written as a "response" to her readers' letters, appreciation, and questions about *Les mots pour le dire*, Cardinal incorporates prose meditations on her past, her writing, language, and women's roles alongside the transcription of an interview that Annie Leclerc conducted with her. In this text, Cardinal confirms, in keeping with the critical views of her contemporaries, the vital mother–daughter union. For example, as she describes her reaction to her mother's death, she underscores their physical and emotional connection: "Et mon berceau, son ventre, mon commencement, son lait, mon origine, la lumière entre ses cuisses! Plus jamais?" (196) ("And my cradle, her stomach, my beginning, her milk, my origin, the light between her thighs! Never again?").[7] Despite the maternal–filial tensions that Cardinal frequently outlines in her works, the connection to the mother is visceral—at the core of the daughter's existence.

"Leaving the mother" in *Les mots pour le dire* also means rejecting the mother's values, many of which manifest themselves in the colonialist culture in which the heroine was raised, that of the French *pieds-noirs* in Algeria. Similar to Fallaci's protests against the nuclear family, the Catholic Church, and the state in Italy, Cardinal's denunciations focus on what she sees as hypocritical individual and collective practices in comparable French institutions whose influence encompasses the colonies. Given the mother's bourgeois code of conduct, strong Catholicism, and sense of superiority vis-à-vis the native Algerians, in her character "patriarchal and colonialist ideologies merge" (Hall, *Marie Cardinal* 42). The daughter will therefore have to leave her beloved motherland, Algeria, where French foreign policy promoted occupation of the country and persecution of native Algerians. Le Clézio explains that "[t]he mother's body and the land, Algeria, are metaphorically conjoined as symbols of origins from which the daughter is drastically severed" (385). Thus, in separating from the mother, the heroine overcomes personal, emotional abuse and at the same time tackles societal oppression.[8] The new relationships she forges satisfy the need for connection and love that her mother could never give her and that she lost upon leaving Algeria.

In *Les mots pour le dire*, the story of mother and daughter also allows Cardinal to address fundamental problems facing the autobiographer: the gap between experience and writing; the inscription of the subject; and the search for a structure and language that convey the complexity of the life story. The text has several layers: the narrating "I" in the present recalls the woman who underwent psychoanalysis; the woman in therapy remembers her childhood and adolescence. Although there is a linear progression in the text from sickness to health, Cardinal does not adhere to a strict chronological ordering. Her narrator describes dreams, remembrances, and scenes from her past as they come to her and as they are pertinent to the story. As such, Cardinal employs what Jean Rousset calls "psychic time" (22–29), preferred by several twentieth-century autobiographers, including Carl Jung. This gives Cardinal extraordinary narrative control, for through the reorganization of events a "story" unfolds.

Like many of the writers treated in this study, Cardinal faces the challenge of constructing a female subject, a voice traditionally denied women. The protagonist's difficulty in expressing herself in words, according to Patricia Elliot, reveals her "problematic position as a subject in language" (72). Through analyses of dreams and remembrances, the narrator/protagonist gradually begins to bridge the gap between unconscious and conscious levels of awareness. Elliot links these discoveries to "the intricate connection between language and the unconscious, and between written (or spoken) articulation and subjectivity" (72). The particularly troubled relationship with the mother complicates the daughter's quest to express herself in therapy and in writing.

In the spirit of the *bildungsroman*, Cardinal's structure allows the subject to move gradually toward self-knowledge. Phil Powrie notes that the text presents "a series of obstacles against which the protagonist has to measure herself, as would the protagonist of any *Bildungsroman*" (167). In recounting this journey, Cardinal writes: "Il faut que je me souvienne et que je retrouve la femme oubliée. . . . C'est avec mes yeux, mes oreilles, ma peau, mon coeur que cette femme vivait. Je regarde mes mains, les mêmes mains. . . . Elle et moi" (16–17) ("I must think back to find again the forgotten woman. . . . It is with my eyes, my ears, my skin, my heart that that woman lived. I look at my hands, the same hands. . . . She and I" 8). In this passage, the fluctuation of first- and third-person pronouns emphasizes the dual nature of the individual as object and subject and distinguishes between the "madwoman" and the healthy woman who is telling the story. The narrator must distance herself from her past self in order to trace the developmental journey: "Pour raconter le passage, la naissance, il faut que j'éloigne la folle de moi, que je la tienne à distance, que je me dédouble" (17) ("In order to tell about the journey, the birth, in effect, I have to remove myself from the mad one, to keep her at a distance, to split myself in two" 9). Cardinal shifts between repudiation and nostalgia for "the madwoman," techniques that emphasize the gap between narrator and her protagonist.[9] By the end of the text, however, the narrator can embrace her past self: "Il y a entre celle que j'étais et celle que je suis devenue une distance inestimable. . . . Pourtant la folle et moi nous ne sommes qu'une seule et même personne . . . nous nous aimons, nous vivons bien ensemble" (291) ("There is an inestimable distance between the person I was and the person I have become. . . . The madwoman and I, however, are but one and the same person . . . we love each other, we live together happily" 270). Such reconciliation indicates an evolution in self-understanding and maturity. Fittingly, once the protagonist is able to find harmony within herself, she is able to spiritually reconcile with the mother as well.

We note a marked shift from the nineteenth-century texts that suppress the mad double. In "Mothers, Madness, and the Middle Class," Elaine Martin explains that in twentieth-century works, such as *Les mots pour le dire* and Sylvia Plath's *The Bell Jar*, it is often the protagonists themselves who are "mad" (37). In such a scenario the double is embodied by "society's mores" and symbolized by "society's definition of sanity" (37). Whereas in nineteenth-century works "it was necessary to kill off the mad double because she expressed dangerous, seditious ideas, unacceptable to society," in the majority of twentieth-century texts both the double and the protagonist are saved (37).[10] Martin holds that twentieth-century works tend to "declare society mad and the 'mad' protagonist sane" (37). Hence, whereas in many nineteenth-century texts society "drives women mad," in the twentieth century we often see a progression, if not a reversal. We find many "mad" protagonists frustrated in their female roles, but they go one step further than their female predecessors—they "take on" the antagonist, society, and its values (which are often instilled in the protagonist by the mother[11]) and claim their right to find new avenues of existence. The heroine's survival is an important narrative strategy in contemporary women's writing.[12] The postmodern female protagonist in Cardinal's text goes beyond the limitations of nineteenth-century and early-twentieth-century heroines in other ways as well, for not only does she transgress social limitations and conventions, but her success in doing so is accompanied by both professional and personal satisfaction. As in Fallaci's *Lettera*, the conclusion of *Les mots pour le dire* presents a more aware and complete protagonist who anticipates a full life.

Two turning points are key to the protagonist's healing. The first occurs during the long psychoanalytical journey Cardinal describes. The second comes about when she begins writing. In order to discuss both pivotal moments, it is necessary to understand the heroine's relationship with her parents—connections that are central to Cardinal's life story—and with authority in general.

Both parental figures embody the theme of illness. The mother's neurosis is described indirectly and not treated in detail. She is a perfectionist—fanatically clean and extremely religious. The protagonist's parents divorce when she is young, and the father is an ineffective, often absent figure. The heroine was, instead, raised in a female-dominated universe: "Aucun homme n'est intervenu dans ma jeunesse. J'étais aux mains des femmes: ma mère, ma grand-mère, les 'domestiques,' les bonnes soeurs-professeurs" (61) ("No man intervened in my early years. I was in the hands of women: my mother, my grandmother, the maids and the nuns who were my teachers" 48). Her father is a strange, alien figure to her who makes his daughter uncomfortable in regarding her as a "little woman" rather than a little girl. Part of the main character's naïveté, curiosity, and fear of men stems from this perplexing, mysterious father figure. His tuberculosis continues the illness/death theme (the protagonist's sister also died of the disease, something that the mother can never overcome). Though at times as a young girl she experienced the desire to be loved and protected by her father (73; 60),[13] this affection is quite foreign to her: "j'ai longtemps cherché à me rapprocher du Père. Mais, ne sachant rien de lui j'ai dû abandonner mes recherches, lasse, même pas triste" (73–74) ("for a long time I tried to get closer to the Father. But, not knowing him, weary, even a little sad, I had to abandon my investigations" 60–61). Such an abstract description of the father reflects the protagonist's empty affective universe, which will ultimately be filled with other relationships—with her husband, her children, her doctor, her writing.

Much of the daughter's hatred for her mother stems from her mother's account of her "failed abortion," or attempts to miscarry. The narrator does not blame her mother so much for her desire to terminate an unwanted pregnancy, as for telling her vulnerable adolescent daughter of the horrendous episode. After we hear of the mother's efforts to destroy her fetus, ranging from bicycling to quinine ingestion, the narrator explains:

Ce que j'ai appelé la saloperie de ma mère ce n'était pas d'avoir voulu avorter . . . sa saloperie c'était au contraire de n'avoir pas été au bout de son désir profond, de n'avoir pas avorté quand il le fallait; puis d'avoir continué à projeter sa haine sur moi alors que je bougeais en elle, et enfin de m'avoir raconté son crime minable, ses pauvres tentatives de meurtre. Comme si ayant raté son coup elle le reprenait quatorze ans après, en sécurité, sans risque d'y laisser sa propre peau. (159–60)
(What I have referred to as beastliness in my mother is not because she wanted an abortion . . . on the contrary, her beastliness consisted in not having followed through on her desire to have an abortion. Then, in having continued to project her hatred onto me when I was inside her, and, finally, in having chosen to speak of her wretched crime, her weak attempts to murder me. It was as if, having bungled it, she were starting up again, fourteen years later, without risking her own skin, in comparative safety. 140)

Because of her internalization of the mother's desire to abort, one symptom of the protagonist's illness is an abnormal menstrual flow, a phenomenon that renders her experience particularly female.[14] In an interview, Cardinal expands on the impact in her own life of her mother's inner desire to lose the child in her womb: "I shouldn't have been born. My mother didn't want me. She did everything possible to miscarry. She didn't pull it off. . . . But I have remained that miscarried child. Yes, I will die like that now" (personal interview).[15] Françoise Lionnet reads the "failed abortion" scene allegorically, noting that it "prefigures the violence of war and its attendant mutilations and monstrosities. France wants to abort its colonial progeny, the *pieds-noirs* being a burden and an embarrassment. The mother, like the *métropole*, kills and mutilates with language that tortures" (204). The mother projects her hatred, violence, and neurosis onto the daughter. We read: "Dites ma mère, saviez-vous que vous la poussiez dans la folie?" (159) ("Tell me, Mother, did you know that you were pushing her into madness?" 140). Much of the protagonist's mother complex stems from a self-image informed by maternal rejection and the impossible endeavor to win her mother's love.

The first turning point in the protagonist's life is intimately linked to her relationship with her parents and revolves around the discovery of her body. Gradually, she comes to understand through therapy the events in her youth that sparked her neurosis. The doctor notices that the word "tuyau" ("tube") seems to be particularly bothersome for his patient. Slowly but surely, the protagonist pieces together the memory of when she was a little girl traveling with her family. During a train ride, she has to go to the bathroom—a simple event that becomes a major ordeal for her neurotic mother. Everything must be deodorized, sanitized, cleansed completely, not to mention the fact that the little girl must be accompanied by her nanny and her mother to the bathroom in the train corridor. As occurs often in the protagonist's therapy, the adult woman suddenly transforms herself into the little girl. The "I" of the adult and of the child become blurred, as in the following passage: "J'avais quatre ans, j'avais trente-quatre ans. J'étais encore écartelée sur le cabinet du train, j'étais allongée sur le divan de l'impasse" (169–170) ("I was four years old, I was thirty-four. I was still torn apart in the bathroom on the train, I was lying on the couch in the cul-de-sac" 151). Such shifting from the time of therapy to the moment of childhood trauma emphasizes the fear and vulnerability that accompany recalling painful events. The memory of the bathroom on the train then leads to a recollection of an even more distant past incident. The protagonist tells her doctor that she recalls herself as a little girl of one year old, walking in a forest with her father and her nanny. She must do "'number one, please'" (171).[16] Suddenly, she hears a tapping noise and turns to see her father behind her taking a photo. As a child, she is mortified to be photographed in such a way. The judgmental eye of the camera, "une sorte d'animal en fer qui a un oeil au bout d'un tuyau" (171) ("a sort of metal animal which has an eye at the end of a tube" 152), of her father, and by extension of other authoritative forces—her mother, God, and society—sees her in all of her glory. Her violent reaction toward the father ("Je le bats tant que je peux. . . . Je veux le tuer!" 171) ("I strike him with all of my strength. . . . I want to kill him!" 152) reveals her passionate side, which so often had to be suppressed because of familial and social conventions—rules that explain the child's embarrassment in the first place. After recalling this scene, the protagonist realizes that she has unmasked the hallucination that has troubled her for so long. As she deals with past events and rids herself of their harmful effect on her, the little girl can return to the past. The protagonist has come back "de très loin" (172) ("from very far away" 153) and feels the "perfection" (172) ("perfection" 153) of her body for the first time. The doctor has helped her "accoucher d'[elle]-même" (172) ("give birth to [her]self" 153). Carolyn Durham notes the reversal of typical male and female roles as the doctor serves as a "midwife" assisting the protagonist's "birth" (222).[17] The heroine is born again, feels new and whole. From this moment of liberation comes a new discovery: "Je passais mes journées à m'amuser avec ce jouet extraordinaire: mon corps" (178) ("I spent days amusing myself with that extraordinary toy: my own body" 160).

Elliot discusses the split between the ideal daughter Cardinal would have wanted to be in order to please her mother and the "humanly flawed, therefore [abject] self" (79). This division is exemplified in Cardinal's description of two little girls, one obedient, ignorant, and locked in her past, and the other terribly aware and coming to life through psychoanalysis. Cardinal describes the child's "eye," which distinctly saw the mother's neurosis, which saw "clairement, durement même, *sa mère* et ce qui l'entourait. Elle voyait *sa mère* lui faire manger son vomi de soupe, *sa mère* se laissant aller à la vulgarité de la pauvre vieille de Jehan Rictus. . . . Un oeil, surtout, qui était sensible à la chose . . . qui avait vu la chose dans *sa mère*" (217; emphasis added) ("with clarity and harshness even *her mother* and her surroundings. She could see *her mother* making her eat her own vomit of soup, *her mother* indulging herself in the vulgarity of Jehan Rictus's story of the old woman. . . . An eye which was above all sensitive to the Thing . . . an eye which had seen the Thing in *her mother*" 199; emphasis added). Cardinal's frequent use of anaphora lulls the reader with its rhythmical cadences and, in the preceding example, points to the source of the main character's illness. However, Elliot explains that in continuing to locate the conflict "*between* her mother and herself," Cardinal is blind to "her own implication in the process of repression" (78). Only later in the text, when the heroine becomes capable of separating from her mother, will she no longer consider herself as victim and her mother as villain; when she is able to distinguish "her own eye/I from that of her mother . . . she can begin to reconstitute herself as subject" (80).

The initial refusal to accept an affinity between mother and daughter is illustrated by the account of the protagonist's first nervous crisis at a Louis Armstrong concert when she is a university student.[18] As she listens to the rhythm of the jazz music, her heart starts beating uncontrollably to a point where she has an intense sense of suffocation and fear of death (52–53; 39–40). She runs home and cries to her mother that she is going to die. Rather than being alarmed by her daughter's terror, however, the mother offers a controlled, unruffled response: "'C'est une angoisse, c'est rien, n'aie pas peur . . . c'est nerveux.' Je n'aimais pas son calme. . . . Je n'aimais pas cette complicité entre nous" (54–55) ("'It's an anxiety attack, it's nothing, don't be afraid . . . it's your nerves.' I didn't like her composure. . . . I didn't like this complicity between us" 41). The mother's recognition of the protagonist's symptoms signals to the daughter the root of a sickness they both share. This leaves no room for the daughter to consider her fears "normal." Cardinal writes: "On aurait dit qu'elle faisait ma connaissance et qu'en même temps elle me reconnaissait" (55) ("It was as if she were making my acquaintance and at the same time recognizing me" 42). Her mother's suspicions leave the daughter feeling betrayed. We realize, however, that in order to heal, the protagonist can no longer blame her mother alone for her anxieties. She must face the fearful project of confronting herself and her own repressed desires.

Part of the protagonist's breaking away from her mother and her social milieu involves sexuality. For example, in revolting against puritanical Christian standards and bourgeois principles, the main character makes the conscious decision to lose her virginity with a boy whom she does not love (56–59; 43–46). Through active effort and an impulse from within, the protagonist is able to move beyond the restrictions imposed by her class and trace her own developmental path. Another example that illustrates the protagonist's renewed sense of her body/her "self" revolves around an erotic dream in which a dashing equestrian both charms and frightens her (191–93; 172–74). She recognizes the two worlds that were constantly at odds during her youth: "L'un que je connaissais bien, celui de mon milieu, l'univers de ma mère. . . . L'autre que je ne connaissais pas, mais qu'inconsciemment je désirais . . . celui de l'aventure, de l'homme, du sexe . . . l'univers de la rue" (192) ("One, which I knew well, from my own background, was the world of my mother. . . . The other, which I didn't know but which, unconsciously, I desired . . . was the world of adventure, the world of men and sex . . . the world of the street" 174). Through therapy, the protagonist faces the childhood traumas that impact her adult life. Once she is able to identify the sources of her illness, she can let go of the terrified little girl, reconcile her internal divisions, and continue her development toward womanhood. A final example of growth through sexual liberation occurs through the protagonist's discoveries of her fear of eroticism and masculine power, of "la mort que l'homme donne à la femme" (275) ("the death which a man inflicts upon a woman" 254). Key dreams and remembrances dramatize such fears. For example, she recalls her childhood revolt when the men in her mother's life threatened to become "her new fathers" (277–79; 256–58). She is astonished to realize as an adult the impact her mother's sensuality had on her as a child, impressions that had been repressed before analysis. Following an important dream concerning female vulnerability, the protagonist feels acutely aware that women are "[t]outes pareilles, toutes trouées. . . . Quelle femme peut empêcher un homme qui le veut vraiment de la pénétrer et de déposer en elle sa semence étrangère? Aucune" (280–81) ("[a]ll the same, all having holes in them. . . . What woman can oppose a man who really wants to from penetrating her and depositing in her his alien seed?" 259–60).[19] Is this fear of sexuality, she asks, linked to "une peur essentielle, vieille comme l'humanité, inconsciemment subie, oubliée? Une peur que les femmes seraient seules à ressentir?" (280) ("the essential fear as old as humanity, unconsciously submitted to and forgotten? A fear which women alone could feel?" 259). Biology is not the only explanation for this feminine fear, however—culture is equally responsible: "[u]ne peur inventée par les femmes, enseignée aux femmes par les autres femmes" (281) ("[a] fear invented by women and taught to them by other women" 260). This identification with women as a collective emphasizes the fact that Cardinal is writing from a woman's perspective. Her experiences with mental illness, the healing process, and her writing are intimately linked to the sense of continuity she feels with her mother, for better or for worse, and to her effort to communicate with sisters, daughters, and future generations of women.

The mother's death represents the final and necessary rupture for the protagonist. As is common in women's self-portraiture, the end of the mother's life shortly precedes the end of the autobiography.[20] As such, it underscores the daughter's sense of mortality. When the main character is established with her own family in Paris, both the mother and the grandmother come to live with her. The grandmother dies shortly after, and the protagonist's relationship with her mother becomes more and more estranged. The mother has lost much of her motivation for living since leaving Algeria and the poor she served there, and she will slowly, but surely, abandon herself to "the Thing," which the protagonist understands only too well. The daughter, however, recovering nicely and learning to appreciate life once again, no longer desires any association with that former world she had abandoned. She states: "je n'aurais pas voulu lui consacrer une seule heure de mon temps. J'avais trop à apprendre" (297) ("I had no wish to devote even an hour of my time to it. I had too much to learn" 276). After one of several of the mother's crises in which she becomes drunk and intolerable, the protagonist and her husband take the mother to see a doctor. At the initial interview, the mother recounts the important events in her life (echoing, in reduced form, the protagonist's sessions with her therapist). As the daughter listens to her mother's "autobiography," she is able to understand better her mother and separate herself from her. The mother becomes *other*, can be externalized and finally *named*: "Pour moi elle n'avait pas de nom c'était: ma mère. Dans ce cabinet de médecin parisien je rencontrais pour la première fois Solange de Talbiac" (308) ("For me, she had no name, it was: my mother. In this Parisian doctor's office, I met for the first time Solange de Talbiac" 287). The mother dies soon after, provoking great upheaval for the protagonist, followed by a sense of relief and freedom. It was as if "tout était en ordre. Elle en avait fini et moi aussi. Elle était libre et moi aussi. Elle était guérie et moi aussi" (310) ("everything had fallen into place. She was through with it and so was I. She was free and so was I. She was healed, and so was I" 290).

Reconciliation with the mother and acceptance of her death lead the protagonist to the point where she can finally construct her own universe, a journey that culminates in finding a home in writing. When she is able to accept her mother's failings and embrace her, the protagonist can visit her mother's grave, recall certain happy childhood experiences, and tell her mother: "Je vous aime" (312) ("I love you" 292). Yalom comments that the scene at the mother's tomb "satisfies both the narrator's personal need for the reconciliation of conflicting sentiments and the artistic need for literary resolution" (58). The text concludes on a positive note of "psychological and spiritual well-being," which derives partly from "the protagonist's mental resolution of antagonistic maternal images. Because the mother is internalized at the core of the daughter's being, making peace with the mother is tantamount to making peace with herself" (Yalom 58). Critics have discussed the exposition of the mother–daughter conflict and reconciliation in *Les mots pour le dire* as pivotal in Cardinal's career. Colette Hall associates the author's capacity for expression with self-discovery: "Once she has broken the silence surrounding her life, Cardinal can start naming things the way they are" ("*L'écriture féminine*" 236). Elliot explains that for Cardinal, learning to deal with, discuss, and write about maternal rejection ultimately leads to the ability to say "I."

"Leaving the motherland," French-occupied Algeria, is also integral to the protagonist's *bildung*. She will live out internally and personally the France/Algeria opposition. As stated previously, Algeria is the warm and welcoming maternal figure for her that evokes fond, youthful memories: "Il me semble que la chose a pris racine en moi d'une façon permanente, quand j'ai compris que nous allions assassiner l'Algérie. Car l'Algérie c'était ma vraie mère" (106) ("It seems to me that the Thing took root in me permanently when I understood that we were to assassinate Algeria. For Algeria was my real mother" 88). Yet it is also the land that emphasizes her exclusion. This conflict is apparent as the protagonist is, on one hand, a resident of Algeria and involved in North African culture, and, on the other, French and influenced by the colonial code of behavior. She is taught when she is young, for example, that there is an insurmountable distance between herself and the Algerian children. Her mother is generous in helping the poor of this country yet continues to establish a strict distance between Algerians and the French *pieds-noirs*. Though the protagonist is in favor of Algerian independence, she is still French and privileged. The opposition between France and Algeria, between the dominant power and the colonized country, implies issues of hierarchy, patriarchal values, and conventional social structures against which the protagonist must fashion herself. It also reflects the hypocrisy the protagonist will refuse when she rejects the values of her mother, her class, and her country. The parallel between her own separation from her milieu and the social revolt and change of the 1960s is underscored by the last chapter of the text, one line that states: "Quelques jours plus tard c'était Mai 68" (317) ("A few days later it was May '68"; translation mine),[21] an evocation of the month of student and workers' riots that encapsulated the counterculture in France.

Resolution of the mother–daughter relationship and the protagonist's ensuing independence are reflected in the ability to develop her own individual voice. This process, the discovery of "[sa] personne" (194) ("[her] self" 175), is linked to the second turning point in *Les mots pour le dire*, which revolves around the birth of the writer. For the heroine, writing her life experiences, struggling to write her "self," is tied to the therapeutic process and part of the cure.

Cardinal stresses the "fiction" that surfaces in the gaps between living, telling, and writing personal events. She emphasizes the modifications inherent in the lapse of time between experiences and the recounting of them—whether it be the protagonist speaking to her doctor or the autobiographer speaking to her readers. In *Autrement dit*, Cardinal elaborates on the difference between living through mental illness and psychoanalysis and writing about them: "Longtemps après la fin de ma psychanalyse j'ai décidé de l'écrire . . . car, entre-temps, j'étais devenue écrivain (ce qui fait déjà de moi une femme différente de celle du livre) et c'est en écrivain que j'ai vu cette histoire, pas en témoin" (27) ("Long after the end of my psychoanalysis I decided to write it . . . because in the meantime I had become a writer [which already makes me a different woman than the one in the book], and it is as a writer that I saw this story, not as a witness"). In creating *Les mots pour le dire* from the writer's point of view, Cardinal explains that she suppressed certain episodes, such as her mother's constant beatings, and emphasized others. Whereas discussion of the mother's "failed abortion" occupied very little time during her actual therapy, it became central to the protagonist's analysis in *Les mots pour le dire*. Cardinal explains: "Je me suis rendu compte en l'écrivant que cette histoire-là valait toutes les raclées du monde ... elle marquait mieux le rejet de la petite fille" (*Autrement dit* 28) ("I realized in writing it that that story was worth all of the beatings in the world ... it showed better the rejection of the little girl").

In *Les mots pour le dire* this fictive, creative zone becomes the locus of healing. For example, as the narrator recalls her first visit with her therapist, she feels like a movie director with a camera who is "capable aussi bien de descendre filmer en gros plan les détails énormément grossis d'un visage, que de s'élever au-dessus du plateau pour saisir l'ensemble d'une scène" (21) ("capable of descending to shoot closeups and of drawing back in order to take in the action of the scene" 12). The metaphor of the filmmaker who can zoom in to capture minute details or film an entire scene from a distance evokes the writer who can use various narrative techniques to describe specific moments in great detail or who can gloss and summarize. Cardinal develops the scene by employing a focusing technique in which she incorporates physical metaphors gradually culminating in the portrait of the ill woman curled up like a fetus. In this way, she leads the reader to the core of the image and the root of the heroine's mother–daughter conflict:

Ainsi, pour cette première visite, je vois Paris ... et, dans Paris, le quartier d'Alésia, et dans ce quartier l'impasse, et dans l'impasse la petite maison, et dans la petite maison le bureau éclairé doucement où parlent un homme et une femme, et cette femme, dans cet ensemble, sur un divan, recroquevillée, comme un foetus dans une matrice. (21)
(So it was for this first visit I see Paris ... and, in Paris, the Alesia district, and in this district the dead end, and on the dead end the little house, and inside the little house the softly lit office where a man and a woman are speaking, and this woman, on a couch, curled up, like a fetus in the womb. 12)

In shaping the scene to culminate in the fetus simile, common in Cardinal's texts, she emphasizes the movement not only into memory, the past, and the origins of life but also into the unconscious. It suggests the protagonist's future rebirth as well. Cardinal concludes: "Mais, à cette époque, je ne savais pas que je commençais à peine à naître et que je vivais les premiers instants d'une lente gestation de sept ans. Embryon gros de moi-même" (21) ("But at that time, I didn't know that I had hardly begun to be born again and that I was experiencing the first moments of a long period of gestation lasting seven years. Huge embryo of myself" 13). We note both the metaphor of the seven-year gestation (the length of time the protagonist was in therapy), representing the healing process through which the healthy woman is "born," and the double image of mother/daughter giving birth to herself.

In another scene that emphasizes narrative control, the narrator recounts to her therapist a nightmare in which she and a community of women—her mother, older Algerian women dressed in black, adolescent girls—fear the aggression of three partisans fighting for Algerian independence. We read: "Nous étions là, serrées les unes contre les autres, des jeunes, des vieilles, des adolescentes . . . toutes avec la peur au ventre et des récits terribles en tête, des histoires de femmes violées et éventrées" (271) ("We were huddling together, young and old, adolescents . . . all of us with fear in our bellies and terrible stories in our heads, stories of women raped and disemboweled" 251). Despite her advocacy of Algerian independence, the patient realizes that in the nightmare she is still an outsider, *other* to those who are fighting for freedom. With her doctor's help, she ultimately concludes that her dream, which sets so many vulnerable women in a dangerous situation, has to do with a hitherto undiscovered fear of male power. After recounting the nightmare, the narrator reflects:

Se remémorer les images d'un rêve comme on regarde un film et entendre sa propre voix raconter ce rêve, cela équivaut à vivre deux moments complètement différents et pourtant il s'agit de la même histoire. Ainsi je me suis entendue, avec étonnement, donner plein de détails sur le début du rêve. . . . Le film, lui, serait passé en quelques secondes, un simple flash, là où mes mots s'attardaient, insistaient. Pourquoi? (272–73)
(To recall images in a dream, as one looks at a film, and to hear one's own voice recounting this dream, is equivalent to living through two completely different moments, and yet they come out of the same event. So I listened with astonishment to my own account of the beginning of the dream. . . . If it had been a film, it would have been over in a few seconds, while my words were so long in coming. Why? 252)

We see that the recent past of recalling dream images and the present of recounting the dream, "deux moments complètement différents" are connected by the common "histoire" ("story").[22] The passage once again emphasizes that the narrator can attribute greater importance to certain parts of her dream. Further, just as she is the "listener" to her own discourse, so the autobiographer is the first reader of her text. Through recounting the dream, expressing herself, fears are uncovered. Yet her words "s'attardaient, insistaient," a lapse of time that indicates that her long-awaited utterances will form a "different" account. This "fictional space," the space in between experience and the "story" of it, allows for learning and growth.

Cardinal expands on the notion of the gap between events and creatively verbalizing or writing them by highlighting the distinction between visual images and words. The metaphor of the film director trying to capture precise moments, scenes, and sensations that would come together as an ensemble on screen reappears in *Les mots pour le dire*. One finds similar themes in Cardinal's *Comme si de rien n'était* (1990; *As If It Were Nothing*). The work consists of fragments of many individual lives, those of two female cousins in particular, within the larger context of historical events of 1989. One of the cousins, Simone (whose life bears some resemblance to Cardinal's), is a teacher who has left her work and studies to raise her five children. Her husband, Georges, with his advanced studies in grammar, "s'était enfoncé dans la philologie, il en avait fait sa spécialité" (79) ("had plunged himself into the study of philology, he had made it his specialization"). The narrator describes how the husband and wife experience reality in different ways, one being more attached to words and the other to images. For instance, consider the following passage, in which Simone explains to her cousin her reaction to the latest televised political events in Rumania: "Georges . . . n'écoute et ne voit que les mots; tout ce qui est écrit sur les pancartes, les banderoles, sur les monuments, ce que disent les gens qui s'expriment en roumain. Moi, ce sont les images qui m'empoignent: l'histoire se voit" (88) ("George . . . only listens to and sees words; everything which is written on road signs, banderoles, on monuments, what people who express themselves in Rumanian say. Me, it's images which grab me: history is seen"). Both the "History" of 1989 and the stories ("histoires") of the individual lives in the text are implied here. The passage echoes the theme of "translating" impressions of important events into words—tasks that are given to characters in *Comme si de rien n'était* and that Cardinal the author takes on in her narrative.

The protagonist's growing wellness and increased creativity in *Les mots pour le dire* are punctuated by key phrases. Toward the end of Chapter 10 we read: "J'allais mieux" (194) ("I was getting better" 175). Chapter 12 closes with: "J'étais presque construite" (232) ("I was almost complete" 213). Structurally, inserting these lines toward the end of chapters heightens our anticipation of the ultimate conclusion that sets the healthy protagonist free to live her life on her own terms. The preceding quotations, which structure the heroine's journey toward wellness, occur shortly before the opening of a "new chapter" in the text and in the protagonist's life. We learn the following toward the beginning of Chapter 13: "la nuit et le matin très tôt, j'écrivais" (234) ("At night and very early in the morning, I wrote" 215). She shows her husband the pages she has written—a problematic moment in which she constantly questions exposing her writing, what she labels as "ce que j'ai fait de plus important dans toute ma vie" (245) ("the most important thing I have ever done in my life" 226). His positive reaction—"'C'est bien, c'est épatant, c'est un livre. C'est même un beau livre que tu écris'" (246) ("'It's good, it's amazing, it's a book. It's even a fine book that you're writing'" 227)—and the approval of the man in her life affirm to her that she is a writer. More importantly, the ability to connect with another person (as she does with her doctor) allows her to grow: "A partir de ce jour-là Jean-Pierre et moi nous avons commencé à former un bloc. . . . Cette réunion de nos deux existences est, pour nous, un trésor inestimable, un festin délicieux dont nous ne parvenons pas à nous rassasier" (249) ("From that day on Jean-Pierre and I began to form a unit. . . . The rejoining of our separate worlds offered incalculable treasure, a delicious feast from which we could never get enough" 229). Her relationship with her children has improved as well.[23] The description of the lovemaking that follows Jean-Pierre's reading of his wife's work is described through natural metaphors and lyrical, fluid phrases that emphasize the protagonist's feeling of liberation: "Viens. . . . Je connais un passage de sable blanc . . . où tu n'auras qu'à te laisser aller. Rappelle-toi, mon doux, mon beau, que la mer est bonne si tu ne la crains pas. . . . Accroche-toi à la mousse.... Plonge!" (247–48) ("Come.... I know a stretch of white sand ... where you can just let yourself go. Remember my sweet, my beauty—the sea is kind if you do not fear her.... Catch the foam.... Dive!" 228). The feminine and sexual symbol of the ocean communicates the protagonist's sensuality, and the use of imperative forms is inviting rather than intimidating. The protagonist's renewed bond with her husband underscores the healing that accompanies communion with others.

In another example that links creativity to growth the protagonist is asked to write advertising copy for a milk factory. She is so happy to have surmounted both her fear of traveling to a northern suburb of Paris and her repugnance for milk that she permits herself a degree of artistry in her project. She brings the piece to a colleague, who is amused by her style: "il s'était tourné vers moi avec un air moqueur: 'Alors, madame fait du Jean Cau maintenant?'" (244) ("[he] turned to me with a look of mockery. 'So, Madame is doing a Jean Cau now?'" 225). When the protagonist realizes that Jean Cau had won the prestigious Goncourt literary prize, she begins to give form to her "gribouillis" (244) ("scribblings" 225) and to type the material from her hidden notebooks. The recognition that she has artistic skill akin to that of a famous writer allows the protagonist to feel self-confident, and therefore she begins to take her own work more seriously. Furthermore, earning a living through writing is "un élément capital de [son] équilibre. Comment, sans cela, aurai[t]-[elle] pu vivre et payer le docteur?" (243) ("central to [her] equilibrium. Without it, how could [she] have lived and paid the doctor?" 224).

When her first book is accepted for publication, the protagonist realizes that her life has been "entièrement transformée" (250) ("completely transformed" 230) because, through writing, she has found the "moyen de [s']exprimer" (250) ("way to express [herself]" 230) and a path that has taken her away from her family's milieu and toward her own world. Cardinal again allows her structure to express new beginnings: toward the opening of Chapter 14 she writes: "Je suis devenue responsable" (252) ("I was becoming responsible" 232). Then, she adds: "Cette unité de mon être ... me permettait d'aller vers les autres. ... J'étais heureuse, j'avais confiance en moi, je savais que j'irais jusqu'au bout" (270) ("This unity of my being ... permitted me to move out towards other people. ... I was happy, I had confidence in myself, I knew that I would go the whole way" 249). Therefore, not only artistic expression heals the protagonist but the fact that creative production opens the door to exchange and communion with others. Her early, secret writings are shared only with her husband; her first book will be shared with society.

Language in psychoanalysis and the creative language of writing are implicitly juxtaposed in *Les mots pour le dire*. Psychoanalytical language involves deciphering words, images, and symbols in order to arrive at specific problems.[24] Writing, on the other hand, allows for invention and fancy: "Les divagations de mes carnets étaient faites d'éléments de ma vie que j'arrangeais comme cela me plaisait, j'allais où je voulais, je vivais des instants que je n'avais pas vécus mais que j'imaginais" (234) ("The divagations in the notebooks were made up of the elements of my life which were arranged according to my fancy: going where I pleased, living out moments I had only imagined" 215). Writing, then, allows for fiction, and this capacity for invention incites a healing liberation: "je n'étais pas tenue par le carcan de la vérité comme avec le docteur. Je me sentais libre comme je ne l'avais jamais été" (234) ("I was not in the yoke of truth, as in analysis. I was conscious of being more free than I had been" 215).

Cardinal's treatment of language in *Les mots pour le dire* is intimately tied to her views on gender relations. Unlike Hélène Cixous and Luce Irigaray, Cardinal is opposed to the creation of a separate *écriture féminine* for fear that "it would further alienate women from society" (Hall, "*L'écriture féminine*" 237). Instead, she encourages women to shock and avoid euphemisms. In *Autrement dit*, for example, Cardinal writes that "il faut écrire brutalement et irrespectueusement" (90) ("one must write brutally and disrespectfully"). In response to critics' suggestions that she use proper terms such as "sanies" ("pus") instead of "crotte" ("excrement, dung") in *Les mots pour le dire*, Cardinal proclaims: "Je refuse ces fioritures hypocrites! Les femmes savent mieux que les hommes ce que c'est que la merde, ne serait-ce que parce qu'elle est le baromètre de la santé de leurs enfants" (*Autrement dit* 86) ("I refuse these hypocritical embellishments! Women know better than men what shit is, if only because it is the barometer of the health of their children"). Cardinal advocates the use of "a transformed traditional language to give visibility to women's experiences" (Hall, "*L'écriture féminine*" 237). She posits that if women use traditional "male language" to describe their lives, its inadequacies will prove that language must evolve. According to Trinh T. Minh-ha, Cardinal wants to maintain our current terminology in order to denounce "the gaps in existing language and its failure to translate women's truths" (52). Minh-ha describes Cardinal's views in this way: "No language to be used among us, women! says Cardinal. Let us use the same words without inhibition or compromise. . . . [T]he public will ultimately change and give words the meanings we desire" (47). Cardinal suggests the following strategy: "[C]'est de nous mettre au ras de notre corps, d'exprimer l'inexprimé et d'employer le vocabulaire tel qu'il est, directement, sans l'arranger. . . . Le langage se féminisera . . . s'enrichira" (*Autrement dit* 89) ("[I]t is to put ourselves at the level of our bodies, to express the unspoken and to use vocabulary as it really is, directly, without altering it. . . . Language will become feminized . . . will enrich itself"). For Cardinal, the ideal language is not a separate female discourse, but rather a medium broad enough to be suitable for all people.

While Cardinal does not advocate an *écriture féminine*, she believes that women and men have different stories to tell. In her texts, she reaches out to ordinary women, like those she met during her years struggling to raise a family. She claims to write for women who "ne savent pas traduire en mots ce que leur corps sait: la lenteur des gestations, la viscosité féconde, l'épaisseur nourrissante. . . . L'archaïsme de nos vies de femmes" (*Autrement dit* 81) ("do not know how to translate into words what their bodies know: the slowness of gestations, the fertile stickiness, the nourishing thickness. . . . The archaism of our lives as women"). Cardinal wants to give these women "des mots qui seront des armes" (*Autrement dit* 81) ("words to be used as arms"). In attributing to her literary projects this political significance, Cardinal communes with other women in a way that allows her to continue her own healing process. Thus, the cathartic function of expression that began in psychoanalysis continues in her various writings. In *Autrement dit*, Cardinal explains the importance of such sharing: "pour moi c'est l'échange qui est important. Je suis très marquée par les dix-sept années où j'ai trimé comme une dingue pour survivre et je me sens plus proche des femmes avec lesquelles j'ai partagé ces années que des autres. C'est pour elles que j'ai envie d'écrire" (66–67) ("for me it is the exchange which is important. I am very influenced by the seventeen years in which I ran around like a nut in order to survive, and I feel closer to the women with whom I shared those years than to others. It is for them that I want to write"). Cardinal's desire to give language to the hitherto silenced *others*, to subvert, and to break down linguistic barriers also constitutes a contemporary female strategy to express what women "are not allowed to say." It is therefore an effort to change women's traditionally submissive role. In order to articulate female experiences, Minh-ha finds that many women "refuse . . . this loss of the substance of words, this division between the Sensory and the Intelligible" (53). This fullness of language that Cardinal and many contemporary women writers and critics seek is necessary if women are to encapsulate their experiences, "write" the body, and persuade others to champion progress for women.

It is interesting to note that *Les mots pour le dire*, a text about the "rebirth" of the protagonist as woman and writer, recalls not only Boileau's seventeenth-century *L'Art poétique* (*The Art of Poetry*)[25] but also Sartre's personal narrative *Les mots* (*Words*). Sartre's text inscribes recollections of the protagonist's actual birth (16–17) as well as the coming to writing. Cardinal builds on the two sections of Sartre's autobiography—"lire" ("to read") and "écrire" ("to write")—with "dire" ("to say") in *Les mots pour le dire*. The evocation in her title of the *parole* (spoken word or speech), the only "language" to which many women have had access in the past, emphasizes the work's feminist slant. Cardinal has been concerned, after all, with giving voice to those women who have been denied the power of the pen.

In several of her texts, Cardinal expresses solidarity with other women through honoring traditional female craftsmanship. She communes with ordinary women, for example, by valorizing the arts of cooking and weaving.[26] In an interview, she states that "there is a sort of hierarchy in the West. It's certain that writing is better than cooking. *I* don't think so. Cooking is an art" (qtd. in Marrone, "Entretien" 119). Cardinal celebrates this basic capacity for creation by crafting her own semiautobiographical/semifictional texts. Carolyn Durham explains that through blending autobiography and fiction Cardinal "restores the female text to its original definition as artisanal activity: *text*, 'woven thing,' from the Latin *texere*, to weave, fabricate" (46–47). Durham continues that "this connection to *fabricate*, 'to construct by putting together finished parts,' . . . reminds us that 'fabrications' or 'fictions' (*fictio*, a making, fashioning) did not begin as falsehoods but, like Cardinal's fusion of autobiography and novel, as carefully crafted constructions" (47). For Cardinal, creativity invokes a community of artisans. Her writing helps her to heal her own wounds but also to connect with other people—particularly other women.[27] This is echoed in *Les mots pour le dire*, in which the personal relationships that writing invites are integral to the protagonist's newfound health.

The heroine's success as a writer affirms her self-worth. We recall that in the female "novel of awakening," development begins within. The protagonist follows an inner impulse that leads to self-understanding.[28] With this renewed sense of self, she can then go beyond societal limitations and embrace her own desires. At this point in the text the protagonist can clearly differentiate herself from "the madwoman." She smiles to herself as she converses with her publisher, thinking of this *other* woman, this former self. Toward the conclusion of Chapter 13 (an ending that connotes separation from the past) we read: "Et s'il avait su qu'il s'adressait à la folle! Je ne pouvais m'empêcher de penser à elle. . . . Je t'ai tirée de là ma vieille, je t'ai tirée de là!" (249–50) ("If only he had known he was addressing a madwoman! I couldn't help thinking of her. . . . It was me who pulled you out of there, my friend. I was the one!" 230). The jovial tone of the direct address to the "madwoman" underscores how much the protagonist has grown through her emotional journey. This rebirth constitutes an important step in the her *bildung*—after discovering and accepting herself, she finds her niche in society.

The protagonist's quest to write and to convey her thoughts and impressions adequately through language is counterbalanced by the importance given to silence in the text. In a scene where the main character describes a partly autobiographical dream, for example, she depicts an enchanting natural setting in which she feels at one with the cosmos: "Impression de participer au Tout, d'être entière. Satisfaction. Silence, parce que l'essentiel est exprimé" (258) ("The impression of being a part of the Whole, of being complete. Satisfaction. Silence, because the essential is expressed"; translation mine). The "impression" of being part of, and at one with, "le Tout" is key here. The author's desire to describe her life, like the protagonist's desire to express her illness and her recovery, can never be completely or perfectly accomplished. Speaking and writing will always constitute that endeavor to express the inexpressible, a communication that one at times experiences in nature, in contact with others, or in one's own thoughts but that is impossible to translate fully into words.

Toward the end of the text, the narrator/protagonist (there is little distance between them at this point) decides that one day she will write her life story. We realize that the newfound means of expression is not enough to sustain the heroine—she must also share her creativity with others in order to fully integrate herself into society. Her decision to write the story of her experience stems from a desire to let others know what mental illness is and to speak to those who have suffered emotional problems: "Pour le leur faire comprendre et pour aider ceux qui vivaient dans l'enfer où j'avais vécu, je me promettais d'écrire un jour l'histoire de mon analyse, d'en faire un roman" (269) ("To make them understand and to help those who lived in the hell where I also lived, I promised myself that I would some day write an account of my analysis, and turn it into a novel" 248). She stresses, however, that an analysis "ne peut pas s'écrire" (269) ("can't be written down" 248), for one would need thousands of pages to express such an overwhelming and multifaceted experience. Instead, her text will be a "novel": "je raconterais *la guérison d'une femme qui me ressemblerait comme une soeur*, sa naissance, sa lente mise au monde" (269; emphasis added) ("I would tell of *the healing of a woman as like me as if she were my own sister*. I would begin with her birth, her slow reentry into the world" 248; emphasis added). The narrator's vision of this future heroine's drama draws our attention to the text we are reading and emphasizes its fictional components. It also stresses the therapeutic aspect of the writer's connection with others, in this case, her readers.

In conclusion, by articulating her pain and finally "leaving the mother," Cardinal's heroine finds her own voice. In doing so, she expresses many of the fears and repressed desires of her female contemporaries. Cardinal's innovative narrative techniques and her bold female protagonist make way for exciting explorations in autobiographical portraiture today, texts that continue to explore self-definition through fragments of past experiences and past texts. In addition, contemporary women writers persist in exploring the mother–daughter relationship and its impact on female identity. Through creativity and sharing her art with others, the heroine of *Les mots pour le dire* forges a new self and a new life.

NOTES

1. Portions of this chapter are based on a conference presentation entitled "The Female Journey: Identity and Development in Marie Cardinal," 45th Annual Foreign Language Conference, Lexington, KY, Apr. 1992. Unless indicated, English translations of quotations from *Les mots pour le dire* are from the following edition: Marie Cardinal, *The Words to Say It: An Autobiographical Novel by Marie Cardinal*, trans. Pat Goodheart (Cambridge, MA: VanVactor and Goodheart, 1983).

2. Carolyn Durham includes an extended analysis of Cardinal's practice of "autocitation" in *The Contexture of Feminism*.

3. As in *Les mots pour le dire, Amour . . . amours . . .* depicts a female protagonist born in Algeria to a French *pied-noir* family. The heroine also writes.

4. See Ramsay (7) for a discussion of such generic maneuverings in contemporary autobiography.

5. Consider, for example, Irigaray's *Et l'une ne bouge pas sans l'autre* (*And One Does Not Move without the Other*) and Chodorow's *The Reproduction of Mothering*.

6. Le Clézio discusses, for example, Hyvrard's *Mère la mort* (*Mother Death*) and *Les prunes de Cythère* (*Cythera's Plums*).

7. English translations throughout this chapter of quotations from *Autrement dit* are

mine.

8. Françoise Lionnet sees Algeria as a central character in the text, "the alter ego of the narrator" (202), and identifies a connection between the psychological *repression* suffered by the protagonist and the political *oppression* of Algeria. See the development of Lionnet's argument (194–206).

9. See Lejeune's discussion in *L'autobiographie en France* of the techniques of nostalgia and repudiation in life writing (75).

10. Martin notes the exception of Joan Gilling in Plath's *The Bell Jar*.

11. Martin explains that the heroines' hate and desire to suppress the mother in order to survive in *Les mots pour le dire* and in *The Bell Jar* result in an "alienation from the mother and from society" (33).

12. As noted in my Introduction, Felski discusses the survival of the heroine in the works of contemporary writers (134).

13. The first set of page numbers refers to the French edition of *Les mots pour le dire*, and the second to the English translation in this and subsequent examples that refer to scenes without offering specific quotations.

14. Cardinal calls on women readers in particular to identify with her struggle and sympathize with the main figure. When the protagonist first deals with the excessive bleeding, for example, she repeats gestures familiar to a female readership: "j'allais constamment surveiller mon état. . . . Selon les circonstances ma main glissait par-devant sur mes poils durs et frisés jusqu'à ce qu'elle rencontre le lieu chaud, doux et humide de mon sexe, puis elle se retirait aussitôt" (13) ("I went to check my condition. . . . Depending on the circumstances, my hand would slip down to my pubic hair, tough and curly, to find the warm, soft, moist place of my genitals, only to quickly take it away again" 5). Likewise, she calculates her cycles, a task at which women are "experts": "'Si mes règles se terminent aujourd'hui, les prochaines reviendront le. . . . Voyons, est-ce que ce mois a trente ou trente et un jours?'" (14) ("'If my period ends today, the next one will be on. . . . Let's figure it out. Does this month have thirty days or thirty-one?'" 6). These passages underscore both a particular female contact with the body and women's unique relationship to time.

15. Excerpts of my interview with Cardinal, "Un Entretien avec Marie Cardinal," have appeared in *Women in French Studies* 4 (1996): 119–31. English translations of quotations from the interview are mine.

16. The English phrase is used in the original French edition of *Les mots pour le dire*.

17. Lionnet also compares the analyst to a midwife (195).

18. Toni Morrison is struck by this moment in Cardinal's text and discusses it in relation to "the way black people ignite critical moments of discovery or change or emphasis in literature not written by them" (viii).

19. Goodheart does not translate the final one-word sentence: "Aucune" ("Not any").

20. Other examples include Sand's *Histoire de ma vie* and Ernaux's *Une femme*. The latter opens and closes with the mother's death. It is interesting to note that in *Autrement dit* Cardinal reserves discussion of her mother's death for the final pages. See in particular 195–205. This structure is discussed further in the next chapter on Ernaux.

21. For some reason, Goodheart does not include the last line of the text in her translation.

22. Goodheart translates "histoire" as "event" in the preceding quotation, but "story" communicates better the potential for fictionalizing the account.

23. In *Autrement dit*, Cardinal notes the following: "C'est la psychanalyse qui m'a

fait retrouver les chemins de ma personne et mes enfants qui m'ont mise au monde" (202) ("It is psychoanalysis which allowed me to find my way and my children who gave birth to me").

24. Key words, for example, that the protagonist shares with her doctor represent traumatic happenings or periods in her life. We read: "Mots clés que nous avions, le docteur et moi, détachés de mon vocabulaire habituel et qui, dans leur concision, servaient à désigner une zone entière, parfois très vaste, de mon individu. . . . Ainsi 'Tuyau' s'attachait à l'avortement raté de ma mère, 'Chien' à la peur d'être jugée et abandonnée" (254–55) ("Key words which the doctor and I had separated out from my usual vocabulary, and which in their conciseness served to designate a vast area of my life. . . . Thus, 'tube' was associated with my mother's attempted abortion, 'dog' with my fear of being judged and abandoned" 234). As the protagonist is able to understand the various terms that link the conscious and the subconscious, she can better understand herself.

25. Ce que l'on conçoit bien s'énonce clairement,
    Et les mots pour le dire arrivent aisément. (160)
    (What one understands well articulates itself clearly,
    And the words to say it come easily.)

26. Consider the role of the embroiderer in *Le passé empiété*.

27. Cardinal continually highlights her commonalities with other women in her works. She attempts to understand women through a reconsideration of traditional historical record, as in *Comme si de rien n'était*, and through revisions of classical myths, exemplified in her portrait of Clytemnestra in *Le passé empiété* and in her study of Medea in *La médée d'Euripide* (*Euripides' Medea*).

28. See Felski (134).

8

Annie Ernaux's Auto/biographies: Unfinished Stories?

> J'ai tracé avec vérité, je crois, le caractère de ma mère, je ne puis passer outre, dans le récit de ma vie, sans me rendre compte . . . de l'importance que ce caractère exerça sur le mien.
> (I think I have truthfully sketched my mother's character, and I cannot proceed further in the recital of my life without taking into account . . . the importance her character had in forming my own.)
> —George Sand, *Histoire de ma vie*

> Je te ressemble, tu me ressembles. . . . Mais je suis sortie de toi, et là, sous tes yeux, je suis une autre toi vivante.
> (I resemble you, you resemble me. . . . But I came from you, and there, before your eyes, I am another living you.)
> —Luce Irigaray, *Et l'une ne bouge pas sans l'autre*

Annie Ernaux's *Une femme* (1987) and *"Je ne suis pas sortie de ma nuit"* (1997) portray a critical moment in female maturation—when a daughter must cope with the loss of her mother.[1] The mother–daughter bond so integral to Marie Cardinal's life writing is again at the forefront of Ernaux's auto/biographies. Characteristic of Ernaux's writing, which often pens connections with significant others, the loss of the mother conjures up feelings of guilt, shame, and love. Familiar to readers is Ernaux's uneasiness regarding her working-class background and the linguistic patterns of her childhood milieu, both analyzed as early as 1974 with the publication of her first novel, *Les armoires vides*. The recent *La honte* (1997; *Shame*) again concerns itself with a daughter's discomfort regarding her roots, this time through the painful memory of an argument in which her father attempts to kill her mother. Readers are also accustomed to Ernaux's tributes to lost "loves": before the homage to her mother in *Une femme*, Ernaux had celebrated her father's life in *La place*

(1983; *A Man's Place*), and the two are often read as companion texts; after *Une femme* came the tribute to Ernaux's former lover in *Passion simple* (1991; *Simple Passion*). With the addition of *"Je ne suis pas sortie de ma nuit"* to her corpus, Ernaux once again celebrates the crucial maternal influence and attempts to reconcile an underprivileged childhood with the cultured life she, the writer, has created for herself. Yet with this recent text Ernaux also proclaims that "leaving the mother," leaving behind the relationship that is so significant to women's identity formation, is an unending process. Common in today's autobiographical musings, the life story is never finished, and it cannot be written only once. Like Cardinal and Marguerite Duras, Ernaux constantly returns in her works to significant events and relationships from her past.

Both *Une femme*, Ernaux's most celebrated text, and *"Je ne suis pa sortie de ma nuit"* offer a daughter's account of her mother's life and, as such, are "biographical." Each text also portrays an inward reflection on the part of its first-person narrator, thus constituting "autobiographical" expression as well.[2] *Une femme* opens and closes with the mother's death and, through remembrances and flashbacks, portrays the full life span of the maternal subject. This includes childhood, marriage, advancement in the social hierarchy, and motherhood, the latter experience characterized by ambitions for the daughter's success. Although this text concerns the same biographical subject and autobiographical voice as *"Je ne suis pas sortie de ma nuit," Une femme* is a highly crafted, literary piece that sets the mother–daughter story in a broad cultural context. *"Je ne suis pas sortie de ma nuit"* is more limited in that it focuses on the end of the mother's life—her slow deterioration and eventual death because of Alzheimer's disease—and employs flashbacks to elucidate selected past moments in the lives of mother and daughter. The inscription of the autobiographical subject is most provocative when the two works are compared.

Ernaux's six-page introduction to *"Je ne suis pas sortie de ma nuit"* was written in 1996 and published in the 1997 edition of the auto/biography. According to this introduction, the story that follows represents Ernaux's original notes and thoughts from the onset of her mother's illness in 1983 through the time of her death in 1986. She writes: "C'est dans la période où elle était encore chez moi que je me suis mise à noter sur des bouts de papier, sans date, des propos, des comportements de ma mère qui me remplissaient de terreur" (10–11) ("It is during the period when she was still at my house that I began noting on pieces of paper, without dates, my mother's remarks, behaviors which filled me with terror"). She states that she wished to modify nothing of the transcription of those last moments with her mother. She renders these pages "telles qu'elles ont été écrites, dans la stupeur et le bouleversement que j'éprouvais alors" (13) ("as they were written, in the stupor and the utter distress that I felt then"). Whether or not this is entirely true is less significant than the fact that Ernaux exploits the autobiographical subgenre of the diary to experiment with narrowing the distance between lived experience and writing—a space that often engenders fiction. In the diary excerpts that make up the text proper of *"Je ne suis pas sortie de ma nuit,"* the narrator considers writing her mother's life story one day, perhaps when she is more distanced from the emotional turmoil at hand. She muses, "Je me demande si je pourrais faire un livre sur elle. . . . Il n'y avait pas de réelle distance entre nous. De l'identification" (35–36) ("I wonder if I could write a book about her. . . . There was not a real distance between us. Identification"). Eventually, Ernaux did create her mother's life story in *Une femme*, written after the mother's death and published in 1987. Yet even in the opening pages of *Une femme*, the narrator fears that she is too close to her subject emotionally: "Peut-être ferais-je mieux d'attendre que sa maladie et sa mort soient fondues dans le cours passé de ma vie . . . afin d'avoir la distance qui facilite l'analyse des souvenirs" (22) ("Perhaps I should wait until her illness and death have merged into the past . . . so that I feel the detachment which makes it easier to analyse one's memories" 12). By the time Ernaux writes the 1996 introduction to *"Je ne suis pas sortie de ma nuit,"* it becomes evident that the "distance" needed to analyze the memory of the mother may never be achieved. In this introduction, she claims that she never reread the original notes taken during the mother's illness, notes that resulted in the recent publication. In my view, somewhere "in between" *Une femme* and *"Je ne suis pas sortie de ma nuit"* lies the writer/narrator's journey toward selfhood—a voyage that remains incomplete. In the continuum from the sketchy diary entries of *"Je ne suis pas sortie de ma nuit"* (1983–86), to the lyrical life story Ernaux offers in *Une femme* (published in 1987), and finally to the 1996 introduction to *"Je ne suis pas sortie de ma nuit,"* Ernaux's voice matures; we hear a more experienced speaker whose views on relationships, selfhood, and literature have evolved. In addition, by 1996, the seasoned artist challenges one single version of the story of mother and daughter.

In a narrative structure that underscores the daughter's identification with the mother and sense of mortality, numerous women's life stories, including these two texts by Ernaux, Sand's *Histoire de ma vie*, Simone de Beauvoir's autobiographical series closing with *Une mort très douce* (*A Very Sweet Death*), and Cardinal's *Les mots pour le dire*, conclude shortly after the mother's passing. Throughout *"Je ne suis pas sortie de ma nuit,"* the mother–daughter identification is heightened because of the mother's impending death. The daughter Annie's[3] feelings are intensified upon witnessing her mother's decay into a forgetful invalid who can no longer groom herself, eat alone, or control her bladder. We read: "Son corps est blanc et mou. . . . Et c'est aussi mon corps que je vois" (20) ("Her body is white and lifeless. . . . And it's also my body that I see"); then, "Jamais femme ne sera plus proche de moi, jusqu'à être comme en moi" (22) ("Never will a woman be closer to me, to the point of being in me"); and finally, "Au moment où elle entre dans la salle à manger, je suis 'elle.' Immense douleur de voir sa vie finir ainsi" (23) ("When she enters the dining room, I am 'she.' Immense sadness to see her life finish like this"). In the preceding passage, quotation marks around "elle" express both the ambiguity of the self/other differentiation ("je" now becomes "elle") and also the distance between the mother's past and present "selves" ("elle"—she has become an unrecognizable woman). As the mother's illness progresses, she and the daughter exchange roles. The daughter cares for her sick parent as she would a baby, a common occurrence in women's and men's adult lives and frequently described in female autobiographical texts.[4] The daughter further expresses that one day she might be the old woman alone in a nursing home. This identification with the maternal figure confirms to the daughter that the mother's passing ultimately equals her own eventual death. We read: "Elle est le *temps*, pour moi. Elle me pousse aussi vers la mort" (74) ("She is *time* for me. She pushes me too toward death"). The daughter realizes that she participates in a cycle of generations, in a female continuity that goes beyond her own life: "Ce n'est pas seulement le sentiment du temps qui passe, quelque chose d'autre, de mortel: je suis maintenant un être dans une chaîne, une existence incluse dans une filiation continuant après moi" (86) ("It is not only the feeling of time which passes, something else, something mortal: I am now part of a chain, an existence included in a succession continuing after me").

For a time, writing allows for release, for grieving, and for holding onto the slippery moments of life. The lifeline that writing represents for Ernaux is clear through the narrator's thoughts shortly following her mother's death: "Attendre de m'être évadée de ces jours. Mais ce sont eux la vérité. . . . Quand j'écrivais sur elle après les visites, est-ce que ce n'était pas pour retenir la vie?" (104) ("To wait until I have escaped from these days. But they represent truth. . . . When I wrote about her after the visits, wasn't it to cling to life?"). Writing is also a bridge to the future. As in *Une femme*, *"Je ne suis pas sortie de na nuit"* creates a literary afterlife for the mother and secures a place in "History" for this "ordinary" woman. Ernaux thus participates in the project of "recovery" dear to many twentieth-century women writers. She also grants a voice to this "powerless" woman, akin to Cardinal's attempt to "arm" women through words.[5] In *"Je ne suis pas sortie de ma nuit,"* the narrator desires, yet fears, contemplating these final moments with the mother: "Un jour, peut-être pourrai-je lire les notes écrites au retour des visites, elles m'apparaîtront dans une continuité, la vie et la mort. En ce moment, je suis dans la rupture" (105) ("One day, maybe I will be able to read the notes written after returning from the visits, they would appear to me in a continuity, life and death. Now, I'm in a moment of rupture"). Unable to reconcile her final Sunday visit with her mother and the mother's death the next day, she explains: "Un jour . . . tout sera lié, *comme une histoire. Pour écrire, il faudrait que j'attende que ces deux jours soient fondus dans le reste de ma vie*" (106–7; emphasis added) ("One day . . . all will be connected, *like a story. To write, I would have to wait for these two days to be fused into the rest of my life*"; emphasis added). That *story*, that work that was supposed to represent Ernaux's healing, growth, and acceptance of her mother's passing, was offered to readers with *Une femme*. At the end of that text, the narrator recalls the same two days (the day before the mother's death and the day of her death) and proclaims, "Maintenant, tout est lié" (103) ("Now everything is one" 89). If the end of *Une femme* represented closure, why, then, did Ernaux need to publish another story?

In comparison to *"Je ne suis pas sortie de ma nuit,"* *Une femme* has a broader scope. Ernaux offers more details about the mother's life and the daughter's childhood. She also includes more extensive background regarding her parents' era, mentioning Léon Blum, economic crises, life during World War

II, the Algerian War, and the May 1968 riots. She discusses the depressed region in Normandy where her parents managed to leave factory work to open their own café-grocery store and quotes current articles from the French press concerning the lack of education still today in that area. For example, Ernaux includes the following information in a footnote:

Dans *Le Monde* du 17 juin 1986, on lit à propos de la région de ma mère, la Haute-Normandie: "Un retard de la scolarisation qui n'a jamais été comblé, malgré des améliorations, continue de produire ses effets (. . .). Chaque année, 7 000 jeunes sortent du système scolaire sans formation. . . . La moitié d'entre eux, selon un pédagogue, ne 'savent pas lire deux pages conçues pour eux.'" (30)
(In an article published by the French newspaper *Le Monde*, dated 17 June 1986, the Haute-Normandie, where my mother was brought up, is subjected to severe criticism: "Despite recent improvements, this region is still suffering from appallingly low schooling standards. . . . Every year the French educational system turns out 7,000 unskilled school-leavers. . . . According to an academic expert, half of them 'are unable to understand even two pages written to their standard.'" 19)

She thus includes "documentation" (a newspaper entry) and authoritative commentary (by "un pédagogue") in her text, which not only lend authenticity to the narrative but also allow her to venture into the realms of sociology, ethnography, history, and culture. Indeed, Ernaux expresses her desire to produce a work "au-dessous de la littérature" (23) ("a cut below literature" 13). We read: "Je voudrais saisir aussi la femme qui a existé en dehors de moi. . . . Ce que j'espère écrire de plus juste se situe sans doute à la jointure du familial et du social, du mythe et de l'histoire" (23) ("I would also like to capture the real woman, the one who existed independently from me. . . . The more objective aspect of my writing will probably involve a cross between family history and sociology, reality and fiction" 13). Carol Sanders comments that in her later novels, including *Une femme*, Ernaux strives for "a new form which combines social history with authorial reflexion, alongside its autobiographical and fictional elements. This is a form that is close to the 'ethnobiography,' or 'autoethnography'" ("Stylistic Aspects" 22). Commenting on her narrative choices, Ernaux states in an article, "The *I* that I use seems to me an impersonal form, hardly sexed, sometimes even more the speech of 'the other' than 'my' speech: a transpersonal form, in sum" ("Vers un *je* transpersonnel" 221).[6] Ernaux's desire to move beyond the personal and individual spheres is, in fact, key to the healing process described in *Une femme*. She explains: "Cette façon d'écrire, qui me semble aller dans le sens de la vérité, m'aide à sortir de la solitude et de l'obscurité du souvenir individuel, par la découverte d'une signification plus générale" (52) ("This way of writing, which seems to bring me closer to the truth, relieves me of the dark, heavy burden of personal remembrance by establishing a more objective approach" 40–41). In essence, moving beyond the mother's life to the lives of others in the same socioeconomic class allows the narrator to understand her mother's attitudes (e.g., about sexuality, marriage, and work), her religious fervor, her roughness, her desires. It allows her to intellectualize and therefore to deal with death more easily. However, as a daughter, she can never fully remove herself from the individual she loves: "Mais je sens que quelque chose en moi résiste, voudrait conserver de ma mère des images purement affectives, chaleur ou larmes, sans leur donner de sens" (52) ("And yet something deep down inside refuses to yield and wants me to remember my mother purely in emotional terms—affection or tears—without searching for an explanation" 41). Furthermore, with the publication of *"Je ne suis pas sortie de ma nuit,"* it is clear that the healing begun in *Une femme* was incomplete. In sum, *Une femme* is an ambitious text, offering a fuller, more complete life story than *"Je ne suis pas sortie de ma nuit."* The latter is rather a meditation on a particular, painful moment. This is echoed in the titles: *Une femme* anticipates a woman's life portrait, while *"Je ne suis pas sortie de ma nuit,"* a title drawn from the last sentence the ill mother wrote in a letter to a friend, reflects an instant, one line extracted from a longer tale, a fragment of a woman's life.[7]

In *Une femme*, Ernaux employs what has become her characteristic sober, simple style since the publication of *La place* in 1983. Danièle Mazingarbe describes "the Ernaux style. . . . The precise word, the clear sentence, the minimum. Without emotion."[8] Ernaux does not mimic the linguistic nuances of the working class in an overly sentimental fashion, but at the same time she refuses an embellished, affected literary style that denies the everyday realities of ordinary people. Christine Fau discusses Ernaux's refusal of a hypocritical, bourgeois language (509). Jérôme Garcin echoes Fau, stating that, according to Ernaux, "art is a betrayal of reality and beauty a bourgeois distortion of truth" (75). Further, style is a "privilege of a cultural elite . . . a way of denying 'the most common things'" (Garcin 75). In an interview, Ernaux elaborates: "My texts are a search for reality . . . through verifiable *facts* and real words, economic and cultural behaviors" (qtd. in Tondeur, "Entretien" 38). Although *Une femme* exemplifies Ernaux's plain, uncomplicated style, it is actually a very artful, literary piece in the spirit of such writers as Albert Camus and Ernest Hemingway—authors dear to Ernaux. *"Je ne suis pas sortie de ma nuit"* again exemplifies a sober, unadorned style. However, a comparison of the two works illustrates the literary superiority of *Une femme*.

First, *Une femme* enters into a tradition of noted French biographies and autobiographies. I have already mentioned Beauvoir's *Une mort très douce*, another autobiographical rendering of a daughter's experience of her mother's death. Next, *Une femme* draws on literary fathers as well. *Une femme* opens with "Ma mère est morte le lundi 7 avril à la maison de retraite . . . où je l'avais placée il y a deux ans" (11) ("My mother died on Monday 7 April in the old people's home . . . where I had installed her two years previously" 1). As Sanders has noted, this opening automatically recalls the beginning of *L'étranger* (*The Stranger*) by Camus (" Stylistic Aspects" 22). That work begins: "Aujourd'hui, maman est morte" (9) ("Today, mother died"). Additional literary echoes resonate in Ernaux's structure. The opening chapters of *Une femme*, following the account of the mother's death, flash back to a traditional story line in life writing: narrating the family history. In Ernaux's case we learn of her proud, severe grandparents, her spirited, ambitious mother, and her humble, loving father. Finally, in publishing more than one version of the mother's story, Ernaux enters into a tradition of "autocitation," discussed in the previous chapter, dear to such contemporary women writers as Cardinal and Marguerite Duras—either quoting directly or revising material from one work for a future publication.[9]

The careful fabrication of *Une femme* in comparison to the unpolished writing of *"Je ne suis pas sortie de ma nuit"* is also reflected in the examination of specific narrative techniques used in the two texts. First, Ernaux shifts adeptly from present to past in *Une femme*, even more frequently than in *"Je ne suis pas sortie de ma nuit."* In the former text, her meditations on time (now her mother "was" rather than "is") render her grief more poignant.[10] Next, in *"Je ne suis pas sortie de ma nuit,"* Ernaux explains that she wrote "très vite, dans la violence des sensations, sans réfléchir ni chercher d'ordre" (11) ("very fast, in the violence of sensations, without thinking or seeking structure"). Words, fragments, and memories are jotted down quickly, at times in a disconnected fashion. Consider, for example, the following passage: "Elle a perdu son dentier du bas. La garde: 'Ça n'a pas d'importance, elle ne mange que du mixé!' Aujourd'hui, elle était joyeuse. (C'est pire)" (57) ("She lost her bottom dental plate. The nurse: 'It doesn't matter, she only eats soft foods!' Today, she was joyful. [It's worse]"). The narrator adds no commentary regarding the nurse's insensitivity. Further, she jumps quickly to a reference about her mother's mental state and then to an undeveloped thought: "(C'est pire)." In another passage, we read: "Sa façon de me toiser, hautaine, parfois, comme si elle ne me reconnaissait pas. Elle mange l'éclair seule, en s'en mettant partout. C'est toutefois le gâteau qu'elle mange le plus facilement. Une chanson des années soixante, à la télévision. . . . Ma vie depuis ce temps" (87) ("Her manner of eyeing me scornfully, haughty at times, as if she didn't recognize me. She eats the éclair on her own, getting it all over herself. And yet it's the pastry she eats the most easily. A song from the sixties, on television. . . . My life since then"). Not only does Ernaux employ fragments, but she shifts from one topic to the next without transitions. Ernaux's unfinished style is also apparent in the blatant contradictions in *"Je ne suis pas sortie de ma nuit."* On page 50, we read: "[ma mère] ne parle jamais de mon père" ("[my mother] never speaks about my father"). On the very next page, Ernaux includes the following quotation, attributed to the mother, regarding the daughter's Renaudot prize: "'Si son père le savait il le dirait à tout le monde'" ("'If her father knew he would tell everyone'"). In contrast to the disjointed and at times careless construction of *"Je ne suis pas sortie de ma nuit,"* Ernaux seeks a perfect structure in *Une femme*. We read:

Au début, je croyais que j'écrirais vite. En fait je passe beaucoup de temps à m'interroger sur l'ordre des choses à dire, le choix et l'agencement des mots, comme s'il existait un ordre idéal, seul capable de rendre une vérité concernant ma mère . . . et rien d'autre ne compte pour moi, au moment où j'écris, que la découverte de cet ordre-là. (43–44)
(Initially, I thought I would find it easy to write. In actual fact, I spend a lot of time reflecting on what I have to say and on the choice and sequence of words, as if there existed only one immutable order which would convey the truth about my mother. . . .

When I am writing, the only thing that matters to me is to find that particular order. 32–33)

As in *"Je ne suis pas sortie de ma nuit,"* Ernaux employs fragments in *Une femme*, but in the latter they often evoke a mood or an image and emerge rhythmically in a tightly constructed narrative. In a recollection of her mother's childhood, for example, we read: "la chambre commune pour tous les enfants, le lit partagé avec une soeur, des crises de somnambulisme où on la retrouvait debout, endormie, les yeux ouverts, dans la cour" (27–28) ("—the six children packed into one room, sharing a bed with one of her sisters, the bouts of sleepwalking, when she was found standing in the courtyard, sound asleep, her eyes wide open" 17). In *Une femme*, Ernaux's skillful use of fragments, along with her conversational, yet poetic, tone, creates mental pictures for the reader. At other moments, Ernaux erects an accumulation of images, as in the following passage:

Images d'elle, entre quarante et quarante-six ans: . . .
  un été, au bord de la mer, elle pêche des moules. . . .
  à l'église, elle chantait à pleine voix. . . .
  elle avait des robes vives et un tailleur noir en "grain de poudre." (48–49)
(Images of her, aged between forty and forty-six: . . .
– at the seaside one summer, she is fishing for mussels. . . .
– in church, she sang . . . in a loud, booming voice. . . .
– she wore brightly coloured dresses and a black woolen suit. 37–38)

The use of indentation (in the original French version of the text) and the lack of capitalization in the above passage, along with the frequent use of parentheses and fragments elsewhere in the text, reflect an effort to find a precise language and a new form, beyond conventional style, to mirror past experiences. In *Une femme*, Ernaux employs these varied techniques artfully. She achieves both a certain cadence that conjures up the maternal image and a particular voice that lulls the reader into an understanding of the daughter's mental state. Finally, although Ernaux employs direct discourse in both texts, in *Une femme*, quotations from the mother are more frequently introduced without the typical tags ("she said," "she claimed"), allowing the "real" woman's voice to come forth. Consider the following example: "Elle me battait facilement, des gifles surtout, parfois des coups de poing sur les épaules ('je l'aurais tuée si je ne m'étais pas retenue!')" (51) ("She would often hit me, usually by slapping my face, or occasionally punching my shoulders ['I could have killed her!']" 39).[11] It is clear from Ernaux's repetition of such phrases that the internal quotation in the previous passage is attributed to the mother. In a realist mode, the narrator steps back and allows the mother's voice to emerge and come to life. Other internal quotations are more ambiguous—are they her mother's words or the choral voice of puritanical, provincial France in the 1940s and 1950s? We read: "Personne ne 'poussait' ses enfants, il fallait que ce soit 'dans eux'" (29) ("In those days, nobody 'pushed' their children, they had to 'have it in them'" 18). Although we see some of these narrative techniques in *"Je ne suis pas sortie de ma nuit,"* they are more refined and expertly manipulated in *Une femme*.

A comparison of specific scenes found in both texts also illustrates how they differ. For example, in *"Je ne suis pas sortie de ma nuit,"* Ernaux recounts a dream as follows: "Début janvier, ce rêve, où je suis dans une rivière, entre deux eaux, avec des filaments sous moi. Mon sexe est blanc et j'ai l'impression que c'est aussi le sexe de ma mère, le même. Oser creuser cela" (54). ("Beginning of January, this dream, where I'm in a river, between two currents, with filaments beneath me. My genitals are white, and I have the impression that they are also my mother's genitals, the same. Dare to look deeply into that"). The passage is characterized by choppy language and, again, fragments. Though there is a strong female, sexual symbol—the filaments that grow beneath the woman recall the umbilical cord, the childbirth process, and the mother–daughter dyad—the image is undeveloped. Do the filaments grow from the genitals? Do they emerge from the river? The passage is simply a glimpse, a flash, a hurried sketch. It is interrupted in the text by the repeated query of one of the mother's demented companions in her nursing home: "'Qui chante?'" (54) ("'Who's singing?'"). In *Une femme*, on the other hand, this same scene matures and unfolds in this way:

Pendant les dix mois où j'ai écrit, je rêvais d'elle presque toutes les nuits. Une fois, j'étais couchée au milieu d'une rivière, entre deux eaux. De mon ventre, de mon sexe à nouveau lisse comme celui d'une petite fille partaient des plantes en filaments, qui flottaient, molles. Ce n'était pas seulement mon sexe, c'était aussi celui de ma mère. (104)
(Throughout the ten months I was writing this book, I dreamed of her almost every night. Once I was lying in the middle of a stream, caught between two currents. From my loins, smooth again like a young girl's, from between my thighs, long tapering plants floated limply. The body they came from was not only mine, it was also my mother's. 89–90)

In this "revision" the passage is much more fluid. The anaphora creates a rhythmical balance, most apparent in the original French version: ("De mon ventre, de mon sexe"). The visual images are also stronger: from "des filaments sous moi. Mon sexe est blanc" in *"Je ne suis pas sortie de ma nuit,"* Ernaux generates in *Une femme*: "De mon ventre, de mon sexe à nouveau lisse comme celui d'une petite fille partaient des plantes en filaments, qui flottaient, molles." There is increased description in this version of the passage. In addition, the sexual image is perfected as the plants emerge clearly from the genital region.

"Je ne suis pas sortie de ma nuit" is not without literary merit,[12] but one wonders why Ernaux chose to publish this diary, which, as a "repetition" of a once so moving story, seems like a daughter's betrayal. How can this meager collection of journal notes carry the same emotional impact created by *Une femme*?[13] After all, did not *Une femme* reflect the "work—the effort and the suffering—of writing [that] is born of this questioning about its own *meaning*, about a direction, an object and a significance which are never acquired in advance, but progressively and doubtfully generated" (Mall 46)? Is it not such careful crafting that creates "literature"? Is *"Je ne suis pas sortie de ma nuit"* merely a facile attempt to weave a text without the necessary creative labor?

Several critics express disappointment with *"Je ne suis pas sortie de ma nuit,"* which at times goes beyond plain style to bad style. Garcin writes that "in wanting to strip writing bare . . . and reduce its function to the act of naming, the writer ends up being nothing but an accountant of facts, a clerk of sentiments" (75). Anne Thébaud adds: "It is no longer a question of a work of introspection but of notes taken from real life" (13). With regard to content, Marie-Laure Delorme discusses the "uneasiness" one experiences in reading *"Je ne suis pas sortie de ma nuit,"* as well as *La honte*, "[a]s if it were time for the author to move on to another story" (73). Although Delorme finds "moments of truth" in *"Je ne suis pas sortie de ma nuit,"* she counters that "moments do not make a book" (73). Hence, critics agree that *"Je ne suis pas sortie de ma nuit,"* begun as something very personal, penned in the heat of distress, contrasts sharply with the carefully woven *Une femme*. In the words of Renaud Matignon, "what was rigor becomes self-satisfaction; what was exorcism turns to exhibition."

After comparing the two texts, one might ask, Why is it important that *Une femme* is the more polished, finished one? Is it not logical that notes written during intense emotional hardship would be very different from a literary endeavor intended for publication? Is Ernaux's *"Je ne suis pas sortie de ma nuit"* an attempt to hug the moment of loss most intensely by refusing to alter her original writing? In my view, the difference between these two auto/biographies speaks to Ernaux's views on literature and life writing, and this recalls the issue raised earlier about the evolution of the writer/narrator's voice in these works.

Why did Ernaux choose to publish *"Je ne suis pas sortie de na nuit"* and to offer it to the reading public as "literature"? On the last page of *Une femme* Ernaux writes, "Il fallait que ma mère, née dans un milieu dominé, dont elle a voulu sortir, devienne histoire, pour que je me sente moins seule et factice dans le monde dominant des mots et des idées où, selon son désir, je suis passée" (106; emphasis added) ("My mother, born into an oppressed milieu from which she wanted to escape, had to become history so that I felt less alone and artificial in *the dominant world of words and ideas*, where, because of her desire, I now live" translation mine; emphasis added). First, might not *"Je ne suis pas sortie de ma nuit"* be Ernaux's heightened revolt against "le monde dominant des mots et des idées"? Is she finally strong enough (famous enough?) to throw bare feelings at her readers, at the writing elite, without revising her inscription of them in any fashion? Barbara Havercroft writes that *"Je ne suis pas sortie de ma nuit"* can be read as "the absent unspoken element of *Une Femme*, what was omitted from it: intense and raw emotion."[14] Toward the conclusion of *"Je ne suis pas sortie de ma nuit,"* the narrator struggles with the mother's death. We read: "Au téléphone, Annie M. m'a dit qu'on ne peut transcrire directement ce qu'on sent, il faut un détour. Je ne sais pas" (103) ("On the telephone, Annie M. told me that one cannot transcribe directly what one feels, only indirectly. I don't know"). Does this comment on Ernaux's experiment with an immediate "transcription" of pain? The narrator questions whether or not she is too vulnerable to write about the mother's death. Yet she perseveres in her project because it is precisely those painful days of loss that are "la vérité, bien [qu'elle] ne sache pas laquelle" (104) ("truth, though [she] does not know which one"). Hence, on a hunch about "truth," something nagging, she searches the unknown. She brutally writes her sorrow.

From her earliest works, Ernaux has been concerned with challenging "the notion of high culture as representing the supreme Good and Truth" (qtd. in Sanders, "Afterword" 124). In a discussion of *Les armoires vides*, Ernaux explains that, in writing her first novel, she avoided the "refined style that [she uses] as a teacher of literature" but employed rather an idiom that, "by being brutally direct, working-class and sometimes obscene, would take issue with the French tradition of the polished sentence, of 'good taste' in literature" (qtd. in Sanders, "Afterword" 125). Although brimming with the "classic" use of striking metaphors, Ernaux's run-on sentences, digressions, and graphic language in *Les armoires vides* seem to achieve her aims. While still challenging "bourgeois language," Ernaux's style evolves into a controlled, polished prose in *Une femme*. With *"Je ne suis pas sortie de ma nuit,"* however, the author seems to recall her earlier rebellion against "correct" writing in the days of *Les armoires vides*. Although in a different style than her first novel, this recent publication nevertheless echoes Ernaux's desire to transgress the boundaries of "'good taste' in literature." A passage from *La honte* is telling regarding Ernaux's need to be shamelessly honest: "J'ai toujours eu envie d'écrire des livres dont il me soit ensuite impossible de parler, qui rendent le regard d'autrui insoutenable" (132) ("I always wanted to write books about which it would later be impossible for me to speak, which render the gaze of others unbearable"). Such frankness can manifest itself thematically, and Ernaux has certainly been forthright about such issues as sexuality and abortion since the time of her first publication. Such candor can also display itself linguistically, in an even stronger refusal of "poetic" language than we saw in *Une femme*. This appears to be the case in *"Je ne suis pas sortie de ma nuit."* The simple, yet "literary," *Une femme* had to make way for the raw cry of *"Je ne suis pas sortie de ma nuit."*

The second reason for Ernaux's publication of *"Je ne suis pas sortie de ma nuit,"* in my view, relates to the mother–daughter story. In the 1996 introduction to *"Je ne suis pas sortie de ma nuit,"* Ernaux offers intriguing insights:

Longtemps, j'ai pensé que je ne . . . publierais jamais [ce journal des visites]. Peut-être désirais-je laisser de ma mère et de ma relation avec elle, une seule image, une seule vérité, celle que j'ai tenté d'approcher dans *Une femme*. Je crois maintenant que l'unicité, la cohérence auxquelles aboutit une oeuvre . . . doivent être mises en danger toutes les fois que c'est possible. En rendant publiques ces pages, l'occasion s'en présente pour moi. (12–13)
(For a long time, I thought I would never publish [these diary entries]. Maybe I wanted to leave behind a single image, a single truth about my mother and my relationship with her, that which I tried to approach in *Une femme*. I now believe that the uniqueness, the coherence toward which a work progresses . . . must be continually challenged. In publishing these pages, such an opportunity arises for me.)

Critics confidently proclaimed that with *Une femme* Annie Ernaux had finally come to terms with her past, including her working-class background, and had at last accepted her mother's death. We now find, however, with the publication of *"Je ne suis pas sortie de ma nuit"* that Ernaux has not resolved issues regarding her past or her emotional connection to her mother. Ernaux's "present" is troubling; she does not feel comfortable in her privileged environment, and she does not fully understand her "self." The daughter has still not overcome her "nuit," her suffering concerning the mother's passing.[15] Therefore, she needs to offer her public *another* version of the mother–daughter story. In a recent interview, Ernaux states: "It's the very uncomfortable position of being between two worlds. My gaze will remain different. I am exiled from my own milieu. I will never depart from that. My gaze is formed by this internal exile" (Tondeur, "Entretien" 38; translation mine).[16] Ironically, though she feels fixed in an "internal exile," that tension sparks her continuous psychological and literary journey—not entirely unlike the voyages of her autobiographical predecessors who struggled with "leaving the country" or "leaving the family" and then inscribing those displacements. The writer/narrator's voice in the introduction to *"Je ne suis pas sortie de ma nuit"* reveals an ongoing process of *bildung*: the maturation of the daughter as she endeavors to "leave the mother" is still incomplete, and the filial–maternal auto/biography is not yet finished. There may be another text to come. . . . Ernaux forewarned us in *Une femme*: "Je vais continuer d'écrire sur ma mère" (22) ("I shall continue to write about my mother" 12). However, this does not necessarily mean that postmodern autobiographical subjects can never experience unity or that the publication of *"Je ne suis pas sortie de ma nuit"* reflects the impossibility of self-understanding. Instead, Ernaux's works reflect the impulse to continue to move *toward* self-knowledge and to strive to express the "real." The writer/narrator we hear in the introduction to *"Je ne suis pas sortie de ma nuit"* has, indeed, evolved from the voices echoing from the pages of *Une femme* and the diary excerpts of *"Je ne suis pas sortie de ma nuit."* Like so many contemporary women autobiographers, she is eager to travel forward in her personal search. Where this journey leads, however, is still unknown.

NOTES

1. This chapter is based, in part, on my conference presentation entitled "Annie Ernaux's Auto/biographies," NEMLA, Baltimore, Apr. 1998. English translations of quotations from *Une femme* are taken from the following edition: Annie Ernaux, *A Woman's Story*, trans. Tanya Leslie (New York: Four Walls Eight Windows, 1991). English translations of quotations from *"Je ne suis pas sortie de ma nuit"* are mine.

2. See my discussion of such creative auto/biographies as Anna Banti's *Artemisia* and Eunice Lipton's *Alias Olympia* in "Women Writing Auto/biography."

3. The daughter is identified by her first name in the text in the following example: "—j'entends: 'Annie!'" (21) ("—I hear: 'Annie!'").

4. Consider the difficulty Cardinal's protagonist experienced in caring for her aging, ill mother in *Les mots pour le dire*.

5. See Cardinal's *Autrement dit* (81).

6. Note the use of the terms "parole" ("speech" or "spoken word") and "forme transpersonnelle" ("transpersonal form") in the original French quotation: "Le *je* que j'utilise me semble une forme impersonnelle, à peine sexuée, quelquefois même plus une parole de 'l'autre' qu'une parole de 'moi': une forme transpersonnelle, en somme."

7. The phrase "je ne suis pas sortie de ma nuit," attributed to the mother, also appears in *Une femme* (90). Leslie translates this as "I am still lost in my world of darkness" (*A Woman's Story* 77). In addition, recall that Fallaci's contemporary text *Lettera a un bambino mai nato* also focuses on a particular life phase.

8. Several critics comment on Ernaux's unadorned style. See, for example, Fau, Mall, and Tondeur, "Relation mère/fille."

9. Durham's discussion of "autocitation" in Cardinal's works can be found in *The Contexture of Feminism*.

10. Ernaux writes, for example, "Mon premier mouvement, en parlant d'elle, c'est de la fixer dans des images sans notion de temps" (22) ("When I speak of her, my first impulse is to 'freeze' her in a series of images unrelated to time" 12).

11. Also see Mall (52) on Ernaux's use of direct discourse in *Une femme*.

12. See, for example, Havercroft's discussion of the use of euphemisms and synecdoches in the text.

13. Marie-Laure Delorme finds that with *"Je ne suis pas sortie de ma nuit,"* "l'émotion devient un procédé" (73) ("emotion becomes a method").

14. A precise page number is not yet available as Havercroft's publication is forthcoming.

15. Havercroft discusses the title's double resonance and concludes that with this publication, the daughter has finally accepted the mother's death. My conclusion is slightly different, emphasizing the ongoing nature of the daughter's struggle.

16. See also Tondeur's *Annie Ernaux ou l'exil intérieur*.

Conclusion

Where does the journey in women's autobiographical writing leave us today? In the texts I have examined, French and Italian women writers offer several examples of protagonists whose development unfolds through separation from oppressive social and familial structures. This process is highlighted when the texts are read as *bildungsromane*, since novels of development stage in a dramatic way women's struggles, successes, and desires for change. As Carol Lazzaro-Weis states, the *bildungsroman* "has always exposed the tensions, contradictions, and difficulties involved in linking problems of subjectivity and representation to the criticism of social and political structures" ("The Female *Bildungsroman*" 26). After tracing protagonists' movements through various developmental stages on the road to maturity and self-realization, it becomes apparent, particularly in the postmodern period, that the representation of a coherent self toward which many autobiographers aspire is not always within reach. However, the ardent desire to comprehend the self as well as the unique pleasure of writing one's story clearly persist. This is evidenced by the explosion of autobiographical narratives being written today.

In the texts analyzed in this study, the autobiographical journey has taken various forms. In *Souvenirs dans l'exil*, Cristina di Belgiojoso voyages far from home and is able to reflect, via letter writing, on her past. Through an examination of others, particularly other women, she analyzes her own character. Writing her experiences allows her gradually to recognize the wisdom that emerges from struggling to live in other countries. At the same time, life in exile compels her to treasure her friends back home. In *Emina*, which also emanated from the princess' exilic sojourn, Belgiojoso once again contemplates European problems from a distance. Through portraying extreme examples of gender prejudice in the Middle East, she indirectly comments on the need for female liberation at home. Céleste Mogador, too, "leaves the country" in search of a new life in

Australia. *Mémoires de Céleste Mogador* is not only the "confession" of a "fallen" woman but the story of her resurrection as a contributing member of society as well as her debut as a writer. At the same time, *Mémoires* presents her lover Lionel's *bildung* as a male counterpart to this woman's autobiography. In the sequel, *Un deuil au bout du monde*, the former prostitute, now the married Countess of Chabrillan, has "reformed." In a text that again treats the interconnected journeys of Céleste and Lionel, we see both individuals become productive society members—she as an accomplished author and he as a French consul—albeit far from France. At the turn of the century, Sibilla Aleramo again depicts separation from an oppressive environment in *Una donna*, but this time it is the family that must be abandoned. In writing this story of liberation, Aleramo portrays a "modern woman" in search of a new identity not bound to maternal models of self-sacrifice. In her contemporary *Lettera a un bambino mai nato*, Oriana Fallaci responds to many of the questions put forth in Aleramo's text. In Fallaci's narrative, public expectations regarding marriage and maternity continue to pose a threat to the unmarried, pregnant protagonist. She, too, resists patriarchal family structures and separates herself from conventional patterns of motherhood. As she strives to live freely, she proposes revisionist familial and societal models. With Marie Cardinal's *Les mots pour le dire*, the quest for selfhood involves an even more significant form of displacement. Her heroine must separate from the mother, the individual most closely tied to a daughter's identity, and find her own voice both to express the trauma of her youth and to write her own future. Through creativity and also through connection with others, the protagonist is able to express herself, gain confidence, and heal. As opposed to Aleramo's heroine, who had to choose between family and carreer, Cardinal's protagonist maintains both. Annie Ernaux's companion auto/biographies *Une femme* and *"Je ne suis pas sortie de ma nuit"* illustrate once again the significance of the mother–daughter relationship as well as the postmodern practice of incessantly rewriting the life story. Such a trend points to the uncertainty of the autobiographical project but also to a persistent belief that self-knowledge is possible. Ernaux's texts portray an evolution on the part of the writer/narrator with regard to both personal understanding and the hierarchy of the literary world.

One might conclude that, chronologically, these women's texts reveal a movement first away from society and then away from those most intimately connected to the self. Separation from the larger community of the country in the nineteenth century would appear to make way for detachment from the smaller unit of the family in the twentieth century. Eventually, it is the mother in particular who must be "left behind" in the daughter's quest for selfhood. It might seem logical that women first had to establish their place within society before they could effectively redefine female roles within the family. They also needed to gain power within the family before they could challenge the values embodied by the mother. Yet, women's movements away from oppressive structures cannot be so neatly or chronologically summarized. Their journeys are, in fact, much more complicated, often involving multiple forms of displacement.

A historical overview of voyages in life writing demonstrates that escape from one's country, family, or mother, indeed, is not limited to one particular time period. For example, modern heroines in the texts of Anna Banti, Cardinal, Nancy Huston, Leïla Sebbar, and Maryse Condé "leave the country" as did their nineteenth-century predecessors. Today's political dissidents experience the same pressures to flee their homelands as did their female forebears. In addition, postcolonial texts prove that, through a rejection of the colonizers' values, "leaving the country" merges with another form of displacement—"leaving the mother" or "motherland." However, importantly, the reasons for undertaking such journeys change over time. The movements staged in the autobiographies I have considered arise from particular historical and cultural circumstances. Belgiojoso left Italy not only because of her subversive political views but in order to conquer unknown lands with the missionary zeal that inspired her nineteenth-century socialist sisters. For Lady Hester Stanhope, Flora Tristan, and Amalia Solla Nizzoli, to name only a few, the time was ripe to take a political, humanitarian, *and* feminist message abroad. Yet nineteenth-century European society eyed these strong, independent figures warily. Far from their homelands, they could comment on problems in Europe more freely. Similarly, Céleste Mogador's need to flee the place of her past transgressions would not be an uncommon sentiment among contemporary women. But Mogador's choice to voyage to a new land at a time when travel by sea could prove perilous was a drastic one. Today, regret because of illicit sexual behavior would not necessitate self-imposed exile in another country, though it might create personal anxiety similar to that experienced by the heroine of *Mémoires*.

Just as separation from one's homeland is not limited to the nineteenth century, neither is the resistance toward patriarchal family structures found in Aleramo's turn-of-the-century *Una donna* restricted to a particular era. Aleramo's account of "leaving the family," fleeing an abusive marriage, follows nineteenth-century works such as George Sand's *Indiana* and Belgiojoso's *Les deux femmes d'Ismaïl Bey* (*The Two Wives of Ismaïl Bey*), which voiced concerns about unfair marriage practices. Further, marital abuse is certainly not absent in modern-day women's texts or lives. But women today have more legal options that guarantee custody rights and personal safety. They need not bemoan permanent detachment from their children because of separation or divorce but, rather, grapple with changing family constellations or single parenthood.

Resistance toward patriarchy's fixed roles, as exemplified in Fallaci's postmodern text, was not foreign to earlier female authors either. Sand, Tristan, Neera, and the Marchesa Colombi, for example, denounced women's limited roles in the nineteenth century. However, Fallaci puts forth a contemporary vision of family and motherhood. Like Cardinal, Ernaux, and Dacia Maraini, Fallaci celebrates her sexuality and personal preferences in her life writing. Her protagonist exercises choice, expresses anger, and condemns injustice in a new voice—that of the modern, liberated woman. She does not need to ask for freedom; she demands it.

Finally, the mother–daughter relationship so central to Cardinal and Ernaux's contemporary autobiographies was equally significant to life stories over a century ago (illustrated by Sand's *Histoire de ma vie*) or several decades ago (exemplified in Colette's *Sido*). However, "leaving the mother" in postmodern texts occurs within a specific historical context and consciousness, and this awareness sheds new light on the daughter's liberation. For example, contemporary research on the impact of the preoedipal phase of parent–child bonding informs our appreciation of how girls mature and how their sense of identification with the mother informs their adult lives. In addition, today's fertility choices, including surrogate motherhood, are engendering new types of maternal–filial relationships. As such, the mother–daughter split in today's narratives is not just a repetition of a prior literary scene but a new act charged with its own significance.

Although the journey toward selfhood may involve several forms of displacement, many contemporary female authors *choose* to focus on "leaving the mother" because of its vital significance in understanding womanhood. The enormous interest in the mother–daughter relationship in the postmodern period and the outpouring of texts on the subject reveal an endeavor on the part of women writers to explore their origins from their own perspective. In their desire to understand the maternal, women writers position themselves within a continuity. This is highlighted in Simone de Beauvoir's moving tribute to her mother, *Une mort très douce*. Beauvoir writes of her sister's reaction to their mother's death: "'La seule chose qui me console . . . c'est que moi aussi je passerai par là. Sans ça, ça serait trop injuste!'" (143) ("'The only thing which consoles me . . . is that I, too, will go through it. Without that, it would be too unjust!'"). One hears echoes of the mother–daughter interconnection portrayed in Annie Ernaux's postmodern auto/biographies.

As we see in Ernaux's maternal–filial stories *Une femme* and *"Je ne suis pas sortie de ma nuit,"* the journey toward selfhood may be an ongoing one that unfolds through the creation of multiple personal narratives. In fact, women writers continually challenge autobiographical conventions, experiment with language, and create new forms. They practice novel representations of the self, including "collective" autobiographies, hybrid texts, and multivoiced narratives. In this way, women participate in redefining life writing. The momentum that stirs today's abundant production of innovative autobiographies demonstrates that existing expressions of selfhood are but early chapters in an unfinished volume.

Works Cited

Abel, Elizabeth, Marianne Hirsch, and Elizabeth Langland, eds. *The Voyage In: Fictions of Female Development*. Hanover, NH: UP of New England, 1983.
Albistur, Maïté, and Daniel Armogathe. *Histoire du féminisme français: Du moyen âge à nos jours*. Paris: des femmes, 1977.
Aleramo, Sibilla. *Un amore insolito: Diario 1940–1944*. Ed. Alba Morino. Milan: Feltrinelli, 1979.
———. *Una donna*. 1906. Milan: Feltrinelli, 1985.
———. *Il passaggio*. 1919. Ed. Bruna Conti. Milan: Serra e Riva, 1985.
———. *A Woman*. Trans. Rosalind Delmar. Berkeley: U of California P, 1980.
Amoia, Alba. *Twentieth-Century Italian Women Writers: The Feminine Experience* Carbondale: Southern Illinois UP, 1996.
Anderson, Linda. "At the Threshold of the Self: Women and Autobiography." *Women's Writing: A Challenge to Theory*. Ed. Moira Monteith. London: Harvester, 1986. 54–71.
Angelini, Franca. "Un nome e una donna." Buttafuoco and Zancan 64–72.
Angelone, Matilde. *In difesa della donna: La condizione femminile in 'Una Donna' di Sibilla Aleramo. Fortuna del romanzo nel mondo anglosussone*. Naples: Conte, 1990.
Aricò, Santo L. *Oriana Fallaci: The Woman and the Myth*. Carbondale: Southern Illinois UP, 1998.
Atwood, Margaret. *Surfacing*. New York: Simon and Schuster, 1972.
Augustine, Saint. *Confessions*. Trans. Maria Boulding. New York: Vintage, 1998.
Avila, Saint Teresa of. *The Life of Saint Teresa of Jesus: The Autobiography of Saint Teresa of Avila*. Trans. and ed. E. Allison Peers. Garden City, NY: Image, 1960.
Bair, Deirdre. *Simone de Beauvoir: A Biography*. New York: Summit, 1990.
Balzac, Honoré de. *A Harlot High and Low*. Trans. Rayner Heppenstall. Harmondsworth: Penguin, 1970.
———. *Illusions perdues*. 1837–43. Paris: Gallimard ("folio" collection), 1972.
———. *Le lys dans la vallée*. Paris, 1835.

———. *Splendeurs et misères des courtisanes.* Paris, 1845–47.
Banti, Anna. *Artemisia.* 1947. Milan: Bompiani, 1994.
Barbiera, Raffaello. *La Principessa Belgiojoso: I suoi amici e nemici—il suo tempo.* Milan: Treves, 1902.
Barthes, Roland. *Roland Barthes par Roland Barthes.* Paris: Seuil, 1995.
Bassanese, Flora A. "*Una donna*: Autobiography as Exemplary Text." Testaferri 131–52.
Baudelaire, Charles. *Les fleurs du mal.* 1857. Ed. Claude Pichois. Paris: Gallimard 1972.
Beauvoir, Simone de. *Le deuxième sexe.* Paris: Gallimard, 1949.
———. *Une mort très douce.* Paris: Gallimard ("folio" collection), 1964.
Belgiojoso, Cristina Trivulzio di (Cristina di Belgiojoso). "Della presente condizione delle donne e del loro avvenire." *Nuova Antologia di scienze, lettere ed arti.* Vol. 1. no. 1. Florence, 1866. Rpt. in *Il 1848 a Milano e a Venezia.* Ed. Sandro Bortone. Milan: Feltrinelli, 1977. 169–85.
———. "Les deux femmes d'Ismaïl Bey." *Récits turcs. Revue des Deux Mondes* 1 and 15 July 1856. "Les deux femmes d'Ismaïl Bey." *Scènes de la vie turque.* Paris: Michel Lévy, 1858.
———. "Emina." *Récits turcs. Revue des Deux Mondes* 1 and 15 Feb. 1856. *Emina.* Paris, 1856. *Emina. Scènes de la vie turque.* Paris: Michel Lévy, 1858.
———. *Oriental Harems and Scenery.* Trans. from the French of Cristina Trivulzio di Belgiojoso. New York: Carleton, 1862.
———. "Un prince kurde." *Récits turcs. Revue des Deux Mondes* 15 Mar. and 1 Apr. 1856. "Un prince kurde." *Scènes de la vie turque.* Paris: Michel Lévy, 1858.
———. "Souvenirs dans l'exil." *Le National* 5 Sept. and 12 Oct. 1850: 1–39. *Souvenirs dans l'exil.* Paris, 1850.
———. *La vie intime et la vie nomade en Orient. Revue des Deux Mondes* 1855. Rpt. as *Asie mineure et Syrie, souvenirs de voyages.* Paris: Michel Lévy, 1858.
Benstock, Shari, ed. *The Private Self: Theory and Practice of Women's Autobiographical Writings.* Chapel Hill: U of North Carolina P, 1988.
Bernheimer, Charles. *Figures of Ill Repute: Representing Prostitution in Nineteenth-Century France.* Cambridge: Harvard UP, 1989.
———. "Prostitution in the Novel." Hollier 780–85.
Blelloch, Paola. *Quel mondo dei guanti e delle stoffe . . . : Profili di scrittrici italiane del '900.* Verona: Essedue, 1987.
Bloom, Lynn Z. "Promises Fulfilled. Positive Images of Women in Twentieth-Century Autobiography." *Feminist Criticism: Essays on Theory, Poetry and Prose.* Ed. Cheryl L. Brown and Karen Olsen. Metuchen, NJ: Scarecrow, 1978.
Boileau, Nicolas. *L'art poétique.* 1674. *Oeuvres complètes.* Ed. Françoise Escal. Paris: Gallimard, 1966. 155–85.
Bonal, Denise. *Passions et prairie; Légère en août.* Paris: EDILIG, Théâtrales, 1988.
Borghi, Liana, Nicoletta Livi Bacci, and Uta Treder, eds. *Viaggio e scrittura: Le straniere nell'Italia dell'ottocento.* Florence: Librerie delle donne, 1993.
Boulenger, Marcel. *Souvenirs du marquis de Floranges.* Paris: Ollendorff, 1906.
Bowman, Frank Paul. "Suffering, Madness, and Literary Creation in Seventeenth-Century Spiritual Autobiography." *French Forum* 1.1 (1976): 24–48.
Brée, Germaine. Foreword. Brodzki and Schenck ix–xii.
Bretonne, Restif de la. *Monsieur Nicolas.* Ed. Pierre Testud. 2 vols. Paris: Gallimard, 1989.
Brodzki, Bella, and Celeste Schenck, eds. *Life/Lines: Theorizing Women's Autobiography.* Ithaca, NY: Cornell UP, 1988.

Brombert, Beth Archer. *Cristina, Portraits of a Princess*. New York: Knopf, 1977.
Brontë, Charlotte. *Jane Eyre*. 1847. Ed. Q. D. Leavis. Harmondsworth: Penguin Books, 1985.
Bucci, Celia. "Historical Reference in a 'Lightly Fictionalized Memoir': Sibilla Aleramo's *A Woman*." *Romance Language Annual* 2 (1990): 200–204.
Buckley, Jerome Hamilton. *Season of Youth: The Bildungsroman from Dickens to Golding*. Cambridge: Harvard UP, 1974.
Burton, Richard F., trans. *Tales from the Arabian Nights*. Ed. David Shumaker. New York: Avenel, 1978.
Butler, Judith. *Bodies That Matter*. New York: Routledge, 1993.
Buttafuoco, Annarita. "Vite esemplari. Donne nuove di primo Novecento." Buttafuoco and Zancan 139–63.
Buttafuoco, Annarita, and Marina Zancan, eds. *Svelamento: Sibilla Aleramo: Una biografia intellettuale*. Milan: Feltrinelli, 1988.
Camus, Albert. *L'étranger*. Paris: Gallimard, 1942.
Cardinal, Marie. *Amour . . . amours. . . .* Paris: Grasset, 1998.
———. *Autrement dit*. Paris: Grasset (Livre de poche), 1977.
———. *La clé sur la porte*. Paris: Grasset, 1972.
———. *Comme si de rien n'était*. Paris: Grasset, 1990.
———. *Les mots pour le dire*. Paris: Grasset, 1975.
———. *Le passé empiété*. Paris: Grasset, 1983.
———. Personal interview. 30 Apr. 1994.
———. *La souricière*. Paris: Julliard, 1965.
———. *The Words to Say It: An Autobiographical Novel by Marie Cardinal*. Trans. Pat Goodheart. Cambridge, MA: VanVactor and Goodheart, 1983.
Cellini, Benvenuto. *La vita. Opere*. Ed. Bruno Maier. Milan: Rizzoli, 1968. 43–618.
Chabrillan, Céleste de (Céleste Mogador). *Pierre Pascal*. Paris: Michel Lévy, 1885.
———. *La sapho*. Paris: Michel Lévy, 1858.
———. *Les voleurs d'or*. Paris: Michel Lévy, 1857.
Chabrillan, Céleste Vénard de, comtesse (Céleste Mogador). *The French Consul's Wife: Memoirs of Céleste de Chabrillan in Gold-Rush Australia*. Trans. Patricia Clancy and Jeanne Allen. Carlton, Vic.: Melbourne UP, 1998.
Chabrillan, Comtesse Lionel de (Céleste Mogador). *Un deuil au bout du monde: Suite des Mémoires de Céleste Mogador*. Paris: Librairie Nouvelle, 1877.
Charles-Roux, Edmonde, et al. *Les femmes et le travail du moyen âge à nos jours*. Paris: La courtille, 1975.
Chodorow, Nancy. *The Reproduction of Mothering: Psychoanalysis and the Sociology of Gender*. Berkeley: U of California P, 1978.
Cialente, Fausta. *Le quattro ragazze Wieselberger*. Milan: Mondadori, 1976.
Cixous, Hélène. "Le rire de la méduse." *L'Arc* 61 (1975): 39–54.
Clancy, Patricia, and Jeanne Allen. Introduction. *The French Consul's Wife: Memoirs of Céleste de Chabrillan in Gold-Rush Australia*. By Comtesse Céleste Vénard de Chabrillan. Carlton, Vic.: Melbourne UP, 1998. 1–13.
Clément, Catherine, and Hélène Cixous. *La jeune née*. Paris: Union générale, 1975.
Clermont-Tonnerre, François de. Introduction. *Mémoires de Céleste Mogador*. By Céleste Mogador. Paris: Amis de l'histoire, 1968. 7–15.
Colet, Louise. *Lui: Roman contemporain*. Paris: Calmann Lévy, 1880.
———. *Lui: A View of Him*. Trans. Marilyn Gaddis Rose. Athens: U of Georgia P, 1986.
Colette, Sidonie Gabrielle. *Sido*. Paris: Editions Krâ, 1929.

Colombi, Marchesa. *Un matrimonio in provincia.* 1885. Novara: Interlinea, 1993.
Costa-Zalessow, Natalia, ed. *Scrittrici italiane dal XIII al XX secolo: testi e critici.* Ravenna: Lungo, 1982.
Crémieux, Benjamin. *Une conspiratrice en 1830, ou le souper sans la Belgiojoso.* Paris: Pierre Lafitte, 1928.
Curtiss, Mina. *Bizet and His World.* New York: Knopf, 1958.
Deledda, Grazia. *Cosima.* 1937. Trans. Martha King. New York: Italica, 1988.
Delorme, Marie-Laure. "Annie Ernaux: Sans surprise." *Magazine littéraire* Feb. 1997: 73.
Delphy, Christine. "The Invention of French Feminism: An Essential Move." *Yale French Studies* 87 (1995): 190–221.
Derrida, Jacques. *Circonfession. Jacques Derrida.* Paris: Seuil, 1991.
Dickens, Charles. *Great Expectations.* Ed. Margaret Cardwell. Oxford: Clarendon P, 1993.
Drake, Richard. Introduction. *A Woman.* By Sibilla Aleramo. Berkeley: U of California P, 1980. v–xxxvi.
Dumas *fils*, Alexandre. *La dame aux camélias.* 1848. Paris: Garnier-Flammarion, 1981.
Dumas the Younger, Alexandre. *The Lady of the Camillias.* Trans. Edmund Goose. Bath, Eng.: Chivers P, 1983.
Durham, Carolyn. *The Contexture of Feminism: Marie Cardinal and Multicultural Literacy.* Urbana, U of Illinois P, 1992.
Egan, Susanna. *Patterns of Experience in Autobiography.* Chapel Hill: U of North Carolina P, 1984.
Eliot, George. *Middlemarch.* Ed. David Carroll. Oxford: Clarendon P, 1986.
Elliot, Patricia. "In the Eye of Abjection: Marie Cardinal's *The Words to Say It*." *Mosaic: A Journal for the Interdisciplinary Study of Literature* 20.4 (1987): 71–81.
Ernaux, Annie. *Les armoires vides.* Paris: Gallimard, 1974.
———. *Cleaned Out.* Trans. Carol Sanders. Normal, IL: Dalkey Archive, 1990.
———. *Une femme.* Paris: Gallimard, 1987.
———. *La honte.* Paris: Gallimard, 1997.
———. *"Je ne suis pas sortie de ma nuit."* Paris: Gallimard, 1997.
———. *A Man's Place.* Trans. Tanya Leslie. New York: Four Walls Eight Windows, 1992.
———. *Passion simple.* Paris: Gallimard, 1991.
———. *La place.* Paris: Gallimard, 1983.
———. "Vers un *je* transpersonnel." *Autofictions et Cie.* Ed. Serge Doubrovsky, Jacques Lecarme, and Philippe Lejeune. Paris: U of Paris X, 1993. 219–21.
———. *A Woman's Story.* Trans. Tanya Leslie. New York: Four Walls Eight Windows, 1991.
Faà, Caterina Camilla. "Storia di donna Camilla Faà di Bruno Gonzaga." *Rivista di Storia, Arte, Archeologia della provincia di Alessandria* 10.4 (1895): 90–99.
Fallaci, Oriana. *Letter to a Child Never Born.* Trans. John Shepley. New York: Simon and Schuster, 1976.
———. *Lettera a un bambino mai nato.* Milan: Rizzoli, 1975.
———. *Il sesso inutile.* Milan: Rizzoli, 1961.
———. *Un uomo: Romanzo.* Milan: Rizzoli, 1979.
Fau, Christine. "Le problème du langage chez Annie Ernaux." *The French Review* 68.3 (1995): 501–12.
Fauchery, Antoine. "Lettres d'un mineur en Australie." *Le Moniteur* 1858.

Felski, Rita. "The Novel of Self-Discovery: A Necessary Fiction?" *Southern Review* 19 (1986): 131–48.
Ferguson, Mary Anne. "The Female Novel of Development and the Myth of Psyche." Abel, Hirsch, and Langland 228–43.
Ferrero, Guglielmo. *L'europa giovane*. Milan: Treves, 1898.
Finucci, Valeria. "Re-Membering the 'I': Faà Gonzaga's *Storia* (1622)." *Italian Quarterly* 28.107 (1987): 21–32.
Flaubert, Gustave. *L'éducation sentimentale*. 1869. Ed. Edouard Maynial. Paris: Garnier, 1964.
———. *Madame Bovary*. 1857. Paris: Garnier, 1971.
French, Marilyn. *The Women's Room*. New York: Ballantine, 1993.
Freud, Sigmund. "A Special Type of Choice of Object Made by Men." *On Creativity and the Unconscious*. Trans. I. F. Grant Duff. New York: Harper, 1958.
Friedman, Susan Stanford. "Women's Autobiographical Selves: Theory and Practice." Benstock 34–62.
Frye, Joanne S. *Living Stories, Telling Lives: Women and the Novel in Contemporary Experience*. Ann Arbor: U of Michigan P, 1986.
Fuderer, Laura Sue. *The Female Bildungsroman in English: An Annotated Bibliography of Criticism*. New York: MLA, 1990.
Garcin, Jérôme. "La haine du style." *Le nouvel observateur* 16–22 Jan. 1997: 75.
Garner, Shirley Nelson, Claire Kahane, and Madelon Sprengnether, eds. *The (M)other Tongue: Essays in Feminist Psychoanalytic Interpretation*. Ithaca, NY: Cornell UP, 1985.
Gattey, Charles Neilson. *A Bird of Curious Plumage: Princess Cristina di Belgiojoso*. London: Constable, 1971.
Gilbert, Sandra M., and Susan Gubar. *The Madwoman in the Attic: The Woman Writer and the Nineteenth-Century Literary Imagination*. New Haven, CT: Yale UP, 1979.
Girardin, Madame Emile de, et al. *La croix de Berny*. Paris: Librairie nouvelle, 1871.
Glasgow, Janis, ed. *George Sand: Collected Essays*. Troy, NY: Whitston, 1985.
Glidden Parker, Marcia. "Céleste de Chabrillan, Nineteenth-Century French Theatre: Woman and Character." Diss. U of Wisconsin-Madison, 1993.
Goethe, Johann Wolfgang von. *Wilhelm Meister's Apprenticeship*. 1795–1796. Trans. H. M. Waidson. New York: Riverrun, 1978–79.
Goldsmith, Elizabeth C. "Giving Weight to Words: Madame de Sévigné's Letters to Her Daughter." Stanton 96–103.
Gregory, Heather, trans. *Selected Letters of Alessandra Strozzi*. By Alessandra Macinghi Strozzi. Berkeley: U of California P, 1997.
Guyon, Jeanne Marie Bouvier de La Mothe. *La vie de Madame Guyon écrite par elle-même*. 1720. Paris: Dervy-Livres, 1983.
Haldane, Charlotte. *Daughter of Paris: The Life Story of Céleste Mogador Comtesse Lionel de Moreton de Chabrillan*. London: Hutchinson, 1961.
Hall, Colette. "*L'écriture féminine* and the Search for the Mother in the Works of Violette Leduc and Marie Cardinal." *Women in French Literature*. Ed. Michel Guggenheim. Saratoga, CA: Anma, 1988. 231–38.
———. *Marie Cardinal*. Atlanta: Rodopi, 1994.
———. "'*She* Is Me More than *I*': Writing and the Search for Identity in the Works of Marie Cardinal." *Redefining Autobiography in Twentieth-Century Women's Fiction: An Essay Collection*. Ed. Janice Morgan and Colette T. Hall. New York: Garland, 1991. 57–71.

Hamalian, Leo. Introduction. *Ladies on the Loose: Women Travellers of the 18th and 19th Centuries.* Ed. Leo Hamalian. New York: Dodd, Mead, 1981. ix–xii.

Hastier, Louis. *Piquantes aventures de grandes dames.* Paris: Arthème Fayard, 1959.

Havercroft, Barbara. "Auto/biographie et agentivité au féminin dans *'Je ne suis pas sortie de ma nuit'* d'Annie Ernaux." *Femmes de lettres et le français hors frontière.* Ed. Lucie Lequin and Catherine Mavrikakis. Montreal: L'Harmattan (forthcoming).

Heilbrun, Carolyn G. *Writing a Woman's Life.* New York: Ballantine, 1988.

Hirsch, Marianne. "Mothers and Daughters: A Review Essay." *Signs: Journal of Women in Culture and Society* 7.1 (1981): 200–222.

———. *The Mother/Daughter Plot: Narrative, Psychoanalysis, Feminism.* Bloomington: Indiana UP, 1989.

———. "The Novel of Formation as Genre: Between Great Expectations and Lost Illusions." *Genre* 12 (1979): 293–311.

———. "Spiritual *Bildung*: The Beautiful Soul as Paradigm." Abel, Hirsch, and Langland 23–48.

Hobbes, Thomas. *The Life of Mr. Thomas Hobbes of Malmesbury; and, Thomas Hobbes II Malmesburiensis Vita.* Exeter, Eng.: The Rota, 1979.

Hollier, Denis, ed. *A New History of French Literature.* Cambridge: Harvard UP, 1989.

Holmes, Diana. *French Women's Writing: 1848–1994.* London: Athlone P, 1996.

Houssaye, Arsène. *Les Confessions, souvenirs d'un demi-sièle.* 6 vols. Geneva, Slatkine, 1971.

Hugo, Victor. *Marion de Lorme, Le roi s'amuse, Lucrèce Borgia.* Paris: Ollendorff, 1908.

Hutcheon, Linda. "Feminism and Postmodernism." Testaferri 25–37.

Hyvrard, Jeanne. *Mère la mort.* Paris: Minuit, 1976.

———. *Les prunes de Cythère.* Paris: Minuit, 1975.

Irigaray, Luce. *Ce sexe qui n'en est pas un.* Paris: Minuit, 1977.

———. *Et l'une ne bouge pas sans l'autre.* Paris: Minuit, 1979.

———. *Speculum of the Other Woman.* Trans. Gillian C. Gill. Ithaca, NY: Cornell UP, 1985.

Jelinek, Estelle C. *The Tradition of Women's Autobiography: From Antiquity to the Present.* Boston: Twayne, 1986.

Johnson, Edward Gilpin. Introduction. *The Private Memoirs of Madame Roland.* By Madame Roland. New York: AMS, 1976.

Jost, François. "La tradition du *Bildungsroman*." *Comparative Literature* 21.2 (1969): 97–115.

Kamuf, Peggy, "Replacing Feminist Criticism." *Diacritics* 12 (1982): 42–47.

Kempe, Margery. *The Book of Margery Kempe.* Ed. Sanford B. Meech. London: Humphrey Milford, 1940.

Knibiehler, Yvonne. "Du nouveau sur la Princesse Belgiojoso." *Rassegna storica del Risorgimento* 58 (1971): 199–213.

Kristeva, Julia. "Woman's Time." Trans. Alice Jardine and Harry Blake. *Feminisms: An Anthology of Literary Theory and Criticism.* Ed. Robyn R. Warhol and Diane Price Herndl. New Brunswick, NJ: Rutgers UP, 1997. 860–77.

Lafayette, Marie-Madeleine, Comtesse de. *La princesse de Clèves.* 1678. Paris: Garnier-Flammarion, 1966.

Lazzaro-Weis, Carol. "The Female *Bildungsroman*: Calling It into Question." *NWSA Journal* 2.1 (1990): 16–34.

———. *From Margins to Mainstream: Feminism and Fictional Modes in Italian*

Women's Writing, 1968–1990. Philadelphia: U of Pennsylvania P, 1993.

Leclerc, Annie. Postscript. *Autrement dit.* By Marie Cardinal. Paris: Grasset (Livre de poche), 1977. 209–22.

Le Clézio, Marguerite. "Mother and Motherland: The Daughter's Quest for Origins." *Stanford French Review* 5.3 (1981): 381–89.

Leduc, Violette. *La bâtarde.* Paris: Gallimard, 1964.

Lejeune, Philippe. *L'autobiographie en France.* Paris: Armand Colin, 1971.

———. *Le pacte autobiographique.* Paris: Seuil, 1975.

Lionnet, Françoise. *Autobiographical Voices: Race, Gender, Self-Portraiture.* Ithaca, NY: Cornell UP, 1989.

Lipton, Eunice. *Alias Olympia: A Woman's Search for Manet's Notorious Model and Her Own Desire.* New York: Charles Scribner's Sons, 1992.

Macciocchi, Maria Antonietta. Preface. *Una Donna.* By Sibilla Aleramo. Milan: Feltrinelli, 1985. 5–12.

Mall, Laurence. "'Moins seule et factice': La part autobiographique dans *Une Femme* d'Annie Ernaux." *The French Review* 69.1 (1995): 45–54.

Manzoni, Alessandro. *I promessi sposi.* Ed. Lanfranco Caretti. Torino: Einaudi, 1971.

Maraini, Dacia. *Donna in guerra.* Torino: Einaudi, 1975.

Marotti, Maria. "Filial Discourses: Feminism and Femininity in Italian Women's Autobiography." *Feminine Feminists: Cultural Practices in Italy.* Ed. Giovanna Miceli Jeffries. Minneapolis: U of Minnesota P, 1994. 65–86.

Marrone, Claire. "Autobiography." Sartori 28–31.

———. "Cristina Trivulzio di Belgiojoso's Western Feminism: The Poetics of a Nineteenth-Century Nomad." *Italian Quarterly* 34.133–34 (1997): 21–32.

———. "Un Entretien avec Marie Cardinal." *Women in French Studies* 4 (1996): 119–31.

———. "Male and Female *Bildung*: The *Mémoires de Céleste Mogador*." *Nineteenth-Century French Studies* 25.3–4 (1997): 335–47.

———. "Women Writing Auto/biography: Anna Banti's *Artemisia* and Eunice Lipton's *Alias Olympia*." *Life Writing/Writing Lives.* Ed. Bette H. Kirschstein. Melbourne, FL: Krieger P (forthcoming).

Martin, Elaine. "Mothers, Madness, and the Middle Class in *The Bell Jar* and *Les Mots pour le dire*." *The French-American Review* 5.1 (1981): 24–47.

———. "Theoretical Soundings: The Female Archetypal Quest in Contemporary French and German Women's Fiction." *Perspectives on Contemporary Literature* 8 (1982): 48–57.

Mason, Mary G., and Carol Hurd Green, eds. *Journeys: Autobiographical Writings by Women.* Boston: G. K. Hall, 1979.

Matignon, Renaud. "Annie Ernaux: L'arrière-cuisine de l'enfance." *Le Figaro* 16 Jan. 1997: 33.

May, Gita. "Madame Roland devant la génération romantique." *The French Review* 36 (1963): 459–68.

Mazingarbe, Danièle. "Récits: La Honte, Je ne suis pas sortie de ma nuit d'Annie Ernaux." *Madame Figaro* Jan. 1997.

McCallum Schwartz, Lucy. "George Sand et le *roman intime*, Tradition and Innovation in 'Women's Literature.'" Glasgow 220–26.

McClary, Susan. *Georges Bizet "Carmen."* Cambridge, Eng.: Cambridge UP, 1992.

Michaud, Stéphane. *Muse et Madone: Visages de la femme de la Révolution française aux apparitions de Lourdes.* Paris: Seuil, 1985.

Milanese, Flavia, trans. *Emina*. By Cristina di Belgiojoso. Ed. Mirella Scriboni. Ferrara: Luciana Tufani, 1997.
Miller, Christopher L. "Orientalism, Colonialism." Hollier 698–705.
Miller, Nancy K. *Getting Personal: Feminist Occasions and Other Autobiographical Acts*. New York: Routledge, 1991.
———. "Representing Others: Gender and the Subject of Autobiography." *Differences* 6.1 (1994): 1–27.
———. "The Text's Heroine: A Feminist Critic and Her Fictions." *Diacritics* 12 (1982): 48–53. Rpt. in *Subject to Change: Reading Feminist Writing*. New York: Columbia UP, 1988. 67–76.
———. "Women's Autobiography in France: For a Dialectics of Identification." *Women and Language in Literature and Society*. Ed. Sally McConnell-Ginet, Ruth Borker, and Nelly Furman. New York: Praeger P, 1980. 258–73. Rpt. as "Writing Fictions: Women's Autobiography in France." *Subject to Change: Reading Feminist Writing*. New York: Columbia UP, 1988. 47–64.
Mills, Sara. *Discourses of Difference: An Analysis of Women's Travel Writing and Colonialism*. New York: Routledge, 1991.
Milner, Max, and Claude Pichois, eds. *Littérature française: De Chateaubriand à Baudelaire 1820–1869*. Vol. 7. Paris: Arthaud, 1985. 9 vols.
Minh-ha, Trinh T. "L'Innécriture: Féminisme et littérature." *French Forum* 8.1 (1983): 45–63.
Mogador, Céleste (Comtesse de Chabrillan). *Adieux au monde: Mémoires de Céleste Mogador*. 1st ed. 5 vols. Paris, 1854. *Mémoires de Céleste Mogador*. 2nd ed. 4 vols. Paris, 1858. *Mémoires de Céleste Mogador*. 2 vols. Paris, 1876. *Mémoires de Céleste Mogador*. Paris: Amis de l'histoire, 1968.
Moi, Toril. *Sexual/Textual Politics: Feminist Literary Theory*. London: Methuen, 1985.
Monicat, Bénédicte. "Ecritures du voyage et féminismes: Olympe Audouard ou le féminin en question." *The French Review* 69.1 (1995): 24–36.
———. *Itinéraires de l'écriture au féminin: Voyageuses du 19e siècle*. Atlanta: Rodopi, 1996.
———. "Problématique de la préface dans les récits de voyages au féminin du 19e siècle." *Nineteenth-Century French Studies* 23.1–2 (1994–95): 59–71.
Morandini, Giuliana. *La voce che è in lei. Antologia della narrativa femminile italiana tra '800 e '900*. Milan: Bompiani, 1980.
Moravia, Alberto. *La ciociara*. Milan: Bompiani, 1957.
Moretti, Franco. *Il romanzo di formazione*. Milan: Garzanti, 1986.
Morrison, Toni. *Playing in the Dark: Whiteness and the Literary Imagination*. New York: Vintage, 1993.
Moser, Françoise. *Vie et aventures de Céleste Mogador*. Paris: Albin Michel, 1935.
Mueller, Janel M. "Autobiography of a New 'Creatur': Female Spirituality, Selfhood, and Authorship in 'The Book of Margery Kempe.'" Stanton 57–69.
Musset, Alfred de. *Louison*. Paris: Charpentier, 1849.
———. *Poésies complètes*. Ed. Maurice Allem. Paris: Gallimard, 1957.
Neera (Anna [Zuccari] Radius). "A Luigi Capuana." *Il castigo*. By Neera. Torino: L. Roux, 1891. 7–60.
Ollivier, Daniel, ed. *Correspondance de Liszt et de Madame d'Agoult*. 2 vols. Paris: Grasset, 1933.
Olney, James, ed. *Autobiography: Essays Theoretical and Critical*. Princeton: Princeton UP, 1980.

Parati, Graziella. *Public History, Private Stories: Italian Women's Autobiography.* Minneapolis: U of Minnesota P, 1996.
Parent-Duchâtelet, Alexandre. *De la prostitution dans la ville de Paris.* 1836. *La prostitution à Paris.* Fort, 1900. Abridged as *La prostitution à Paris au XIXe siècle.* Ed. Alain Corbin. Paris: Seuil, 1981.
Passerini, Luisa. *Autobiography of a Generation: Italy 1968.* Trans. Lisa Erdberg. Hanover, NH: U of New England P, 1996.
———. *Autoritratto di gruppo.* Florence: Giunti, 1988.
Petacco, Arrigo. *La Principessa del Nord. La misteriosa vita della dama del Risorgimento: Cristina di Belgioioso.* Milan: Mondadori, 1993.
Pickering-Iazzi, Robin. Afterword. *Unspeakable Women: Selected Short Stories Written by Italian Women during Fascism.* Trans. Robin Pickering-Iazzi. New York: Feminist P, 1993. 101-14.
———. "Designing Mothers: Images of Motherhood in Novels by Aleramo, Morante, Maraini, and Fallaci." *Annali d'italianistica* 7 (1989): 325-40.
———. Preface. *Unspeakable Women: Selected Short Stories Written by Italian Women during Fascism.* Trans. Robin Pickering-Iazzi. New York: Feminist P, 1993. xi-xiii.
Planté, Christine. *La petite soeur de Balzac: Essai sur la femme auteur.* Paris: Seuil, 1989.
Plath, Sylvia. *The Bell Jar.* New York: Harper and Row, 1971.
Pougy, Liane de. *Mes cahiers bleus.* Paris: Plon, 1977.
Powrie, Phil. "Reading for Pleasure: Marie Cardinal's *Les Mots pour le dire* and the Text as (Re)play of Oedipal Configurations." *Contemporary French Fiction by Women: Feminist Perspectives.* Ed. Margaret Atack and Phil Powrie. Manchester: Manchester UP, 1990. 163-76.
Pratt, Annis, et al. *Archetypal Patterns in Women's Fiction.* Bloomington: Indiana UP, 1981.
Ramsay, Raylene L. *The French New Autobiographies: Sarraute, Duras, and Robbe-Grillet.* Gainesville: UP of Florida, 1996.
Riccoboni, Madame. *Lettres de Mistress Fanni Butlerd.* 1757. Ed. Joan Hinde Stewart. Geneva: Droz, 1979.
Rich, Adrienne. *Of Woman Born: Motherhood as Experience and Institution.* 1976. London: Virago, 1977.
Rinci, Dominique, and Bernard Lecherbonnier, eds. *Littérature: Textes et documents,* 19e. Paris: Nathan, 1986.
Robeson Burr, Anna. *The Autobiography: A Critical and Comparative Study.* Boston: Houghton Mifflin, 1909.
Rochefort, Christiane. *Cats Don't Care for Money.* Trans. Helen Eustis. Garden City, NY: Doubleday, 1965.
———. *Les stances à Sophie.* Paris: Grasset, 1963.
Rogers, Juliette M. "Liane de Pougy." Sartori 430-31.
Roland, Madame. *Mémoires de Madame Roland.* Paris: Plon, 1864.
Rosa, Annette. *Citoyennes: Les femmes et la Révolution française.* Paris: Messidor, 1988.
Rosowski, Susan J. "The Novel of Awakening." Abel, Hirsch, and Langland 49-68.
Rousseau, Jean-Jacques. *Les Confessions.* 1782-89. Paris: Gallimard ("folio classique" collection), 1973.
Rousset, Jean. *Narcisse romancier.* Paris: José Corti, 1986.
Said, Edward W. *Orientalism.* New York: Random House, 1979.
Sand, George. *Histoire de ma vie.* 1854-55. *Oeuvres autobiographiques.* Ed. Georges

Lubin. 2 vols. Paris: Gallimard, 1970. I: 1–1453; II: 1–465.

———. *Indiana*. 1832. Paris: Gallimard ("folio" collection), 1984.

———. *Lélia*. 1833, 1839. Ed. Béatrice Didier. 2 vols. Meylan, France: Aurore, 1987.

———. *Lettres d'un voyageur. Oeuvres autobiographiques*. Ed. Georges Lubin. 2 vols. Paris: Gallimard, 1970. II: 633–943.

———. *La petite Fadette*. 1848. Paris: Garnier-Flammarion, 1967.

———. *Story of My Life: The Autobiography of George Sand*. A Group Translation. Ed. Thelma Jurgrau. Albany: State U of New York P, 1991.

Sanders, Carol. Afterword. *Cleaned Out*. By Annie Ernaux. Normal, IL: Dalkey Archive, 1990. 124–27.

———. "Stylistic Aspects of Women's Writing: The Case of Annie Ernaux." *French Cultural Studies* 4 (1993): 15–29.

Sarraute, Nathalie. *Enfance*. Paris: Gallimard ("folio" collection), 1983.

Sartori, Eva Martin, ed. *The Feminist Encyclopedia of French Literature*. Westport, CT: Greenwood P, 1999.

Sartre, Jean-Paul. *Les mots*. Paris: Gallimard ("folio" collection), 1964.

Schor, Naomi. "Idealism." Hollier 769–74.

Scriboni, Mirella. Preface. *Emina*. By Cristina di Belgiojoso. Trans. Flavia Milanese. Ed. Mirella Scriboni. Ferrara: Luciana Tufani, 1997. 9–29.

———. "Il viaggio al femminile nell'Ottocento: La principessa di Belgioioso, Amalia Nizzoli e Carla Serena." *Annali d'italianistica* 14 (1996): 304–25.

Severgnini, Luigi. Introduction. *Ricordi dell'esilio*. By Cristina Trivulzio di Belgiojoso. Trans. and ed. Luigi Severgnini. Cinisello Balsamo: Paoline, 1978. 5–20.

———, trans. *Ricordi dell'esilio*. By Cristina Trivulzio di Belgiojoso. Ed. Luigi Severgnini. Cinisello Balsamo: Paoline, 1978.

Sévigné, Madame de. *Correspondance*. Ed. Roger Duchêne. Paris: Gallimard, 1974–78.

Showalter, Elaine. *A Literature of Their Own: English Women Novelists from Brontë to Lessing*. Princeton: Princeton UP, 1977.

Siena, Caterina da. *The Dialogue*. Trans. Suzanne Noffke. New York: Paulist P, 1980.

Smith, Sidonie. *Subjectivity, Identity and the Body: Women's Autobiographical Practices in the Twentieth Century*. Bloomington: Indiana UP, 1993.

Smith, Sidonie, and Julia Watson, eds. *Women, Autobiography, Theory: A Reader*. Madison: U of Wisconsin P, 1998.

Spigelman, Art. *Maus: A Survivor's Tale*. New York: Pantheon, 1986.

Spinosa, Antonio. *Italiane: Il lato segreto del Risorgimento*. Milan: Mondadori, 1994.

Staël, Madame de. *Corinne ou l'Italie*. 1807. Ed. Simone Balayé. Paris: Gallimard ("folio" collection), 1985.

———. *Dix années d'exil*. Paris: Plon, 1904.

Stanton, Domna C., ed. *The Female Autograph: Theory and Practice of Autobiography from the Tenth to the Twentieth Century*. Chicago: U of Chicago P, 1987.

Stendhal. *Le rouge et le noir*. 1830. Paris: Garnier-Flammarion, 1964.

———. *Vie de Henry Brulard*. Ed. Béatrice Didier. Paris: Gallimard ("folio" collection), 1973.

Stern, Daniel (Marie d'Agoult). *Mes souvenirs*. 1877. Paris: Calmann Lévy, 1880.

Sterne, Laurence. *The Life and Opinions of Tristram Shandy, Gent*. London: G. Routledge, 1893.

Stewart, Grace B. "Mother, Daughter and the Birth of the Female Artist." *Women's Studies* 6 (1979): 127–45.

Suleiman, Susan Rubin. "Writing and Motherhood." Garner, Kahane, and Sprengnether

352–77.
Testaferri, Ada, ed. *Donna: Women in Italian Culture*. Toronto: Dovehouse, 1989.
Thébaud, Anne. "L'Urgence d'Écrire." *La quinzaine littéraire* 16 Feb. 1997: 13.
Tondeur, Claire-Lise. *Annie Ernaux ou l'exil intérieur*. Atlanta: Rodopi, 1996.
———. "Entretien avec Annie Ernaux." *The French Review* 69.1 (1995): 37–44.
———. "Relation mère/fille chez Annie Ernaux." *Romance Languages Annual* 7 (1995): 173–79.
Wittig, Monique. *Le corps lesbien*. Paris: Minuit, 1973.
Wood, Sharon. *Italian Women's Writing: 1860–1994*. London: Athlone P, 1995.
Woolf, Virginia. *A Room of One's Own*. 1929. London: Grafton, 1988.
Worley, Linda Kraus. "Through Others' Eyes: Narratives of German Women Travelling in Nineteenth-Century America." *Yearbook of German American Studies* 21 (1986): 39–50.
Yalom, Marilyn. *Maternity, Mortality, and the Literature of Madness*. University Park: Pennsylvania State UP, 1985.
Zola, Émile. 1880. *Nana*. Ed. Henri Mitterand. Paris: Gallimard ("folio classique" collection), 1977.
Zonana, Joyce. "The Sultan and the Slave: Feminist Orientalism and the Structures of *Jane Eyre*." *Signs: Journal of Women in Culture and Society* 18.3 (1993): 592–617.

Index

Abandonment, of child, 101–104
Abel, Elizabeth, 17, 20
Abortion, 4, 15, 107–117 passim, 122, 126, 132; debate, 18, 109, 116 n.7, 141 n.24, 153
Adams, Henry, 7
Adolescence, 2, 7, 9, 132; and abuse 61
Africa, 9, 86
Agoult, Marie d' (Daniel Stern), 12, 13, 32, 33, 39, 40, 43 n.18, 99, 102
Albustur, Maïté, 64, 76 n.11
Aleramo, Sibilla (Rina Pierangeli Faccio), 4, 7, 14, 15, 19, 22, 59 n.20, 91–105, 107–111, 115, 121, 122, 158, 159; Works: *donna, Una* (*A Woman*), 4, 7, 14, 19, 91–105, 107, 109, 116, 121, 158, 159; *passaggio, Il* (*The Passage*), 92
Algeria, 3, 122, 123, 130; as character 140 n.8; independence of, 133; as mother 131; opposition between France and, 130, 121; war in, 147
Alias Olympia (Lipton), 24 n.12, 154 n.2
Allegory, 92, 126
Allen, Jeanne, 87 nn.1, 2
Alzheimer's disease, 144
Amoia, Alba, 107, 116 n.1
Angelini, Franca, 92, 96, 99
Angelone, Matilde, 92

Anger, 4, 14, 15, 104, 114; previously repressed, 99, 159
Arabian Nights, 46
Argomathe, Daniel, 64, 76 n.11
Aricò, Santo L., 107, 108, 116 n.8, 117 nn.11, 17
art poétique, L' (*Art of Poetry, The*, Boileau), 137, 141 n.25
Artemisia (Banti), 6, 24 n.12, 105 n.4, 154 n.2
Atwood, Margaret, 20
Audouard, Olympe, 30, 58 n.5
Augustine, Saint, 7, 10, 15, 21
Australia, 3, 4, 62, 63, 69, 70, 72–74, 76 nn.15, 23, 77–87 passim, 87 n.1, 158
Authority: nineteenth-century values and, 45; relationship of heroine to, 125; textual, 3, 7, 14, 21
Autobiographical novel, 3, 11, 91, 101
Autobiography, 30, 38, 45, 59 n.18, 61, 62, 66, 67, 77, 96, 104, 122, 139, 144, 152, 157, 158, 160; "collective," 1, 108, 160; common elements with *bildungsroman*, 21–24, 97; definition of, 1, 24 n.1; desire to write, 99, 138–139; fundamental problems in, 123; fused with fiction, 92, 93, 108, 137–139, 147; fused with journalism, 107; mother's death in, 129, 140 n.20,

145; phases of life as opposed to complete, 108, 155 n.7; read as *bildungsroman*, 2–5, 16–20, 24 n.4, 157; spiritual, 10, 25 n.19; story of woman versus women, 116; subjectivity of or subject in, 115, 144; theoretical debates and trends, 1–9, 14, 15, 24 n.3; traditions in French and Italian, 1–9, 10–15, 25 n.18, 76 n.19, 148; unfinished, 144; writer as first reader of, 133

Auto/biography, 1, 107, 122, 143, 152, 154, 154 n.2, 158, 160

"Autocitation," 122, 139 n.2, 155 n.9

Autoritratto di gruppo (*Autobiography of a Generation*, Passerini), 116 n.4

Avila, Saint Teresa of, 10

Awakening. *See* Development

Bair, Deirdre, 117 n.16

Bal Mabille, 61, 75 n.2, 79

Balzac, Honoré de, 32, 33, 41, 53, 59 n.20, 63, 64, 77, 84, 105 n.4

Banti, Anna, 6, 24 n.12, 154 n.2, 159

Barthes, Roland, 7

Bassanese, Flora A., 59 n.3, 92, 97, 105 nn.8, 16

Baudelaire, Charles, 25 n.25, 64, 78

Beauvoir, Simone de, 14, 15, 114, 117 n.16, 145, 148, 160

Belgiojoso, Cristina Trivulzio di, 3, 9, 12, 13, 17, 20, 29–43, 45–59, 62, 63, 85, 92, 102, 107, 110, 111, 157, 159; Works: *Asie mineure et Syrie, souvenirs de voyages* (*Oriental Harems and Scenery*), 32, 42 n.12, 46–48, 51, 55, 58 n.6, 59 n.7; "Della presente condizione delle donne e del loro avenire" ("On the Present Condition of Women and Their Future"), 56, 57; *deux femmes d'Ismaïl Bey, Les* (*Two Wives of Ismaïl Bey, The*), 159; *Emina*, 3, 17, 20, 33, 45–59, 102, 157; "prince kurde, Un" ("Kurdish Prince, A"), 59 n.15; *Récits turcs* (*Turkish Narratives*), 32; *Scènes de la vie turque* (*Scenes from Turkish Life*), 58 n.1, 59 n.15; *Souvenirs dans l'exil* (*Memoirs from Exile*), 3, 29–43, 45, 47, 58, 157;

vie intime et la vie nomade en Orient, La (*see Asie mineure et Syrie*)

Belgiojoso, Emilio, 29, 48

Bell Jar, The (Plath), 125, 140 nn.10, 11

Bernheimer, Charles, 64, 65, 76 n.12, 77, 81

Bildung. *See* Development

Bildungsroman, 45, 49, 50, 61, 68, 94, 124, 138; common elements with autobiography, 21–24, 97; critical studies of nineteenth century, 16–18; critical studies of twentieth century, 18–20, 26 nn.29, 30; definition, 16, 17, 105 n.6; in French tradition, 63, 75 n.8; prototypical male 16–18, 20, 25–26 n.28, 63, 65; reading autobiography as, 2–5, 16–20, 157

Biography, 3, 5, 17, 23, 33, 35, 92, 144; creative, 6; French, 148; partial, 148; potential, 116; subjectivity of, 115

Birth-of-the-artist story. *See* Künstlerroman

Blelloch, Paola, 6

Blood, 140 n.14

Body: control over female, 86; discovery of, 126, 127, 129; female, 14, 25 n.27, 108, 114; female contact with, 140 n.14; as flesh, 103; of mother, 123

Boileau, Nicolas 137, 141 n.25

Bolognini, Pietro, 36

Bonal, Denise, 117 n.14

Book of Margery Kempe, The, 10

Borghi, Liana, 59 n.8

Boulenger, Marcel, 53

Bowman, Frank Paul, 25 n.19

Brée, Germaine, 10

Bretonne, Restif de la, 21

Brodzki, Bella, 7

Brombert, Beth Archer, 32–34, 42 n.5, 47, 48, 52, 53

Brontë, Charlotte, 21, 49, 51, 58 n.2

Brothel, 63, 65, 111

Bucci, Celia, 102

Buckley, Jerome Hamilton, 17, 21, 24 n.4, 105 n.6

Butler, Judith, 24 n.5

Buttafuoco, Annarita, 98, 105 n.10

Caird, Mona, 97

Index

Canada, 9
Canon, 3, 6, 10, 11, 15, 19, 24 n.11, 111
Camus, Albert, 148
Cardinal, Marie, 4, 6, 9, 15, 19, 20, 22, 93, 108, 109, 114, 115, 117 nn.13, 19, 121–141, 143–146, 149, 154 nn.4, 5, 158–160; Works: *Amour . . . amours . . .* (*Love . . . loves . . .*), 122, 139 n.3; *Autrement dit* (*In Other Words*), 123, 131, 132, 136, 137, 139 n.7, 140 n.20, 140–141 n.23, 154 n.5; *Cet été-là* (*That Summer*); *clé sur la porte, La* (*Key in the Door, The*), 122; *Comme si de rien n'était* (*As If It Were Nothing*), 133, 134, 141 n.27; *Médée d'Euripide, La* (*Euripides' Medea*), 141 n.27; *mots pour le dire, Les* (*Words to Say It, The*), 4, 19, 22, 93, 108, 109, 117 nn.13, 19, 121–141, 145, 154 n.4, 158; *passé empiété, Le* (*Encroached Upon Past, The*), 6, 24 n.13; *souricière, La* (*Trap, The*), 122, 137, 141 n.27
Career, 2, 92; combining family life and/or motherhood and, 4, 19, 91, 102, 108, 122, 158; desire for, 101; dichotomy between motherhood and, 93, 102, 109, 112; establishment of, 2; as obstacle, 113; sacrifice of, 116 n.8
Caribbean, islands of, 9
castigo, Il (*Punishment, The*, Neera), 12, 13
Catholicism, 123
Cavendish, Margaret, 7
Cellini, Benvenuto, 21
Cena, Giovanni, 92, 99
Chabrillan, Céleste de, 87 nn.6, 7, 8; Works: *Pierre Pascal*, 83; *sapho, La* (*Sapho*), 84; *voleurs d'or, Les* (*Gold Thieves*), 80, 81, 84, 85. *See also* Chabrillan, Comtesse de; Mogador, Céleste; Vénard, Céleste-Élisabeth
Chabrillan, Comte Lionel de, 61, 76 n.16, 77–87 passim
Chabrillan, Comtesse de, 24 n.10, 61, 68, 74, 77–87, 158; Works: *deuil au bout du monde, Un* (*Mourning at the Ends of the Earth*), 3, 4, 31, 63, 69, 73, 76 nn.16, 17, 77–87, 99, 158; *French Consul's Wife, The* (*see Un deuil au bout du monde*). *See also* Chabrillan, Céleste de; Mogador, Céleste; Vénard, Céleste-Élisabeth
Charles-Roux, Edmonde, 64
Charrière, Isabelle de, 11
Chateaubriand, François-René de, 21, 46, 58 n.4
Child, 8, 22, 26 n.28, 107–117 passim, 123, 160; abandoned, 22; address to, 108; custody, 1, 101, 104, 112, 159; attachment to parents, 68; defining oneself in relation to, 100; loss of, 108, 113; separation between mother and, 104, 159; unborn (*see* Fetus); writing as substitute, 99
Childbirth, 4, 92, 96, 104, 116, 137, 151; images of, 127, 132, 139, 140–141 n.23; risks, 100; technology, 102
Childhood, 2, 67, 94, 123, 144, 150; experiences, 8, 125, 130; milieu, 143; as paradise, 23; trauma in, 127, 129; underprivileged, 144
Chincholle, Charles, 83
Choice, reproductive, 102, 104, 107–117 passim, 159
Chodorow, Nancy, 8, 24 n.15, 122
Christianity, 10, 25 n.25, 55
Church: Catholic 25 n.25, 31, 123; challenging ideals of, 111; in decisions, intrusions of, 109
Cialente, Fausta, 116 n.4
Ciaq-Maq-Oglou, 47, 48
Circonfession. Jacques Derrida (Derrida), 8
Cixous, Hélène, 6, 15, 96, 122, 136
Clancy, Patricia, 87 nn.1, 2
Class, 2, 3, 5, 9, 11, 50, 56, 62, 86; boundaries or restrictions, 30, 128; equality, 98; rejection of values of, 131
Classism, 58, 85, 86, 97
Clermont-Tonnerre, François de, 73, 74, 75 n.2, 76 n.20
Clytemnestra, 6
Cocteau, Jean, 15
Colet, Louise, 33–35, 42 n.15, 43 n.16
Colette, Sidonie Gabrielle, 91, 96, 101, 160

Colonialism, 58 n.4, 123, 131
Colonizer, 45, 54, 159
Colombi, Marchesa, 13, 159
Coming-of-age, 45, 49, 50, 57
Commune, 62
Confession, 62, 68, 82, 92, 158; as genre or structural pattern, 2, 23, 71, 82, 99, 104
Confessions (Augustine), 21
Conversion, 18, 23, 24, 54, 80, 82, 86, 96
Corinne (Staël), 13, 20, 68
Cosima (Deledda), 101
Costa-Zalessow, Natalia, 10, 25 n.22
Courtesan. *See* Prostitute
Crémieux, Benjamin, 54
croix de Berny, La (*Cross of Berny, The*), 53
Curtiss, Mina, 75 nn.4, 6, 9

dame aux camélias, La (Dumas *fils*), 77
Damiani, Felice, 92
Daughter, 5, 10, 11, 15, 109, 123; daughter-artist, 102; ideal, 127; motherless, 67; quest for independence of, 17, 143–155 passim, 160; resentment toward mother, 93, 126, 128; role reversal with mother, 145, 146, 154 n.4; sense of mortality, 129, 145, 146; stifled growth, 121
Death, 2, 19, 59 n.18, 81, 115, 125; death-rebirth rituals, 96; emotional, 102; entrapment and, 102; fear of, 128; of fetus, 113; as insignificant, 116; loss of child versus, 102; of mother, 5, 102, 123, 129, 130, 140 n.20, 143–155 passim, 160; opinions on, 108; preparation for, 2, 143–155 passim, 160; spiritual, 103; tragic literary conclusions, 13, 17, 20, 23, 50, 78
Deconstruction, 6
Deledda, Grazia, 91, 101
Delorme, Marie-Laure, 155 n.13, 152
Delmar, Rosalind, 105 nn.1, 5, 12, 17
Delphy, Christine, 6, 24 n.15
Derrida, Jacques, 8
deuxième sexe, Le (*Second sex, The*, Beauvoir), 14
Development: of exceptional heroine, 61, 74; of fetus, 110, 111; of the imagination, 105 n.6; intellectual, 77, 92, 97; losses in process of, 94, 104, 115, 143; through love relationships, 67, 108; nineteenth-century models of, 49; as ongoing process, 154; parallel stories, 61, 75 n.8, 77; psychological growth or, 2–5, 16–20, 23, 24, 25–26 n.28, 29, 30, 37–40, 49–51, 57, 61, 63, 72, 73, 78, 109, 121, 124, 130, 138; through separation from oppressive structures, 157; through sexual liberation, 129; spiritual awakening or, 105 n.8; of Western versus Oriental girl, 49
Developmental Literature. *See* *Bildungsroman*
Dialogue, 9, 22, 68, 69, 108, 113. *See also* Monologue/Dialogue
Diary, 3, 5, 21, 31, 70, 79, 92, 93, 144, 151
Dickens, Charles, 21, 23, 49
Dieulafoy, Jane, 30, 79
Difference, 2, 6, 9, 110. *See also* Gender
Displacement, 58 n.2; away from oppressive structures, 1, 2, 154, 158–160; that parallels change, 38; within context of cultural or economic divisions, 98. *See also* Movement
Dix années d'exil (*Ten Years of Exile*, Staël), 11
Divorce, 18, 56, 100, 121, 125, 159
Donna in guerra (*Women at War*, Maraini), 109
Doucet, Camille, 62, 71
Drake, Richard, 92, 97, 98, 105 n.7
Dumas, Alexandre, 62, 71, 82, 85
Dumas *fils*, Alexandre, 62, 77
Duras, Madame de, 11
Duras, Marguerite, 15, 122, 144, 149
Durham, Carolyn, 127, 137–138, 139 n.2, 155 n.9

Écriture féminine (Female language or writing), 6, 15, 91, 136
Education, women's advances in, 98
Egan, Susanna, 23
Eliot, George, 18
Elliot, Patricia, 124, 127, 128, 130
Enfance (*Childhood*, Sarraute), 22
Ernaux, Annie, 4, 5, 7, 9, 15, 19, 20, 22,

93, 109, 114, 115, 117 n.19, 122, 140 n.20, 143–155, 158–160; Works: *armoires vides, Les* (*Cleaned Out*), 7, 19, 93, 143, 153; *femme, Une* (*Woman's Story, A*), 4, 5, 117 n.19, 140 n.20, 143–155, 158, 160; *honte, La* (*Shame*), 19, 143, 153; *"Je ne suis pas sortie de ma nuit"* (*"I Have Not Escaped My Misery"*), 4, 5, 117 n.19, 143–155, 158, 160; *Passion simple* (*Simple Passion*), 15, 144; *place, La* (*A Man's Place*), 143–144, 148
Essentialism, 6, 8, 24 n.15
Este, Isabella d', 10
Et l'une ne bouge pas sans l'autre (*And One Does Not Move without the Other*, Irigaray), 139 n.5
étranger, L' (Camus), 148
europa giovane, L' (*Young Europe*, Ferrero), 97
Excision, 86
Exile, 1, 3, 4, 29–32, 37–41, 42 n.3, 47, 48, 77, 78, 157, 159; companion in, 80; internal, 154
Expatriate, 30
Experience: female, 6, 7, 14, 15, 19, 22, 23, 111, 121, 126, 136, 137; of contemporary women, 116; gaps between writing and, 123; marginal, 31; multicultural, 1, 9; postcolonial, 9; time between telling or writing and, 131, 133, 134; traumatic, 39

Faà, Caterina Camilla, 11, 25 n.22
Fallaci, Oriana, 4, 15, 19, 20, 22, 59 n.20, 104, 107–117, 121–123, 125; 155 n.7, 158, 159; Works: *Lettera a un bambino mai nato* (*Letter to a Child Never Born*), 4, 15, 19, 22, 104, 107–117, 121, 125, 155 n.7, 158; *sesso inutile, Il* (*Useless Sex, The*), 107; *uomo, Un* (*A Man*), 107, 116 n.5
Family, 2, 13, 14, 17, 19, 22, 23, 25 n.25; alternative, 110; artistic production and, 122; autobiographical presentations of, 92, 148; career and, 122, 158; conventional or bourgeois, 79, 93; conventions, 127; as ideal or myth, 111; lover as, 68; modification of, 92, 158, 159; nuclear, 123; as oppressive, 99; roles, 57, 98, 158; separation from, 103, 104, 107, 135, 154, 157–159
Fascist period, 101
Father, 112, 143; absence of, 125; as authoritative force, 127; disillusionment with, 93–95; identification with, 93, 96; loss of, 63, 68, 76 n.10; in literary tradition, 15; name of, 99, 105 n.11; relationship with, 17, 25, 125, 126; substitute, 129
Fau, Christine, 148, 155 n.8
Felski, Rita, 19, 20, 26 n.30, 140 n.12, 141 n.28
Female, 8; as concept, 6; continuity, 66, 129, 146, 160; suppression, 4, 57
Feminism, 6–8, 92, 98, 99; birth of, 42 n.4; linked to socialism, 97; radical, 116 n.8; themes or concerns in writing, 4, 14, 30, 31, 56–58, 80, 82, 85, 86, 99, 101, 103, 107, 111, 122, 137; Western, 3, 45, 57
Feminist movement. *See* Women's movement
Feminist revisionist writing: of history, 6, 141 n.27; of mythology, 6, 141 n.27
femme libre, La (*Free Woman, The*), 42 n.4
Ferguson, Mary Anne, 25–26 n.28
Ferrero, Guglielmo, 97
Fertility, choices, 111, 112, 160
Fetus, 4, 107–117 passim, 126, 132
Fiction, 29, 42 n.13, 131, 144; autobiographical, 45, 92, 93, 108, 139, 147; as locus of growth and healing, 132, 133, 136; semifictional forms or texts, 3, 137; structural elements in autobiography and, 23
Finucci, Valeria, 25 n.22
Flaubert, Gustave, 18, 33, 46, 49, 51, 61, 78, 84
Fourier, Charles, 42 n.4
France, 3, 6, 13, 30, 40, 41, 42 n.4, 57, 69, 76 nn.11, 15, 78–81, 85, 86, 102, 122, 158; in the 1940s and 1950s, 150; and the colonies, 126; counterculture in, 131; intellectual elite in, 84; opposition between Algeria and, 130, 131; at turn of century, 101
Francophone, studies, 9

Franco-Prussion War, 62, 76 n.15
Frappier-Mazur, Lucienne, 59 n.17
French, Marilyn, 20
French feminism, 6, 24 n.15
Freud, Sigmund, 68, 123
Fuller, Margaret, 31
Fuderer, Laura Sue, 19
Frye, Joanne S., 21, 23

Garcin, Jérôme, 148, 152
Garibaldi, Giuseppe, 30
Gattey, Charles Neilson, 33, 47
Gautier, Théophile, 53, 62
Gender, 16, 78, 157; and children's lives, 110; identity, 2, 8; and language, 136; limitations, 17; oppression, 4, 7, 13, 49, 58, 86, 98, 111; in relation to power struggle, 8; roles, 14, 18, 48, 56, 111
Genre, 3, 16, 17, 21–23; "female genres," 24 n.6, 31, 42 n.10; "male genres," 13, 42 n.10
Gentileschi, Artemisia, 6
Giacomelli, Antonietta, 13
Girardin, Delphine de, 53, 62, 71, 99
Girardin, Émile de, 62, 71
Glidden Parker, Marcia, 75 nn.3, 5, 76 n.18
Goethe, Johann, 16, 25 n.25, 49, 61, 97
Goodheart, Pat, 139 n.1, 140 nn.19, 21, 22
Grandmother, 109, 125, 129
Great Expectations (Dickens), 21, 23
Guindorf, Marie-Reine, 42 n.4
Guyon, Madame, 10

Haldane, Charlotte, 76 nn.17, 23, 83, 84
Halimi, Gisèle, 114, 117 n.16
Hall, Colette, 123, 130, 136
Harem, 35, 45, 48–53, 56, 57, 59 n.9, 63, 111, 112; member of, 3, 17, 46, 49, 56, 58 n.5; research on, 59 n.20
Harlot. *See* Prostitute
Hastier, Louis, 42 n.14
Havercroft, Barbara, 152, 155 nn.12, 14, 15
Heilbrun, Carolyn G., 15
Hemingway, Ernest, 148
Hirsch, Marianne, 16, 17, 20, 22, 24 n.4, 50, 51, 63, 75 n.8, 101, 102

Histoire de ma vie (*Story of My Life*, Sand), 7, 12, 25 n.24, 17, 67, 93, 140 n.20, 143, 145, 160
Hobbes, Thomas, 21
Home, 26 n.28, 29, 30, 41, 42, 42 n.1, 157; confinement to, 21, 111
Homosexuality, 15
Houssaye, Arsène, 33, 42 n.14
Hugo, Victor, 81
Hurd Green, Carol, 24 n.1
Hutcheon, Linda, 8
Hybrid texts, 1, 116 n.4, 122, 160
Hyvrard, Jeanne, 122, 139 n.6

Identification, 6, 7; with father, 93, 96; feminine, 110, 129, 132, 133, 140 n.14; with mother, 95, 96, 102, 103, 110, 122, 128, 145, 146, 160
Identity, 1, 2, 8, 24, 25 nn.27, 28, 30, 158; assumed between author, narrator and protagonist, 21; in connection with mother, 122; explored through character portrait, 48; female, 2, 6, 9, 14, 19, 20, 109, 139; formation, 22, 144
Indiana (Sand), 159
Irigaray, Luce, 6, 96, 122, 123, 136, 139 n.5, 143
Irony, 17, 26 n.28, 21
Islam, 48, 52; codes of conduct, 45; female education in, 48; marriage laws in, 52, 55, 56; women in, 55
Italian studies, 9
Italian unification, 30, 56, 59 n.19, 100
Italy, 3, 29–32, 38, 40, 41, 42 nn.4, 11, 46, 57, 59 nn.8, 15, 102, 123, 159; divisions between northern, central, and southern, 98; French rule in, 100; intellectual women in, 98; at turn of century, 94, 100; women's right to vote in, 105 n.9

Jane Eyre (Brontë), 21, 49, 58 n.2
Johnson, Edward Gilpin, 12
Jaubert, Caroline, 29, 37, 39–41
Jesus Christ, 110, 112
Jost, François, 16, 21, 24 n.4, 59 n.18
Journey: autobiographical, 1, 15, 24 n.1, 157, 159; emotional, 4, 5, 17, 19, 20, 25–26 n.28, 29, 33, 40, 41, 45, 50, 57,

Index 179

75, 80, 103, 115, 121, 124, 130; toward health, 134, 138; as humanitarian mission, 54; intellectual, 98; physical, 4, 12, 17, 36, 42 n.3, 70, 73–75, 78–81, 98, 103, 107; both psychological and literary, 154; of writer/narrator, 145; youth as, 23;
Jung, Carl, 124

Kamuf, Peggy, 24 nn.11, 14
Kempe, Margery, 10
Knibiehler, Yvonne, 47
Kristeva, Julia, 6, 102
Kulischiff, Anna, 42 n.4
Künstlerroman, 4, 5, 77, 84, 86; of the 1920s, 101

La Fayette, General, 30, 32, 36, 37
Lafayette, Madame de, 91
Lamartine, Alphonse de, 46, 58 n.4
Langland, Elizabeth, 17, 20
Language, 5, 10, 122, 124, 160; in autobiography, search for, 123; bourgeois, 148, 153; empowerment through, 137; gender relations and, 136; graphic, 114, 153; male, 91, 114, 123; psychoanalytical versus creative, 135, 141 n.24; search for new style or, 150, 153; sexual division and, 110; versus silence, 138; spoken, 137, 155 n.6; violence through, 126
Lazzaro-Weis, Carol, 157
Leclerc, Annie, 123
Le Clézio, Marguerite, 122, 123, 139 n.6,
Leduc, Violette, 15
Légère en août (*Light in August*, Bonal), 117 n.14
Lejeune, Philippe, 43 n.17, 140 n.9
Lesbian, 122; identity, 15
Leslie, Tanya, 154 n.1, 155 n.7
Letters, 3, 10, 11, 21, 29–32, 50, 53, 68–70, 78, 86, 91, 157
Lettres de Mistress Fanni Butlerd (*Letters from Mistress Fanni Butlerd*, Riccoboni), 11
Lettres d'un voyageur (*Letters of a Voyager*, Sand), 29
Life, in autobiography, 1, 2, 7, 30

Life and Opinions of Tristram Shandy, The (Sterne), 116 n.6
Life story. *See* Autobiography
Life writing. *See* Autobiography
Lionnet, Françoise, 126, 140 nn.8, 17
Lipton, Eunice, 24 n.12, 154 n.2
Liszt, Franz, 30, 32–34, 39
Locate, 32, 37, 46, 47
Lombroso, Cesare, 97
Louison (Musset), 34
Lui: Roman contemporain (*Lui: A View of Him*, Colet), 33, 42–43 n.15, 43 n.16

Macciocchi, Maria Antonietta, 91, 105 n.2
Macinghi Strozzi, Alessandra, 10, 25 n.21
Madame Bovary (Flaubert), 18, 78, 84, 85
Madness. *See* Mental illness
Male, approval, 81, 85, 112, 117 n.13, 134
Mall, Laurence, 151, 155 nn.8, 11
Manzoni, Alessandro, 23, 49, 53
Maraini, Dacia, 59 n.20, 109, 159
Mariani, Emilia, 42 n.4
Marotti, Maria, 94, 96
Marriage, 2, 13, 48, 75, 79, 86, 101, 144; abusive husband or, 1, 4, 22, 92, 103, 108, 111, 159; alienating or loveless, 20, 97; arranged, 50; bourgeois, 64, 91; civil versus religious, 82; as closure, 23; confinement of, 49–51; disillusionment with, 93, 95; expectations or attitudes toward, 147, 158; laws, 55, 56; monogamous, 54, 58, 59 n.17; proposal, 72; rape followed by, 94; as redeeming, 80; renunciation of, 101, 107; traditional, 1, 121
Marrone, Claire, 24 n.12, 25 n.18, 58 n.1, 75 n.1, 126, 137, 140 n.15, 154 n.2
Martin, Elaine, 19, 124, 140 nn.10, 11
Martineau, Harriet, 31
Mason, Mary G., 24 n.1
Maternal: complex, 5, 126; devotion, 25 n.25; rejection, 130; repression, 51, 102, 140 n.11; substitute, 53. *See also* Mother; Motherhood
Matignon, Renaud, 152
matrimonio in provincia, Un (*Country Marriage, A*, Colombi), 13
Matrophobia, 93

Maturation. *See* Development, psychological growth or
Maus: A Survivor's Tale (Spigelman), 8
Mazzini, Giuseppe, 30
Mazingarbe, Danièle, 148
McCallum Schwartz, Lucy, 25 n.23, 50
McClary, Susan, 64, 75 nn. 4, 6
Memoir, 3, 10, 11, 50, 61. *See also* Autobiography
Mémoires (*Memoirs*, Roland), 11, 12
Menstruation, 126, 140 n.14
Mental illness, 5, 23, 50, 93, 102, 104, 116, 121–141 passim
Méry, 53
Mes cahiers bleus (*My Blue Notebooks*), 87 n.3
Mes souvenirs (*My Memoirs*, Stern), 39, 40
Mezzogiorno, 100
Michaud, Stéphane, 25 n.25
Michel, Louise, 13
Middle East, 3, 29–32, 38, 41, 42 n.3, 45–47, 157
Middlemarch (Eliot), 18
Middleton, Dorothy, 45
Mignet, François, 36, 37
Milan, 30, 32, 36, 93
Milanese, Flavia, 58 n.1
Miller, Christopher L., 58 n.4
Miller, Nancy K., 8, 24 n.11, 26 n.31, 68
Mills, Sara, 79
Minh-ha, Trinh T., 136, 137
Miscarriage, 108, 109, 113, 122, 126
Missionary, nineteenth-century female explorer, social reformer, and/or, 45, 46, 159
Modernism, 101
Mogador, Céleste, 3, 4, 9, 12, 17, 22, 30, 31, 61–76, 77–87, 93, 99, 111, 115, 157–59; Works: *Adieux au monde: Mémoires de Céleste Mogador* (*Goodbye to the World: Memoirs of Céleste Mogador*) 24 n.9, 73 (*see also Mémoires de Céleste Mogador*); *Mémoires de Céleste Mogador* (*Memoirs of Céleste Mogador*), 3, 4, 17, 61–76, 77–87, 99, 158, 159. *See also* Chabrillan, Céleste de; Chabrillan, Comtesse de; Vénard, Céleste-Élisabeth
Moi, Toril, 24 n.14
Monicat, Bénédicte, 31, 42 nn.6, 8, 46, 48, 58 n.5, 59 nn.9, 11, 76 n.19, 79, 80, 87 n.5
Monologue, 108
Monologue/Dialogue, 4, 108, 109
Monogamy, 49, 55, 58, 59 n.17 (*see also* Marriage, monogamous)
Monsieur Nicolas (Bretonne), 21
Morandini, Giuliana, 46
Moravia, Alberto, 105 n.4
Moretti, Franco, 16
Morrison, Toni, 140 n.18
mort très douce, Une (*Very Sweet Death, A*, Beauvoir), 145, 148, 160
Moser, Françoise, 62, 71, 73, 76 nn.10, 17, 18, 20
Motherland, 123; leaving the, 130, 159
Mother, 2, 5, 7, 10, 14, 15, 22, 66, 93, 125; absent, 51; alienation from or disillusionment with, 93, 140 n.11; as authoritative force, 127; death of, 102, 123, 129, 130, 140 n.20, 143–155 passim, 160; inconsistent, 63; loss of, 94; memory of, 101, 102; reconciliation with, 124, 130; relationship with (unborn) child, 107–117 passim, 123, 160; role in family, 57; and sacrifice, 103, 104, 122, 158; separation between child and, 104; sexuality of, 129; split from, 67, 97, 121, 123, 128, 139, 144, 154, 158–160; values of daughter and, 110, 122, 123, 129, 131, 158
Mother–daughter relationship, 4, 5, 10, 15, 17, 18, 26 n.25, 66, 93, 101, 102, 121–141 passim, 143–155 passim, 158, 160
Motherhood, 2, 4, 14, 18, 93 96, 100, 104, 121, 144, 159; break from traditional models of, 92, 158; as choice, 102, 109 (*see also* Choice, reproductive); confinement of, 49, 50; dichotomy between career and, 93, 102, 109 (*see also* Career, combining family life and/or motherhood and); expectations regarding, 158; innovative or regenerative visions of, 109, 111, 116 n.8; as institution, 4, 13, 91, 111; as sacri-

fice, 103, 109; single, 1, 4, 107–109, 111, 115; surrogate, 1, 111, 112, 117 n.14, 160
mots, Les (*Words*, Sartre), 137
Movement: away from oppressive structures, 1, 158, 159; away from society, 158; that parallels or contributes to change, 40, 157; theme of, 2. *See also* Displacement; Separation
Mozzoni, Anna Maria, 42 n.4
Mueller, Janel M., 10
Muslim. *See* Islam
Musset, Alfred de, 30, 32–35, 41, 61, 65, 91

Nana (Zola), 65, 78
Napoleon III, 30, 32
Napoleon, Prince, 73, 82
Narrator, shifting perspectives of, 100, 108, 124
National, Le, 32, 42 n.1
Neera (Anna [Zuccari] Radius), 12, 13, 15, 49, 159; correspondence with Luigi Capuana, 12, 13
Negri, Ada, 91, 101
Nerval, Gérard de, 46
"New autobiographies," 2, 108
Nightingale, Florence, 30
Nizzoli, Amalia Solla, 13, 31, 42 n.7, 46, 159
Nostalgia, 14, 17, 38, 67, 124, 140 n.9; for the homeland, 78; tone, 93
Novel, 1, 17, 62, 93, 122, 138, 139; epistolary (*see* Letters); women writers of, 13, 14, 17, 22
Novel of Awakening. *See Bildungsroman*
Novel of Development. *See Bildungsroman*
Novel of Formation. *See Bildungsroman*
Novel of Self-discovery. *See Bildungsroman*

Object relations psychology, 8
Orient, 3, 31, 41, 46, 47, 51, 58 n.2
Orientalism, 46, 58 n.4
Others: defining or analyzing oneself in relation to, 8, 23, 29, 33, 42 n.2, 59 n.9, 157; as foreign, 30, 48; hitherto silenced, 137; mother as, 130; outsider or, 133; praising oneself through, 85; self merged with, 108

Pact, autobiographical, 62
Parent-Duchâtelet, Alexandre, 64, 76 n.12
Paris, 30, 37, 40, 41, 48, 62, 72, 73, 87 n.3, 129, 132, 135
Passerini, Luisa, 116 n.4
Patriarchy, 75 n.5, 91, 107, 111, 123, 158, 159; challenging structures of, 110, 131, 159; entrapment within, 103
Pen name. *See* Pseudonym
Personal narrative. *See* Autobiography
Petacco, Arrigo, 33, 36–38, 42 n.5, 47
petite Fadette, La (*Little Fadette*, Sand), 59 n.10
Pickering-Iazzi, Robin, 101, 105 nn.14, 15, 109, 111, 113, 115, 116, 116 n.8
Pied-noir, 122, 123, 126, 131
Planté, Christine, 6, 14, 25 n.26, 42 nn.4, 10
Plath, Sylvia, 125, 140 n.10
Polygamy, 48, 49, 54
Postcolonial criticism, 6, 8
Postmodern criticism, 6
Postmodernism, 8
Pougy, Liane de, 87 n.3
Powrie, Phil, 124
Pratt, Annis, 50, 59 nn.12, 14
Pregnancy, 108, 109, 111, 112, 114, 158; unwanted, 122, 126
promessi sposi, I (*Betrothed, The*, Manzoni), 23
Pro-life advocacy, 116 n.8
Prostitute, 3, 4, 17, 37, 38, 61–71 passim, 77–87 passim, 97, 103, 158; as slur, 114
Prostitution, 4, 64, 65, 76 nn.11, 12, 86
Pseudonym, 12, 92, 99
Psyche, myth of, 25–26 n.28
Psychoanalysis, 5, 6, 15, 17, 24 n.15, 121–141 passim

quattro ragazze Wieselberger, Le (*Four Wieselberger Girls, The*, Cialente), 116 n.4
Quest story, 17, 23

Rage. *See* Anger
Ramsay, Raylene L., 24 n.1, 116 n.3, 139 n.4
Rape, 63, 91, 94, 105 n.4, 97, 114
Realism, 23, 48, 150
Recovery, of writers, stories, and literary

texts, 6, 24 n.12, 146. *See also* Feminist revisionist writing
Repudiation, as technique in autobiography, 124, 140 n.9
Resistance movement, 107
Revolution of 1848, 62
Revue des Deux Mondes, 32, 34
Riccoboni, Madame, 11
Rich, Adrienne, 93
"rire de la méduse, Le" ("Laugh of the Medusa, The," Cixous), 15
Risorgimento, 13, 29, 47
Rochefort, Christiane, 19
Rogers, Juliette M., 87 n.3
Roland Barthes par Roland Barthes (*Roland Barthes by Roland Barthes*, Barthes), 7
Roland, Madame, 11, 12
Roman Revolutions, 30, 31, 37, 38
Romantic ideology, 49, 80
Romantic myth, 67, 77
Romantic stereotype, 46
Rome, 31, 32, 37, 47, 102; as cultural or intellectual center, 98, 100, 105 n.8
Room of One's Own, A (Woolf), 14, 101, 102
Rosawki, Susan J., 18, 20
Rousseau, Jean-Jacques, 7, 11, 12, 15, 21, 61, 62, 82
Rousset, Jean, 124

Said, Edward W., 46
Salon, 30
Sand, George, 7, 11–15, 17, 25 n.24, 29, 30, 33, 35, 45, 59 n.10, 67, 84, 91, 93, 99, 102, 140 n.20, 143, 145, 159, 160
Sandeau, Jules, 53, 99
Sanders, Carol, 147, 153
Sarraute, Nathalie, 22
Sartre, Jean-Paul, 137
Schenck, Celeste, 7
Scriboni, Mirella, 42 nn.2, 7, 46, 48, 58 n.4
Self, 1–5, 7, 8, 10, 11, 14, 15, 17, 22, 30, 33, 61, 85, 110, 114, 131, 145, 158, 160; definition of, 122; lack of understanding of, 154; maternal influence on, 121; models of, 87; other as separate from or merged with, 108, 145;

past versus present, 124, 138, 145; postmodern, multiple, and/or fragmented, 7, 100; reformed or new, 79, 129, 138, 139; representation of coherent, 157; woman voyager and, 78
Self-discovery, 2, 4, 19, 61, 94, 117 n.19, 121, 130
Selfhood. *See* Self
Self-realization, 2, 5, 18, 97, 101
Separation: away from oppressive structures or forces, 20, 99, 157, 158; from the past, 138; refusal of, 122; trauma of, 104
Serao, Matilde, 11, 31, 59 n.20
Serena, Carla, 31, 42 n.7, 45, 46
Severgnini, Luigi, 32, 41, 42 n.1, 47
Sévigné, Madame de, 10
Sexuality, 2, 4, 15, 104, 114, 147, 153, 159; and deviance, 77, 78; excluded in autobiography, 12; language and, 122; liberation and, 128, 129; oppression and, 3, 4, 57, 58
Shepley, John, 116 n.2, 117 n.18
Showalter, Elaine, 25 n.16
Sido (Colette), 160
Siena, Caterina da, 10
Smith, Sidonie, 7, 8, 25 n.27
Socialism, 13, 25 n.25, 42 n.4; linked to feminism, 97
Society, 16–22, 26 n.28, 63, 75 n.8, 86, 92, 97, 98, 135; alienation from, 136, 140 n.11; as antagonist, corruptive force, or stifling agent, 22, 30, 65, 66, 125; as authoritative force, 127; entry or reentry into, 2, 139; expectations of women, 16, 37; finding niche in, 138; integration into 18, 21, 97, 138, 158; limited contact with, 95; patriarchal or male-dominated, 94, 110; proper bourgeois, 64, 78; transformation of, 110, 111, 158; values, conventions, or mores of, 124, 125; women's roles in, 98, 103
Souvenirs du marquis de Floranges (*Memoirs of the Marquis of Floranges*, Boulenger), 53
Spigelman, Art, 8
Spinosa, Antonio, 42 n.5

Index

Splendeurs et misères des courtisanes (*A Harlot High and Low*, Balzac), 77
Staël, Madame de, 11, 13, 20, 30, 45, 49, 51, 68
Stages: in female novel of self-discovery, 19, 20; life or developmental, 2, 18, 23, 157
stances à Sophie, Les (*Cats Don't Care for Money*, Rochefort), 19
Stanhope, Lady Hester, 31, 45, 159
Stein, Gertrude, 7
Stelzi, Gaetano, 36
Stendhal, 21, 33, 36
Stern, Daniel. *See* Marie d'Agoult
Subject: autobiographical, 4, 12, 123, 154; biographical, 144, 145; contemporary inscriptions of, 91; defining oneself as, 101, 128; erasure of, 7; female, 1, 15, 19, 24, 124; maternal, 144; object versus, 124
Subjectivity, 25 n.27, 30, 99, 124, 157; female, 7, 15, 101
Suicide, 23, 66, 77, 93, 96, 102, 115, 116; after loss, contemplation of, 113
"Sur une morte" ("About a Dead Woman," Musset), 34
Surfacing (Atwood), 20
Syria, 3, 42 n.3, 47
Svevo, Italo, 21

Teaching, 111; as profession, 57, 98
Thébaud, Anne, 152
Therapy. *See* Psychoanalysis
Thierry, Augustin, 30, 36
Time: narrative, 23, 70, 149; women's relationship to, 140 n.14
Tondeur, Claire-Lise, 148, 154, 155 nn.8, 16
Travel Literature. *See* Travel Writing
Travel Writing, 3, 12, 29–31, 42 n.13, 46, 47, 58 n.4, 70–72, 76 n.19, 77–80, 86
tribune des femmes, La (*Women's Tribune*), 42 n.4
Tristan, Flora, 13, 30, 45
Truth, 1, 8, 11, 19, 36, 152–53; fiction and, 108; relativity of, 115; of women, 136
Turkey, 3, 32, 42 nn.3, 11, 46, 47, 49

Ulysses, 25 n.28

Vénard, Céleste-Élisabeth, 61. *See also* Mogador, Céleste; Chabrillan, Comtesse de; Chabrillan, Céleste de
Véret, Désirée, 42 n.4
Vie de Henry Brulard (*Life of Henry Brulard, The*, Stendhal), 21
Virginity, loss of, 94, 128
vita, La (*Life*, Cellini), 21
vita, La (*Life*, Hobbes), 21
Vivanti, Annie, 91
Voilquin, Suzanne, 13, 42 n.4
Vote for women, 98, 105 n.9
Voyage. *See* Journey

Watson, Julia, 7, 8
White, Barbara, 59 n.12
Wilhelm Meister's Apprenticeship (Goethe), 16
Wittig, Monique, 15
Woman: as concept, 2, 6, 25 n.25; as cultural creation, 14; defining or redefining, 98; as distinct category, 107
Women's literature. *See* Women's writing
Women's movement, 4, 14, 19, 57, 91; at the turn of the century, 98
Women's Room, The (French), 20
Women's studies, 8
Women's writing, 19, 91, 96, 160; during 1920s and 1930s, 101, 102; and autobiography, 1–9, 10–15, 21–24; and the *bildungsroman*, 2–5, 16–20; neglected corpus of, 6, 24 n.12; in the nineteenth century, 14, 23, 30, 84, 91, 99, 102, 111, 114; postmodern or contemporary, 4, 5, 8, 14, 22, 23, 91, 100, 104, 107, 109, 111, 122, 125, 137, 149, 160; tradition of, 6, 7, 25 n.16; at turn of century, 4, 14, 19, 87, 91, 98, 111
Wood, Sharon, 42 n.4, 92, 100, 105 nn.10, 13
Woolf, Virginia, 14, 91, 96, 101
World War I, 102
World War II, 105 n.9, 146–147
Worley, Linda Kraus, 79

Yalom, Marilyn, 123, 130

Zola, Émile, 64, 65, 78
Zonana, Joyce, 58 n.2

About the Author

CLAIRE MARRONE is Associate Professor of French and Italian at Sacred Heart University. She has published numerous articles on 19th- and 20th-century women writers, autobiography, and the *bildungsroman*.